I0318863

William Chambers

Seven pagodas of the coromandel coast

William Chambers

Seven pagodas of the coromandel coast

ISBN/EAN: 9783337413989

Printed in Europe, USA, Canada, Australia, Japan

Cover: Foto ©ninafisch / pixelio.de

More available books at **www.hansebooks.com**

THE
SEVEN PAGODAS.

Descriptive and Historical Papers

RELATING TO

THE SEVEN PAGODAS

ON THE

COROMANDEL COAST.

BY

WILLIAM CHAMBERS, ESQ.; J. GOLDINGHAM, ESQ.;
BENJAMIN GUY BABINGTON, ESQ., M.D., F.R.S.;
REV. G. W. MAHON, M.A.; LIEUTENANT JOHN BRADDOCK;
REV. W. TAYLOR; SIR WALTER ELLIOT, K.C.S.I.;
CHARLES GUBBINS, ESQ.

EDITED BY
CAPTAIN M. W. CARR,
Madras Staff Corps.

MADRAS:
PRINTED FOR THE GOVERNMENT OF MADRAS,
BY CALEB FOSTER, FOSTER PRESS, 23, RUNDALL'S ROAD, VEPERY.
1869.

EDITOR'S NOTE.

THE papers contained in this volume, descriptive of the Sculptures, Inscriptions and Monolithic temples known as the SEVEN PAGODAS, have been reprinted in a collected form, under the orders of the Government of Madras, with a view to promote the intelligent study and examination of these interesting relics of a bygone age. They have been selected as conveying valuable information on the subject, recorded by various competent observers at different times, but so scattered through the published transactions of learned Societies as to be rarely accessible to any one person visiting the spot.*

The origin of the European appellation "Seven Pagodas" cannot satisfactorily be traced. The name may have been given, as stated by Dr. Graul's guide, to the five *Rathas*, the Ganesa temple and the Shore temple.† The story of "magnificent pagodas swallowed up by the sea" is as apocryphal as the legend of the submerged city of Bali.

A matter of greater interest and importance, the age of the Sculptures and Inscriptions at Mâvalivaram, has not, it is to be regretted, been definitely ascertained. No date has—if the record of such exist—been found in any one of the Inscriptions.

* Proceedings of the Madras Government, 1st May 1869.

† Reise nach Ostindien, Vol. III., p. 202.

Mr. Fergusson, writing of the *Rathas*, states as his opinion that they were "carved by the Hindus, probably about 1300 A. D."* The researches of Sir Walter Elliot led him to fix the era of the oldest Tamil Inscription on the rocks of Mávalivaram at the latter part of the 11th century, and that of the rock inscription at *Sáluvan* Kuppam at the commencement of the 12th century.†

The Sanscrit Inscriptions are doubtless anterior in date to those in the Tamil language. The Rev. Mr. Taylor conjectures that the excavations and sculptures, together with these older Inscriptions, were accomplished in the 16th or 17th century. Sir Walter Elliot, on the other hand, is of opinion that they could not have been made later than the 6th century.

The following valuable remarks by Mr. Fergusson explain the style of the monolithic *Rathas* :—

"Although these *Raths*, as they are called locally, are comparatively modern, and belong to a different faith, they certainly constitute the best representations now known of the forms of the Buddhist buildings * * and make their external forms more intelligible than they could otherwise be made from the mere internal copies of them which alone we possess [elsewhere] in the rock-cut examples. There are no essential differences which cannot be accounted for by the consideration that the sacred caves of the Buddhists were designed for a well-understood purpose—the Chaityas as temples, the Viharas as residences—which was the invariable rule in Buddhist times. When their successors the Hindus, began to follow their example, they copied blindly and unmeaningly. * * This * explains many points in the architecture [of the South of India] which without this would be perfectly unintelligible. The Raths are, in fact, transition specimens, and as such link the two styles together, the one serving to explain the peculiarities of the other."‡

* History of Architecture, Vol. II., p. 502.

† See p. 140 f., *infra*.

‡ History of Architecture, Vol. II., p. 504

Some notes, corrective and explanatory, have been added by the Editor; these are distinguished by brackets [ ]. The orthography of Indian names occurring in these papers has been revised, and a uniform system of transliteration adopted.

In the Appendix will be found, among other matters, copies of the Sanscrit Inscriptions made by Mr. Arthur Burnell of the Madras Civil Service. Also a description of the Pagodas by Kávali Lakshmayya, printed in the original language from the Mackenzie MSS. in which it has lain for the last sixty odd years. This document gives a more detailed account of the antiquities at Mávalivaram than is contained in any of the other papers on the subject; its translation, with Braddock's description, will probably be found the most useful guide to a traveller visiting the spot. An Index to the whole has been added.

The English letter press and illustrations have been executed by the Foster Press. The Devanâgarî printing was performed at the Press of the Society for the Promotion of Christian Knowledge.

A sketch map, carefully executed by the Revenue Survey Department, accompanies the volume. It contains ground plans of the monolithic temples and principal excavations.

MADRAS, *September* 1869.

CONTENTS.

PAGE

I.—Some account of the Sculptures and Ruins at Mâvalipuram, a place a few miles north of Sadras, and known to Seamen by the name of the Seven Pagodas. By WILLIAM CHAMBERS, Esq. 1

II.—Some account of the Sculptures at Mahábalipuram; usually called the Seven Pagodas. By J. GOLDINGHAM, Esq. 30

III.—An account of the Sculptures and Inscriptions at Mahâmalaipûr; illustrated by Plates. By BENJAMIN GUY BABINGTON, M.B., F.R.S., Sec. R.A.S. 44

IV.—A Guide to the Sculptures, Excavations, and other remarkable objects at Mâmallaipûr, generally known to Europeans as "The Seven Pagodas," by the late Lieutenant JOHN BRADDOCK, of the Madras Establishment. To which are added some Archæological Notes, by the Reverend WILLIAM TAYLOR, and a Supplementary account

PAGE

of the remains at Sâluvan Kuppam, by Sir WALTER ELLIOT, K.C.S.I., of the Madras Civil Service.—Communicated to the Madras Journal of Literature and Science by the Reverend GEORGE WILLIAM MAHON, A.M., Garrison Chaplain, Fort St. George . . 63

V.—On the Inscription near the Varâhasvâmi Temple, at Mâmallaipuram or the Seven Pagodas, with a transcript and translation. By Sir WALTER ELLIOT, K.C.S.I. 132

VI.—Notes on the Ruins at Mahâbalipuram on the Coromandel Coast. By CHARLES GUBBINS, Esq., Bengal Civil Service 146

Appendix 173

The Sthalapurâna 173
Description of the Pagodas, &c. at Mâvalivaram, written in the Telugu language by Kâvali Lakshmayya in 1803. With a translation 156
Sanscrit sloka 220
The Inscriptions 221
Arjuna's penance 226
Death of Mahishâsura 227
Bibliographical List 230

[illegible] 232

ILLUSTRATIONS.

		PAGE
PLATE I.	Arjuna's Penance	47
II.	(1) Do. (2) Krishna Mandapa	48
III.	(1) Kailâsa (2) Nârâyana	49
IV.	Death of Mahishâsura	49
V.	Varâha Avatâra	50
VI.	Vâmana Avatâra	50
VII.	(1) Bhadrakâlî (2 & 3) Columns	50
VIII.	(1) Devî (2) Dwârapâla	50
IX.	Excavated Temple	50
X.	(1) ? Durgâ (2) ? Durgâ (3) ? Vishnu	50
XI.	(1) Dolotsava Mandapa (2) Shore Temple	51
XII.	Vishnu	51
XIII.	Alphabet of Ancient Tamil	54
XIV.	Ganesa Temple Inscription	57
XV.	Inscription on buried Siva Temple	59
XVI.	Figures on Dharmarâja's Ratha	60
XVII.	Inscriptions on Dharmarâja's Ratha	61
XVIII.	Ancient Sanscrit Alphabets	62
XIX.	The five Rathas	103
XX. & XXI.	Plan of Mâmallaipûr	110
XXII.	The Shore Temple	156
XXIII.	Sketch of Mahâbalipuram	172
XXIV.	Buried Siva Temple at Sâluvankuppam	225

For Corrigenda, &c., see end of Volume.

THE SEVEN PAGODAS.

I.—*Some account of the Sculptures and Ruins at Mávalipuram, a place a few miles north of Sadras, and known to seamen by the name of the Seven Pagodas.* By WILLIAM CHAMBERS, ESQ.

[From the Asiatic Researches, Vol. I. 1788.]

AS amidst inquiries after the histories and antiquities of Asia at large, those of that division of it in which this society* resides, may seem on many accounts to lay claim to a particular share of its attention, a few hints put down from recollection, concerning some monuments of Hindu antiquity, which, though situated in the neighbourhood of European settlements on the Coromandel Coast, have hitherto been little observed, may it is conceived, be acceptable, at least as they may possibly give rise hereafter to more accurate observations, and more complete discoveries on the same subject. The writer of this account went first to view them in the year 1772, and curiosity led him thither again in 1776; but as he neither measured the distances nor size of the objects, nor committed to writing at the time the observations he made on them, he

[* The Asiatic Society of Bengal.]

hopes to be excused if, after the lapse of so many years, his recollection should fail him in some respects, and his account fall far short of that precision and exactness, which might have been expected, had there then existed in India so powerful an incentive to diligent inquiry, and accurate communication, as the establishment of this society must now prove.

The monuments he means to describe, appear to be the remains of some great city, that has been ruined many centuries ago; they are situated close to the sea, between Covelong and Sadras, somewhat remote from the high road, that leads to the different European settlements. And when he visited them in 1776, there was still a native village adjoining to them, which retained the ancient name, and in which a number of Brahmans resided, that seemed perfectly well acquainted with the subjects of most of the sculptures to be seen there.

The rock, or rather hill of stone, on which great part of these works are executed, is one of the principal marks for mariners as they approach the coast, and to them the place is known by the name of the *Seven Pagodas*, possibly because the summits of the rock have presented them with that idea as they passed: but it must be confessed, that no aspect which the hill assumes, as viewed on the shore, seems at all to authorize this notion; and there are circumstances, which will be mentioned in the sequel, that would lead one to suspect, that this name has arisen from some such number of Pagodas that formerly stood here, and in time have been buried in the waves. But, be that as it may, the appellation by which the natives distinguish it, is of a quite different origin: in their language, which is the

Tamil, (improperly termed *Malabar,*) the place is called Mâvalipuram, which, in Sanscrit, and the languages of the more northern Hindus, would be Mahâbalipura, or the City of the great Bali. For the Tamulians, (or Malabars,) having no *h* in their alphabet, are under a necessity of shortening the Sanscrit word *mahâ*, great, and write it *mâ*.* They are obliged also, for a similar reason, to substitute a *v* for a *b*, in words of Sanscrit, or other foreign original that begin with that letter; and the syllable *am*, at the end, is merely a termination, which, like *um* in Latin, is generally annexed to neuter substances.† To this etymology of the name of this place it may be proper to add, that Bali is the name of a hero very famous in Hindu romance; and that the river Mâvaligangâ, which waters the eastern side of Ceylon, where the Tamil language also prevails, has probably taken its name from him, as, according to that orthography, it apparently signifies the Ganges of the great Bali.

The rock, or hill of stone, above mentioned, is that which first engrosses the attention on approaching the place; for, as it rises abruptly out of a level plain of great extent, consists chiefly of one single stone, and is situated very near to the sea-beach, it is such a kind of object as an inquisitive traveller would naturally turn aside to examine. Its shape is also

* They do indeed admit a substitute [magā], but the abbreviation is most used.

† This explains also, why the Sanscrit word *Veda*, by which the Hindus denominate the books of the law of their religion, is written by the Tamulians *Vedam*, which is according to the true orthography of their language, and no mistake of European travellers, as some have supposed; while the same word is called *Bed* by the Bengalis, who have in effect no *V* in their alphabet.—See Dow, Vol. I. Dissert. p. 41.

singular and romantic, and, from a distant view, has an appearance like some antique and lofty edifice. On coming near to the foot of the rock from the north, works of imagery* and sculpture crowd so thick upon the eye, as might seem to favour the idea of a petrified town, like those that have been fabled in different parts of the world by too credulous travellers.† Proceeding on by the foot of the hill, on the side facing the sea, there is a pagoda rising out of the ground, of one solid stone, about sixteen or eighteen feet high, which seems to have been cut upon the spot out of a detached rock, that has been found of a proper size for that purpose.‡ The top is arched, and the style of architecture, according to which it is formed, different from any now used in those parts. A little further on, there appears upon an huge surface of stone, that juts out a little from the side of the hill, a numerous group of human figures in bas relief, considerably larger than life, representing the most remarkable persons, whose actions are celebrated in the Mahâbhârata, each of them in an attitude, or with weapons or other insignia, expressive of his character, or of some one of his most famous exploits.§ All these figures are, doubtless, much less distinct than they were at first; for, upon comparing these and the rest of the sculptures that are exposed to the sea air, with others at the same place, whose situation has afforded them

* Among these, one object, though a mean one, attracts the attention, on account of the grotesque and ridiculous nature of the design; it consists of two monkeys cut out of one stone, one of them in a stooping posture, while the other is taking the insects out of his head.

† See Shaw's Travels, p. 155, et seq.

[‡ The Ganesa temple appears to be referred to.]

[§ Arjuna's penance.—cp. Braddock, *infra.*]

protection from that element, the difference is striking; the former being every where much defaced, while the others are fresh as recently finished. This defacement is no where more observable, than in the piece of sculpture which occurs next in the order of description. This is an excavation in another part of the east side of the great rock, which appears to have been made on the same plan, and for the same purpose that choultries are usually built in that country; that is to say, for the accommodation of travellers. The rock is hollowed out to the size of a spacious room, and two or three rows of pillars are left, as a seeming support to the mountainous mass of stone which forms the roof. Of what pattern these pillars have originally been, it is not easy now to conjecture; for the air of the sea has greatly corroded them, as well as all the other parts of the cave. And this circumstance renders it difficult to discover, at first sight, that there is a scene of sculpture on the side fronting the entrance. The natives, however, point it out, and the subject of it is manifestly that of *Kr*ishna attending the herds of Nanda Ghosha* the Admetus of the Hindus; from which circumstance, *Kr*ishna is also called Gopâla, or the cowherd, as Apollo was entitled Nomius.

The objects which seem next to claim regard, are those upon the hill itself, the ascent of which, on the north, is, from its natural shape, gradual and easy at first, and is in other parts rendered more so, by very excellent steps cut out in several places, where the communication would be difficult or impracticable without them. A winding stair of this sort leads to a kind of temple cut out of the solid rock, with some

[* The cowherd Nanda, the foster and putative father of *Kr*ishna.]

figures of idols in high relief upon its walls, very well finished, and perfectly fresh, as it faces the west, and is therefore sheltered from the sea air.* From this temple again there are flights of steps, that seem to have led to some edifice, formerly standing upon the hill; nor does it seem absurd to suppose, that this may have been a palace, to which this temple, as a place of worship, may have appertained. For, besides the small detached ranges of stairs that are here and there cut in the rock, and seem as if they had once led to different parts of one great building, there appear in many places small water-channels cut also in the rock, as if for drains to an house; and the whole top of the hill is strewed with small round pieces of brick, which may be supposed, from their appearance, to have been worn down to their present form, during the lapse of many ages. On ascending the hill by its slope on the north, a very singular piece of sculpture presents itself to view. On a plain surface of the rock, which may once have served as the floor of some apartment, there is a platform of stone, about eight or nine feet long, by three or four wide, in a situation rather elevated, with two or three steps leading up to it, perfectly resembling a couch or bed, and a lion very well executed at the upper end of it by way of pillow, the whole of one piece, being part of the hill itself. This the Brahmans, inhabitants of the place, called the bed of Dharma-râja, or Yudhishthira, the eldest of the five brothers, whose fortunes and exploits are the leading subject in the Mahâbhârata. And at a considerable distance from this, at such a distance, indeed, as the apartment of the women might be supposed to be from that of

[* Cp. Braddock, No. 2.]

the men, is a bath excavated also from the solid rock, with steps in the inside, which the Brahmans call the bath of Draupadî, the wife of Yudhishthira and his brothers. How much credit is due to this tradition, and whether this stone couch may not have been anciently used as a kind of throne rather than a bed, is matter for future inquiry. A circumstance, however, which may seem to favour this idea is, that a throne in the Sanscrit, and other Hindu languages, is called *siṁhâsana*, which is composed of the words *siṁha*, a lion, and *âsana*, a seat.

These are all that appear on that part of the upper surface of the hill, the ascent to which is on the north; but, on descending from thence, you are led round the hill to the opposite side, in which there are steps cut from the bottom to a place near the summit, where is an excavation that seems to have been intended for a place of worship, and contains various sculptures of Hindu Deities. The most remarkable of these, is a gigantic figure of Vishnu, asleep on a kind of bed, with a huge snake wound about in many coils by way of pillow for his head;* and these figures, according to the manner of this place, are all of one piece, hewn from the body of the rock.

But though these works may be deemed stupendous, they are surpassed by others that are to be seen at the distance of about a mile, or a mile and an half, to the southward of the hill. They consist of two† Pagodas, of about thirty feet long by twenty feet wide, and about as many in height, cut out of the solid rock, and each consisting originally of one

[* Cp. Braddock, No. 19, *infra*.]
[† There are five, the five *Rathas*.]

single stone. Near these also stand an elephant full as big as life, and a lion much larger than the natural size, but very well executed, each hewn also out of one stone. None of the pieces that have fallen off in cutting these extraordinary sculptures are now to be found near or any where in the neighbourhood of them, so that there is no means of ascertaining the degree of labour and time that has been spent upon them, nor the size of the rock or rocks from which they have been hewn, a circumstance which renders their appearance the more striking and singular. And though their situation is very near the sea-beach, they have not suffered at all by the corrosive air of that element, which has provided them with a defence against itself, by throwing up before them a high bank, that completely shelters them. There is also great symmetry in their form; though that of the Pagodas is different from the style of architecture, according to which idol temples are now built in that country. The latter resembles the Egyptian; for the towers are always pyramidical, and the gates and roofs flat, and without arches; but these sculptures approach nearer to the Gothic taste, being surmounted by arched roofs or domes, that are not semi-circular, but composed of two segments of circles meeting in a point at top. It is also observable that the lion in this group of sculptures, as well as that upon the stone couch above mentioned, are perfectly just representations of the true lion; and the natives there give them the name, which is always understood to mean a lion in the Hindu language, to wit, *siṁha;* but the figure, which they have made to represent that animal in their idol temples for centuries past, though it bears the same appellation, is a distorted monster, totally unlike the original; insomuch that it has from hence been supposed that the lion was not anciently known in this country, and that *sinha* was a name given to a monster that existed only in Hindu romance. But it is plain that that animal was well known to the authors of these works, who, in manners as well as arts, seem to have differed much from the modern Hindus.

There are two circumstances attending these monuments, which cannot but excite great curiosity, and on which future inquiries may possibly throw some light. One is, that on one of the Pagodas last mentioned, there is an inscription of a single line, in a character at present unknown to the Hindus.* It resembles neither the *Devanágarí*, nor any of the various characters connected with or derived from it, which have come to the writer's knowledge from any part of Hindostan. Nor did it, at the time he viewed it, appear to correspond with any character, Asiatic or European, that is commonly known. He had not then, however, seen the alphabet of the *Páli*, the learned language of the Siamese, a sight of which has since raised in his mind a suspicion, that there is a near affinity between them, if the character be not identically the same. But as these conjectures, after such a lapse of time, are somewhat vague, and the subject of them is perhaps yet within the reach of our researches, it is to be hoped that some method may be fallen upon of procuring an exact copy of this inscription.

The other circumstance is, that though the outward form of the Pagodas is complete, the ultimate design of them has manifestly not been accomplished,

[* Since deciphered by Dr. Babington, see *infra*.]

but seems to have been defeated by some extraordinary convulsion of nature. For the western side of the most northerly one is excavated to the depth of four or five feet, and a row of pillars left on the outside to support the roof; but here the work has been stopped, and an uniform rent of about four inches breadth has been made throughout the solid rock, and appears to extend to its foundations, which are probably at a prodigious depth below the surface of the ground. That this rent has happened since the work began, or while it was carrying on, cannot be doubted; for the marks of the mason's tools are perfectly visible in the excavated part on both sides of the rent, in such a manner as to show plainly that they have been divided by it. Nor is it reasonable to suppose that such a work would ever have been designed, or begun, upon a rock that had previously been rent in two.

Nothing less than an earthquake, and that a violent one, could apparently have produced such a fissure in the solid rock: and that this has been the case in point of fact, may be gathered from other circumstances, which it is necessary to mention in an account of this curious place.

The great rock above described is at some small distance from the sea, perhaps fifty or an hundred yards,* and in that space the Hindu village before mentioned stood in 1776. But close to the sea are the remains of a Pagoda, built of brick,† and dedicated to *Siva*, the greatest part of which has evidently been swallowed up by that element; for the door of the innermost apartment, in which the idol is placed, and

[* Would be more correctly estimated at half a mile.]
[† A mistake: it is built of stone.]

before which there are always two or three spacious courts surrounded with walls, is now washed by the waves; and the pillar used to discover the meridian at the time of founding the Pagoda*† is seen standing at some distance in the sea. In the neighbourhood of this building there are some detached rocks, washed also by the waves, on which there appear sculptures, though now much worn and defaced. And the natives of the place declared to the writer of this account, that the more aged people among them remembered to have seen the tops of several Pagodas far out in the sea, which being covered with copper (probably gilt) were particularly visible at sunrise, as their shining surface used then to reflect the sun's rays, but that now that effect was no longer produced, as the copper had since become incrusted with mould and verdigris.‡

These circumstances look much like the effects of a sudden inundation; and the rent in the rock above described makes it reasonable to conjecture that an earthquake may have caused the sea to overflow its boundaries, and that these two formidable enemies may have joined to destroy this once magnificent city. The account which the Brahmans, natives of the place, gave of its origin and downfall, partly, it should seem, on the authority of the Mahâbhârata, and partly on that of later records, at the same time that it countenances this idea, contains some other curious particulars, which may seem to render it worthy of attention. Nor ought it to be rejected on account of that

* See Voyage du M. Gentil, Vol. I., page 158.

[† More probably a flag-staff, *dhvajastambha*. It has been taken by some for a *lingam*, which is manifestly an error.—cp. Bp. Heber's Journal and Bruce's Scenes and Sights in the East.]

[‡ Cp. Gubbins, *infra*.]

fabulous garb, in which all nations, but especially those of the East, have always clad the events of early ages.

"Hiranyàksha (said they) was a gigantic prince, "that rolled up the earth into a shapeless mass, and "carried it down to the abyss, whither Vishnu fol- "lowed him in the shape of an hog, killed him with "his tusks, and replaced the earth in its original "situation. The younger brother of Hiranyàksha "was Hiranyakasipu, who succeeded him in his king- "dom, and refused to do homage to Vishnu. He "had a son named Prahlâda, who at an early age "openly disapproved this part of his father's conduct, "being under the tuition of Sukrâchârya. His father "persecuted him on this account, banished him, and "even sought to kill him, but was prevented by "the interposition of heaven, which appeared on the "side of Prahlâda. At length, Hiranyakasipu was "softened, and recalled his son to his court, where, "as he sat in full assembly, he began again to argue "with him against the supremacy of Vishnu, boasted "that he himself was lord of all the visible world, "and asked what Vishnu could pretend to more. "Prahlâda replied, that Vishnu had no fixed abode, "but was present everywhere. Is he, said his father, "in that pillar? Yes, returned Prahlâda. Then let "him come forth, said Hiranyakasipu; and, rising "from his seat, struck the pillar with his foot; upon "which Vishnu, in the Narasimha Avatára, that is "to say, with a body like a man, but an head like a "lion, came out of the pillar, and tore Hiranyakasipu "in pieces. Vishnu then fixed Prahlâda on his "father's throne; and his reign was a mild and vir- "tuous one, and as such was a contrast to that of "his father. He left a son named Namuchi,* who "inherited his power and his virtues, and was the "father of Bali, the founder of the once magni- "ficent city of Mahâbalipura, the situation of which "is said to be described in the following verse, taken "from the Mahâbhârata :—

गङ्गायाः दक्षिणे भागे योजनानां शतद्वयं ।
पञ्चयोजनमात्रेण पूर्वाब्धेश्चैव पश्चिमे ॥

The sense of which is literally this :—

"South of the Ganges two hundred yojanas,
"Five yojanas† westward from the eastern sea."

Such is the Brahman account of the origin of this place. The sequel of its history, according to them, is as follows :—

"The son of Bali was Bânâsura, who is repre- "sented as a giant with a thousand hands. Aniruddha, "the son‡ of Krishna, came to his court in disguise, "and seduced his daughter; which produced a war, "in the course of which Aniruddha was taken prisoner, "and brought to Mahâbalipura;§ upon which Krishna "came in person from his capital Dvârakâ, and laid "siege to the place. Siva guarded the gates, and "fought for Bânâsura, who worshipped him with

[* An error : Virochana was the son of Prahlâda, and father of Bali; Namuchi was the son of Viprachitti by Simhikâ, sister of Hiranya-kasipu.—See the Vishnupurâna.]

† The *yojana* is a measure often mentioned in the Sanscrit books, and, according to some accounts, is equal to nine, according to others twelve English miles. But at that rate the distance here mentioned, between this place and the Ganges, is prodigiously exaggerated, and will carry us far south of Ceylon. This, however, is not surprising in an Hindu poem; but, from the second line it seems pretty clear that this city, at the time this verse was composed, must have stood at a great distance from the sea.

[‡ Aniruddha was the grandson, not the son, of Krishna.]

[§ *Sonitapura*, according to the Vishnupurâna—cp. Wilson's trans., Book V. chap. 33.]

"his thousand hands; but K*ri*sh*n*a found means to "overthrow *S*iva, and having taken the city, cut off "all Bâ*n*âsura's hands, except two, with which he "obliged him to do him homage. He continued in "subjection to K*ri*sh*n*a till his death; after which a "long period ensued, in which no mention is any "where made of this place, till a prince arose, whose "name was Malêcheren,* who restored the kingdom "to great splendour, and enlarged and beautified "the capital. But in his time the calamity is said "to have happened by which the city was entirely "destroyed; and the cause and manner of it have "been wrapped up by the Brahmans in the following "fabulous narration. Malêcheren, (say they,) in an "excursion which he made one day alone, and in dis-"guise, came to a garden in the environs of the city, "where was a fountain so inviting, that two celestial "nymphs had come down to bathe there. The Râjâ "became enamoured of one of them, who condes-"cended to allow of his attachment to her; and she "and her sister-nymph used thenceforward to have "frequent interviews with him in that garden. On "one of those occasions, they brought with them a "male inhabitant of the heavenly regions, to whom "they introduced the Râjâ; and between him and "Malêcheren a strict friendship ensued; in conse-"quence of which he agreed, at the Râjâ's earnest "request, to carry him in disguise to see the court "of the divine Indra, a favour never before granted "to any mortal. The Râjâ returned from thence "with new ideas of splendour and magnificence, which "he immediately adopted in regulating his court, and "his retinue, and in beautifying his seat of govern-

[* The same as Mallêsudu? cp. Taylor, *infra*.]

"ment. By this means Mahâbalipura became soon "celebrated beyond all the cities of the earth; and "an account of its magnificence having been brought "to the gods assembled at the court of Indra, their "jealousy was so much excited at it, that they sent "orders to the God of the Sea to let loose his billows, "and overflow a place which impiously pretended to "vie in splendour with their celestial mansions. This "command he obeyed, and the city was at once over-"flowed by that furious element, nor has it ever "since been able to rear its head."

Such is the mode in which the Brahmans choose to account for the signal overthrow of a place devoted to their wretched superstitions.

It is not, however, improbable, that the rest of this history may contain, like the mythology of Greece and Rome, a great deal of real matter of fact, though enveloped in dark and figurative representations. Through the disguise of these we may discern some imperfect records of great events, and of revolutions that have happened in remote times; and they perhaps merit our attention the more, as it is not likely that any records of ancient Hindu history exist but in this obscure and fantastic dress. Their poets seem to have been their only historians, as well as divines; and whatever they relate, is wrapped up in this burlesque garb, set off, by way of ornament, with circumstances hugely incredible and absurd, and all this without any date, and in no other order or method, than such as the poet's fancy suggested, and found most convenient. Nevertheless, by comparing names and grand events, recorded by them, with those interspersed in the histories of other nations, and by calling in the assistance of ancient monuments, coins, and inscriptions, as occasion shall offer, some probable conjectures, at least, if not important discoveries, may, it is hoped, be made on these interesting subjects. It is much to be regretted, that a blind zeal, attended with a total want of curiosity, in the Muhammadan governors of this country, has been so hostile to the preservation of Hindu monuments and coins. But a spirit of inquiry among Europeans may yet perhaps be successful; and an instance, which relates to the place above described, though in itself a subject of regret, leaves room to hope that futurity may yet have in store some useful discoveries. The *Kázi* of Madras, who had often occasion to go to a place in the neighbourhood of Mahâbalipura, assured the writer of this account, that within his remembrance a ryot of those parts had found, in ploughing his ground, a pot of gold and silver coins, with characters on them which no one in those parts, Hindu or Muhammadan, was able to decipher. He added, however, that all search for them would now be vain, for they had doubtless been long ago devoted to the crucible, as, in their original form, no one there thought them of any value.

The inscription on the Pagoda mentioned above, is an object which, in this point of view, appears to merit great attention. That the conjecture, however, which places it among the languages of Siam, may not seem in itself chimerical, the following passages from some authors of repute are here inserted, to show that the idea of a communication having formerly subsisted between that country and the coast of Coromandel, is by no means without foundation; nay, that there is some affinity, even at this day, between the Pàli and some of the Hindu languages: and that the same mode of worship seems formerly to have prevailed in the Deccan, which is now used by the Siamese.

Monsieur de la Loubère, in his excellent account of Siam, speaks thus of the origin of the Pàli language:—

"The Siamese, says he, do not mention any coun-"try where the Pàli language, which is that of their "laws and their religion, is at present in use. They "suppose, indeed, on the report of some among them, "who have been on the Coast of Coromandel, that "it bears some resemblance to some of the dialects "of that country; but they at the same time allow, "that the character in which it is written is not known "but among themselves. The secular Missionaries "settled at Siam believe that this language is not "entirely a dead one; because they have seen in "their hospital a man from the neighbourhood of "Cape Comorin, who mixed several Pàli words in "his discourse, declaring that they were in use in his "country, and that he himself had never studied nor "knew any other than his mother-tongue. They at "the same time mention, as matter of certainty, that "the religion of the Siamese comes from those parts; "as they have read in a Pàli book that Samana "Kodam,* the idol of the Siamese, was the son of a "king of Ceylon."†‡

[* The Siamese form of *Sramana* Gautama, a name applied to Buddha, signifying 'Gautama the ascetic.']

[† Buddha, according to tradition, was the son of *Suddhodana*, the king of Kapilavastu, a city and State on the borders of Nepal.]

‡ "Les Siamois ne nomment aucun Païs, où la langue Bali qui est "celle de leurs loix et de leur religion, soit aujourd'huy en usage. "Ils soupçonnent à la vérité, sur le rapport de quelques-uns d'entre

The language of the man mentioned in this passage, who came from the neighbourhood of Cape Comorin, could be no other than the Tamil; but the words here alluded to may very possibly have been derivatives from the Sanscrit, common to both that and the Pâli.

In another part of the same work, where the author treats of the history of Samana Kodam at large, on the authority of the Pâli books, he says :—

"The father of Samana Kodam, according to the "same Pâli book, was a king of Teve Lankâ, that "is to say, of the famous Ceylon."*

Here it is observable, that, while the country of Siam seems to be utterly unknown, both to the natives of Ceylon and Hindostan, Ceylon should nevertheless be so well known to the Siamese, and under the same appellation it bears in the Sanscrit. An epithet is also here prefixed to it which seems to be the same as that used by the Hindus in speaking of that island; for they also call it, in Sanscrit, Deva Lankâ, or the Sacred Lankâ. From several passages in the same work it also appears, that the Sanscrit word *mahâ*, which signifies "great" is constantly used

"eux, qui ont été a la côte de Coromandel, que la langue Balie a quel- "que ressemblance avec quelqu'un des dialects de ce pais la: mais "ils conviennent en même temps que les lettres de la langue Balie "ne sont connues que chez eux. Les Missionaires séculiers à Siam "croyent que cette langue n'est pas entièrement morte; parce qu'ils "ont vu dans leur hôpital un homme des environs du Cap de Como- "rin, qui mettoit plusieurs mots Balis dans son langage, assurant "qu'ils etoient en usage en son pais, et que luy n'avoit jamais etudié, "et ne savoit que sa langue maternelle. Ils donnent d'ailleurs pour "certain que la religion des Siamois vient de ces quartiers la, parce "qu'ils ont lu dans un livre Balie que Sommonacodom que les Sia- "mois adorent, etoit fils d'un Roy de l'isle de Ceylone."

* "Le pere de Sommonacodom etoit, selon ce meme livre Bali, un Roy de Teve Lanca, c'est a dire un Roy de la célèbre Ceylan."

in the Páli language in the same sense. And the names of the days of the week are most of them the same in Sanscrit and in Páli, as may be seen in the following comparison of them :—

Sanscrit.	Páli.*	
Áditya-vára,	Van Athit,	Sunday.
Soma-vára,	Van† Tchán,	Monday.
Mańgala-vára,	Van Angkaan,	Tuesday.
Budha-vára,	Van Pout,	Wednesday.
Brihaspati-vára,	Van Prahout,	Thursday.
Sukra-vára,	Van Souc,	Friday.
Śani-vára,	Van Sáoa,	Saturday.

The same author gives, in another place, an account of a pretended print of a foot on a rock, which is an object of worship to the Siamese, and is called Prâbât, or the venerable foot. For *prá*, in Páli he says, signifies "venerable," which agrees with *pará-para* and *parameshtha* in Sanscrit; and *bát* in the same tongue is a foot, as *páda* in Sanscrit. After which he goes on to say :—

"We know that in the island of Ceylon, there "is a pretended print of a human foot, which has "long been held in great veneration. It represents, "doubtless, the left foot; for the Siamese say that "Samana Kodam set his right foot on their Prâbât "and his left foot at Lanká."‡§

From Knox's History of Ceylon it appears, that the impression here spoken of is upon the hill called,

[* The names given are Siamese.]

† Here one Hindu word is substituted for another; for *Chánd* in Hindustani, and *Chandra* in Sanscrit, signify the moon as well as *Soma*.

‡ "On sait que dans l'isle de Ceylan, il y a un prétendu vestige de "pié humain, que depuis long temps y est en grande vénération. Il "représente sans doute le pié gauche; car les Siamois disent que "Sommonacodom posa le pié droit à leur prabat, et le pié gauche à "Lanca."

[§ Cp. Spence Hardy's Manual of Budhism, p. 212.]

by the Singhalese, "Hamalell;" by Europeans, "Adam's Peak;" and that the natives believe it to be the footstep of their great idol Buddou, between the worship of whom, as described by Knox, and that of Samana Kodam, as related by M. de la Loubère, there is a striking resemblance in many particulars, which it may be proper here to enumerate.

1*st.*—Besides the footsteps above mentioned, there is a kind of tree (which, from description, appears to be the Pipal tree* so well known in India) which the Singhalese hold sacred to Buddou, and the Siamese to Samana Kodam; insomuch that the latter deem it meritorious to hang themselves upon it. The Singhalese call it Bogahah;† for *gahah*, in their language, signifies a tree; and *bo* seems to be an abbreviation of Bod or Buddou;‡ and the Siamese call it, in Pâli, Pra si Mahâ Pout, which, according to La Loubère's interpretation, signifies the tree of the great Pout.§ This he supposes to mean Mercury; for he observes that Pout, or Poot, is the name of that planet in the Pâli term for Wednesday; and in another place, he says, Pout is one of the names of Samana Kodam. It is certain that Wednesday is called the name of Bod, or Budd, in all the Hindu languages, among which the Tamil, having no *b*, begins the word with a *p*, which brings it very near the Pâli mode of writing it. It is equally certain

[* Ficus religiosa, called by Buddhists the Bodhi tree, "the tree of wisdom," because under it Gautama became Buddha "the Enlightened."—Cp. Bigandet's life of Gaudama, p. 55.]

[† The 'bo-tree.']

[‡ Fo, Bod, Buddou, Budd, Baoth, Pood, &c., are some of the numerous modes in which Gautama's appellative, Buddha, has been spelt.—See Manual of Budhism, p. 354.]

§ In vulgar Siamese they call it *Ton-pô*.

that the days of the week, in all these languages, are called after the planets in the same order as with us; and that Bod, Budd, or Pood, holds the place of Mercury. From all which it should appear that Pout, which, among the Siamese, is another name for Mercury, is itself a corruption of Buddou, who is the Samana Kodam of the Greeks. And it is singular that, according to M. de la Loubère, the mother of Samana Kodam is called, in Pâli, Mahamania,* or the great Mania, which resembles much the name of Maia, the mother of Mercury. At the same time that the Tamil termination *an*, which renders the word Poodan, creates a resemblance between this and the Woden of the Gothic nations, from which the same day of the week is denominated, and which, on that and other accounts, is allowed to be the Mercury of the Greeks.†

2ndly.—The temples of Samana Kodam are called Pihan; and round them are habitations for the priests, resembling a college; so those of Boddou are called Vihar, and the principal priests live in them as in a college. The word Vihar,‡ or, as the natives of Bengal would write it, Bihar, is Sanscrit; and Ferishtah, in his History of Bengal, says, that this name was given by the Hindus to the Province of Behar, because it was formerly so full of Brahmans, as to be, as it were, one great seminary of learning, as the word imports.

[* Mahâmâyâ, Mahâmâyâdevi, Mâyâ, or Mâyâdevi.]

[† "Much erroneous speculation has originated in confounding Budha, the son of Soma, and regent of the planet Mercury, 'he who knows,' the intelligent, with Buddha, any deified mortal, or 'he by whom the truth is known.'—Wilson's Vishnu Purâna." Spence Hardy, Manual of Budhism, p. 354 n.]

[‡ Vihâra.]

3rdly.—The Siamese have two orders of priests, and so have the worshippers of Buddou. Both the one and the other are distinguished by a yellow habit, and by another circumstance, which must be mentioned in the words of the respective authors. Knox says of the Buddou Priests, "They have the "honour of carrying the Tallipot* with the broad "end over their heads foremost, which none but the "king does." And M. de la Loubère says of the Siamese priests, "To defend themselves from the "sun they have the Talapat, which is their little "umbrella, in the form of a screen."†

The word here used is common to most of the Hindu languages, and signifies the leaf of the Palmyra tree. M. de la Loubère mentions it as a Siamese word, without seeming to know its origin or primary signification.

4thly.—The priests of Buddou, as well as those of Samana Kodam,‡ are bound to celibacy, as long as they continue in the profession; but both the one and the other are allowed to lay it down and marry.

5thly.—They both eat flesh, but will not kill the animal.

6thly.—The priests of either nation are of no particular tribe, but are chosen out of the body of the people.

These circumstances plainly show that this is a system of religion different from that of the Vedas; and some of them are totally inconsistent with the

[* Tâlapât, "palm-leaf."]

† "Pour se garentir du soleil ils ont le Talapat, qui est leur petit "parasol en forme d'écran."

[‡ The same persons: Samana Kodam (Sramana Gautama) was the Buddha, i.e. the "Enlightened." (Max Müller.) See note * at p. 17.]

principles and practice of the Brahmans. And, indeed, it is manifest, from Knox's whole account, that the religion of the Singhalese is quite distinct from that which prevails at this day among the Hindus, nor does it appear that there is such a race of men as that of the Brahmans among them. The only part in which there seems to be any agreement is in the worship of the Devatás, which has probably crept in among them from their Tamil neighbours; but that is carried on in a manner very different from the Brahmanical system, and appears to be held by the nation at large in very great contempt, if not abhorrence. Knox's account of it is this: "Their temples "(*i. e.* those of the Devatás) are, he says, called "Kôvils," which is the Tamil word for Pagoda. He then goes on to say, "A man piously disposed, "builds a small house at his own charge, which is the "temple, and himself becomes priest thereof. This "house is seldom called God's House, but most "usually Yakko,* the Devil's." But of the prevailing religion he speaks in very different terms, and describes it as carried on with much parade and splendour and attended with marks of great antiquity. "The "pagodas, or temples of their gods, says he, are so "many that I cannot number them. Many of them "are of rare and exquisite work, built of hewn stone, "engraven with images and figures; but by whom, "and when, I could not attain to know, the inhabi-"tants themselves being ignorant therein. But sure "I am, they were built by far more ingenious artifi-"cers than the Chingelays† that now are on the land. "For the Portuguese, in their invasions, have defaced "some of them, which there is none found that hath

[* Yaksha.] [† Singhalese.]

"skill enough to repair to this day." In another place, he says, "Here are some ancient writings, "engraven, upon rocks, which puzzle all that see "them. There are divers great rocks in divers parts "in Cande Uda,* and in the northern parts. These "rocks are cut deep with great letters for the space "of some yards, so deep that they may last to the "world's end. Nobody can read them, or make any-"thing of them. I have asked Malabars and Gen-"toos, as well as Chingelays and Moors, but none of "them understood them. There is an ancient temple, "Goddiladenni in Yattanour, stands by a place where "there are of these letters." From all which the antiquity of the nation and their religion is sufficiently evident; and from other passages it is plain, that the worship of Buddou, in particular, has been from remote times a very eminent part of that religion; for the same author, speaking of the tree at Anurodgburro,† in the northern part of the island, which is sacred to Buddou, says, "The due perform-"ance of this worship they reckon not a little meri-"torious; insomuch that as they report, ninety "kings have reigned there successively, where, by "the ruins that still remain, it appears they spared "not for pains and labour, to build temples and high "monuments to the honour of this god, as if they "had been born to hew rocks and great stones, and "lay them up in heaps. These kings are now happy "spirits, having merited it by these labours." And again he says, "For this god, above all other, they "seem to have an high respect and devotion," &c.

And from other authorities it will appear, that this worship has formerly been by no means confined to

[* Kandy.] [† Anurâdhapura.]

Ceylon, but has prevailed in several parts of India prior to that of the Brahmans; nay, that this has been the case even so late as the ninth and twelfth centuries of the Christian Æra.

In the well-known* Anciennes Relations, translated from the Arabic by that eminent orientalist Eusebius Renaudot, the Arabian traveller gives this account of the custom of dancing-women, which continues to this day in the Deccan, but is not known among the Hindus of Bengal, or Hindustan Proper.

"There are in India public women, called women "of the idol, and the origin of this custom is this: "when a woman has made a vow for the purpose of "having children, if she brings into the world a pretty "daughter, she carries it to Bod, (so they call the "idol which they adore,) and leaves it with him."†

This is a pretty just account of this custom, as it prevails at this day in the Deccan; for children are, indeed, devoted to this profession by their parents, and when they grow up in it they are called, in Tamil,‡ *Devadási*, or female slaves of the idol. But it is evident they have changed their master since this Arabian account was written, for there is no idol of the name of Bod now worshipped there. And the circumstance of this custom being unknown in other parts of India, would lead one to suspect that the Brahmans, on introducing their system of religion

* Anciennes Relations des Indes et de la Chine, de deux voyageurs Mohametans, qui y allèrent dans le neuvième siècle. Paris, 1718, 8vo.

† "Il y a dans les Indes des femmes publiques, appellées femmes "de l'idole; l'origine de cette coustume est telle: Lorsqu'une femme a "fait un voeu pour avoir des enfans, si elle met au monde une belle "fille, elle l'apporte au *Bod*, c'est ainsi qu'ils appellent l'idole qu'ils "adorent, auprès duquel elle la laisse, &c. Anc. Rel. p. 109.

[‡ The word is Sanscrit, and common to the vernacular languages.]

into that country, had thought fit to retain this part of the former worship, as being equally agreeable to themselves and their new disciples.

The same Arabian travellers give us an account of a very powerful race of Hindu kings, according to them, indeed, the most powerful in India, who then reigned on the Malabar Coast with the title of Balhâra.* Their dominion appears to have extended over Guzerat, and the greatest part, if not the whole, of the ancient kingdom of Vijayapûr. For the Arabian geographer quoted by M. Renaudot makes Nabelvàrah the metropolis of these princes, which is, doubtless, Nahervalah, the ancient capital of Guzerat; though M. Renaudot seems not to have known that place; and the rest of the description sufficiently shows the great extent of their dominion southward. M. D'Anville speaks of this race of kings on the authority of the Arabian geographer Edrisi, who wrote in the twelfth century, according to whom it appears that their religion was, even so late as that period, not the Brahmanical, but that of which we are now speaking. M. D'Anville's words are these: "Edrisi acquaints "us with the religion which this prince professed in "saying, that his worship was addressed to Bodda, "who, according to St. Jerome and Clemens Alexan-"drinus, was the founder of the sect of the Gym-"nosophists, in like manner as the Brahmans were "used to attribute their institution to Brahmâ."†

[* Cp. Sir H. M. Elliot's History of India, as told by its own Historians, pp. 85—89.]

† "L'Edrisi nous instruit sur la religion que professoit ce Prince, en "disant que son culte s'adressoit à Bodda, que selon St. Jerome and "St. Clement d'Alexandrie, avoit été l'instituteur des Gymnoso-"phistes comme les Brachmanes rapportoient à Brahma leur institut." Ant. Geog. de L'Inde, p. 94.

The authority of Clemens Alexandrinus is also cited on the same subject by Relandus in his 11th Dissertation, where, treating of the language of Ceylon, he explains the word Vihàra, above spoken of, in these terms :—

"Vihâra signifies a temple of their principal god "Buddou, who, as Clemens Alexandrinus has long "ago observed, was worshipped as a god by the "Hindus."*

After the above quotations, the following extract from the voyage of that inquisitive and ingenious traveller M. Gentil, published in 1779, is given as a further and very remarkable illustration of this subject :—

"This system is also that of the Brahmans of our "time; it forms the basis of that religion, which "they have brought with them into the southern "parts of the Peninsula of Hindustan into Madura, "Tanjore, and Mysore.

"There was then in those parts of India, and "principally on the Coast of Coromandel and "Ceylon, a sort of worship, the precepts of which we "are quite unacquainted with. The god, Baouth, "of whom at present they know no more in India "than the name, was the object of this worship; but "it is now totally abolished, except that there may "possibly yet be found some families of Indians "who have remained faithful to Baouth and do not "acknowledge the religion of the Brahmans, and who "are on that account separated from, and despised "by the other castes.

*"*Vehar*, templum dei primarii Buddoo [illegible] quem Indos ut "Deum venerari jam olim notavit Clemens Alexandrinus. Strom. lib. "1. p. 223. Rel. Diss. pars tertia, p. 85.

"I have not, indeed, heard that there are any such "families in the neighbourhood of Pondicherry; "but there is a circumstance well worthy of remark, "which none of the travellers that have treated of "the Coast of Coromandel and Pondicherry seem to "have noticed. It is this, that at a short league's "distance to the south of this town, in the plain of "Virapatnam, and pretty near the river, we find a "statue of granite very hard and beautiful. This "statue, which is from three feet to three and a half "in height, is sunk in the sand to the waist, and "weighs doubtless many thousand weight; it is, as "it were, abandoned in the midst of this extensive "plain. I cannot give a better idea of it, than by "saying, that it exactly agrees with, and resembles "the Samana Kodam of the Siamese; its head is of "the same form, it has the same features, its arms "are in the same attitude, and its ears are exactly "similar. The form of this divinity, which has "certainly been made in the country, and which "in no respect resembles the present idols of the "Gentoos, struck me as I passed this plain. I made "various inquiries concerning this singular figure, "and the Tamilians, one and all, assured me that "this was the god Baouth, who was now no longer "regarded, for that his worship and his festivals had "been abolished ever since the Brahmans had made "themselves masters of the people's faith."*

* "Ce système est aussi celui des Brames de nos jours; il fait la "base de la religion qu'ils ont apportée dans le sud de la presqu' isle "de l'Indostan, le Madure, le Tanjaour, et le Maissour.

"Il y avoit alors dans ces parties de l'Inde, & principalement à la "Côte de Coromandel & à Ceylan, un culte dont on ignore absolument "les dogmes: le Dieu Baouth, dont on ne connoit aujourd'hui, dans "l'Inde, que le nom, etoit l'objet de ce culte; mais il est tout-a-fait

M. Gentil then goes on to say a good deal more upon this subject, in the course of which he supposes that this deity is the Fo of the Chinese, whose worship by their own accounts, was brought from India. And, indeed, the abridgement of the name Pout, mentioned in a note of this paper, which the vulgar Siamese reduce to the single syllable Po, seems to countenance this opinion. But as this is foreign to our present purpose, and the above passages, it is hoped, are sufficient to establish what was proposed, it seems high time to take leave of this subject, with an apology for that prolixity which is inseparable from this kind of discussion.

17th June, 1784.

"aboli, si ce n'est qu'il se trouve encore quelques familles d'Indiens "séparées & méprisées des autres castes, qui sont restées fidèles à "Baouth, & qui ne reconnoissent point la religion des Brames.

"Je n'ai pas entendu dire qu'il y ait de ces familles aux environs de "Pondichery; cependant, une chose tres digne de remarque, & à "laquelle aucun des voyageurs qui parlent de la Côte de Coromandel "& de Pondichery, n'ont fait attention, est que l'on trouve à une "petite lieue au sud de cette Ville, dans la plaine de Virapatnam, "assez près de la rivière, une statue de Granit très dur & très beau: "cette statue, d'environ trois pieds a trois pieds & demi de hauteur, "est enfoncée dans le sable jusqu'à la ceinture, & pese sans doute "plusieurs milliers; elle est comme abandonnée au milieu de cette "vaste plaine: je ne peux mieux en donner une idée, qu'en disant "qu'elle est exactement conforme & ressemblante a Sommonacodom "des Siamois; c'est la même forme de tête, ce sont les mêmes traits "dans le visage, c'est la même attitude dans les bras, & les oreilles "sont absolument semblables. La forme de cette divinité, qui cer- "tainement a été faite dans le pays, & qui ne ressemble en rien aux "divinités actuelles des Gentils, m'avoit frappé lorsque je passai dans "cette plaine; je fis diverses informations sur cette figure singulière, "les Tamoults m'assurèrent tous que c'etoit Baouth qu' on ne regar- "doit plus; que son culte & ses fêtes etoient cessées depuis que les "Brames s'etoient rendus les maîtres de la croyance du peuple."

II.—Some *account of the Sculptures at Mahâbalipuram; usually called the Seven Pagodas.* By J. Goldingham, Esq.

[From the Asiatic Researches, Vol. V. 1798.]

THESE curious remains of antiquity, situate near the sea, are about thirty-eight English miles southerly from Madras. A distant view presents merely a rock, which, on a near approach, is found deserving of particular examination. The attention, passing over the smaller objects, is first arrested by a Hindu pagoda, covered with sculpture, and hewn from a single mass of rock; being about twenty-six feet in height, nearly as long, and about half as broad. Within is the *lingam,** and a long inscription on the wall, in characters unknown.

Near this structure, the surface of the rock, about ninety feet in extent, and thirty in height, is covered with figures in bas-relief. A gigantic figure of the god *Krishna* is the most conspicuous, with Arjuna his favourite, in the Hindu attitude of prayer; but so void of flesh, as to present more the appearance of a skeleton than the representation of a living person. Below is a venerable figure, said to be

[* This temple now contains an image of Ganesa.—Cp. Babington, *infra.*]

the father of Arjuna;* both figures proving the sculptor possessed no inconsiderable skill. Here are the representations of several animals, and of one which the Brahmans name *siṁha*, or lion; but by no means a likeness of that animal, wanting the peculiar characteristic, the mane. Something intended to represent this is, indeed, visible, which has more the effect of spots. It appears evident, the sculptor was by no means so well acquainted with the figure of the lion as with that of the elephant and monkey, both being well represented in this group. This scene, I understand, is taken from the Mahâbhârata, and exhibits the principal persons whose actions are celebrated in that work.

Opposite, and surrounded by a wall of stone, are pagodas of brick, said to be of great antiquity. Adjoining is an excavation in the rock, the massy roof seemingly supported by columns, not unlike those in the celebrated cavern in the Island of Elephanta, but have been left unfinished. This was probably intended as a place of worship. A few paces onward is another, and a more spacious, excavation, now used, and I suppose originally intended, as a shelter for travellers. A scene of sculpture fronts the entrance, said to represent Krishna attending the herds of Ananda.† One of the group represents a man diverting an infant, by playing on a flute, and holding the instrument as we do.‡ A gigantic figure of the god, with the *gopis*, and several good representations of nature, are observed. The columns

[* A Brahman on the spot states that this figure represents Dronâchâryya, the preceptor of the Kauravas and Pândavas.]

[† Nanda?]

[‡ Krishna.]

supporting the roof are of different orders: the base of one is the figure of a Sphynx. On the pavement is an inscription, (see Inscript.) Near is the almost deserted village, which still retains the ancient name Mahâbalipuram. The few remaining Brahmans visit the traveller, and conduct him over the rock.

In the way up the rock a prodigious circular stone is passed under, so placed by nature on a smooth and sloping surface, that you are in dread of its crushing you before you clear it. The diameter of this stone is twenty-seven feet. The top of the rock is strewed with fragments of bricks, the remains, as you are informed, of a palace standing on this site. A rectangular polished slab, about ten feet in length, with the figure of a *siṁha* couchant, at the south end, is shewn you as the couch of the Dharmarâja. A short way further, the bath used by the females of the palace is pointed out. A tale I suspect fabricated by the Brahmans to amuse the traveller. That some of their own caste had chosen this spot, retired among rocks, and difficult of access, to reside in, and that the bath, as it is called, which is only a rough stone hollowed, was their reservoir for water, would have an air of probability. The couch seems to have been cut from a stone accidentally placed in its present situation, and never to have made a part of the internal furniture of a building. The *siṁha*, if intended as a lion, is equally imperfect with the figures of the same animal before mentioned.

Descending over immense beds of stone, you arrive at a spacious excavation; a temple dedicated to Siva, who is represented, in the middle compartment, of a large stature and with four arms; the left foot rests on a bull couchant; a small figure of

Brahmá on the right hand; another of Vishnu on the left; where also the figure of his goddess Pârvati is observed. At one end of the temple is a gigantic figure of Vishnu, sleeping on an enormous cobra-da-capella with several heads, and so disposed as to form a canopy over the head of the god.* At the opposite end is the goddess Sivâ with eight arms, mounted on a *simha*. Opposed to her is a gigantic figure with a buffalo's head and human body. Between these is a human figure, suspended with the head downwards. The goddess is represented with several warlike weapons, and some armed dwarf attendants; while the monster is armed with a club. In the character of Durgá, or protector of the virtuous, the goddess is rescuing from the Yamarâja† (the figure with the buffalo's head) the suspended figure fallen improperly into his hands. The figure and action of the goddess are executed in a masterly and spirited style. Over this temple, at a considerable elevation, is a smaller, wrought from a single mass of stone. Here is seen a slab, similar to the Dharmarája's couch. Adjoining is a temple, in the rough, and a large mass of rock, the upper part roughly fashioned for a pagoda. If a conclusion may be drawn from these unfinished works, an uncommon and astonishing perseverance was exerted in finishing the structures here; and the more so, from the stone being a species of granite, and extremely hard.‡

The village contains but few houses, mostly inhabited by Brahmans, the number of whom has, how-

[* *Sesha*, "the king of the serpent race as a large thousand-headed snake, at once the couch and canopy of Vishnu, and the upholder of the world, which rests on one of his heads."—Wilson.]

[† Should be Mahishásura.]

[‡ Cp. Gabbius, *infra*.]

ever decreased of late, owing to a want of the means of subsisting. The remains of several stone edifices are seen here; and a large tank, lined with steps of stone. A canopy for the pagoda attracts the attention, as by no means wanting in magnificence or elegance.* It is supported by four columns, with base and capital, about twenty-seven feet in height; the shaft tapering regularly upwards is composed of a single stone, though not round, but sixteen-sided; measuring at bottom about five and a half feet.

East of the village, and washed by the sea, which, perhaps, would have entirely demolished it before now but for a defence of large stones in front, is a pagoda of stone, containing the *lingam*, and dedicated to *Siva*. Besides the usual figures within, one of a gigantic stature is observed stretched out on the ground, and represented as secured in that position.† This the Brahmans tell you was designed for a Rájá, who was thus secured by Vishnu; probably alluding to a prince of the Vishnu caste having conquered the country, and taken its prince. The surf here breaks far out over, as the Brahmans inform you, the ruins in the city, which was incredibly large and magnificent. Many of the masses of stone near the shore appear to have been wrought. A Brahman, about fifty years of age, a native of the place, whom I have had an opportunity of conversing with since my arrival at Madras, informed me his grandfather had frequently mentioned having seen the gilt tops of

[* The Dolotsava Mandapam, 'porch of the swinging festival,' where the image of the god used annually to be brought out and swung before the people.]

[† It is an image of Vishnu, in a recumbent position. The folds of his garment were apparently mistaken for fetters.—Cp. other notices, *infra*.]

five pagodas in the surf, no longer visible. In the account of this place by Mr. William Chambers, in the first volume of the Asiatic Researches, we find mention of a brick pagoda, dedicated to *Siva*, and washed by the sea;* this is no longer visible; but as the Brahmans have no recollection of such a structure, and as Mr. Chambers wrote from memory, I am inclined to think the pagoda of stone mentioned above to be the one he means. However, it appears from good authorities that the sea on this part of the coast is encroaching by very slow, but no less certain steps, and will perhaps in a lapse of ages entirely hide these magnificent ruins.

About a mile to the southward are other structures of stone, of the same order as those north, but having been left unfinished, at first sight appear different: the southernmost of these is about forty feet in height, twenty-nine in breadth, and nearly the same in length, hewn from a single mass: the outside is covered with sculpture, (for an account of which see Inscriptions:) the next is also cut from one mass of stone, being in length about forty-nine feet, in breadth and height twenty-five, and is rent through the middle from the top to the bottom; a large fragment from one corner is observed on the ground. No account is preserved of the powerful cause which produced this destructive effect. Beside these, are three smaller structures of stone. Here is also the *simha*, or lion, very large, but, except in size, I can observe no difference from the figures of the same animal northerly. Near the *simha* is an elephant of stone about nine feet in height, and

[* See page 10, *supra*.]

large in proportion. Here, indeed, we observe the true figure and character of the animal.

The Brahman before mentioned informed me that their Purāṇas contained no account of any of the structures here described, except the stone pagodas near the sea and the pagodas of brick at the village, built by Dharmarāja and his brothers. He, however, gave me the following traditional account: That a northern prince (perhaps one of the conquerors) about one thousand years ago was desirous of having a great work executed, but the Hindu sculptors and masons refused to execute it on the terms he offered. Attempting force I suppose, they, in number about four thousand, fled with their effects from his country hither, where they resided four or five years, and in this interval executed these magnificent works. The prince at length discovering them, prevailed on them to return, which they did, leaving the works unfinished as they appear at present.*

To those who know the nature of these people, this account will not appear improbable. At present we sometimes hear of all the individuals of a particular branch of trade deserting their houses, because the hand of power has treated them somewhat roughly; and we observe like circumstances continually in miniature. Why the Brahmans resident on the spot keep this account secret, I cannot determine; but am led to suppose they have an idea, the more they can envelope the place in mystery the more people will be tempted to visit and investigate, by which means they profit considerably.

[*Cp. Gubbins, *infra*.]

The difference of style in the architecture of these structures, and those on the coast hereabouts, (with exceptions to the pagodas of brick at the village, and that of stone near the sea, both mentioned in the Purāṇas, and which are not different,) tends to prove that the artists were not of this country; and the resemblance of some of the figures and pillars to those in the Elephanta cave, seems to indicate they were from the northward.* The fragments of bricks, at the top of the rock, may be the remains of habitations raised in this place of security by the fugitives in question. Some of the inscriptions, however, (all of which were taken by myself with much care,) may throw further light on this subject.

INSCRIPTIONS AT MAHABALIPURAM.†

On the lower Division of the Southern Structure and the Eastern Face.

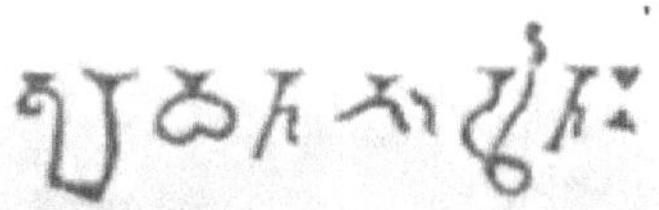

This inscription is above a figure apparently female, but with only *one* breast, (as at the cave in *Elephanta* Island.)‡ Four arms are observed; in one of the hands a battle-axe, a snake coiled up on the right side.

[* "There is nothing here of which the prototype cannot be traced in the caves of the north. In plan and design they resemble the Hindu series at Ellora, though many of their details are only to be found at Ajunta and Salsette."—Fergusson, Jour. R. A. S. Vol. VIII, p. 88.]

[† Cp. Babington, *infra.*]

[‡ Arddhanárisa, a form of *Siva*, half male, half female.]

Above a male figure with four arms.

Northern Face.

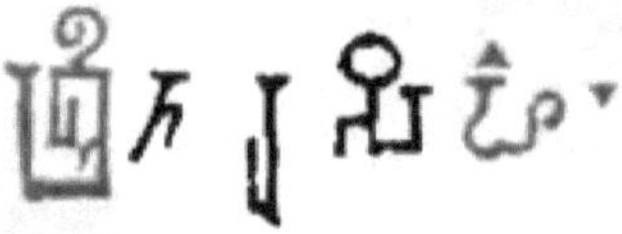

Above a male figure with four arms; a battle-axe in one of the hands.

Southern Front.

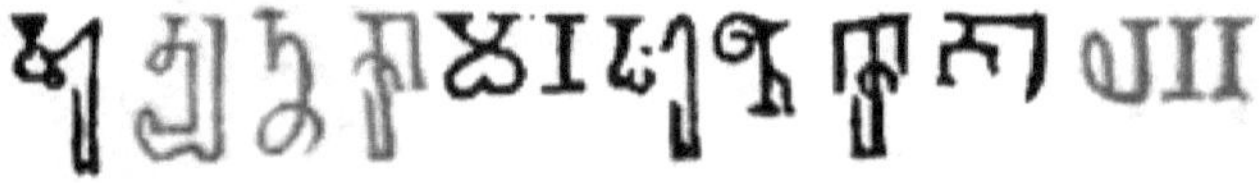

Above a male figure, with four arms.

Above a male figure.

On the Middle Division, Eastern Face.

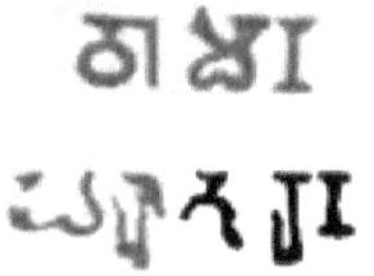

Above a male.

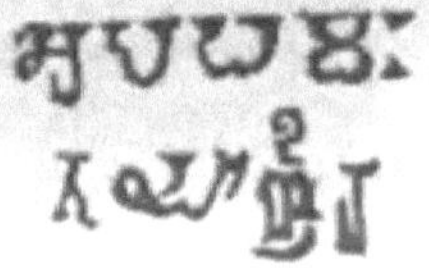

Above a male, bearing a weapon of war on the left shoulder.

Northern Face.

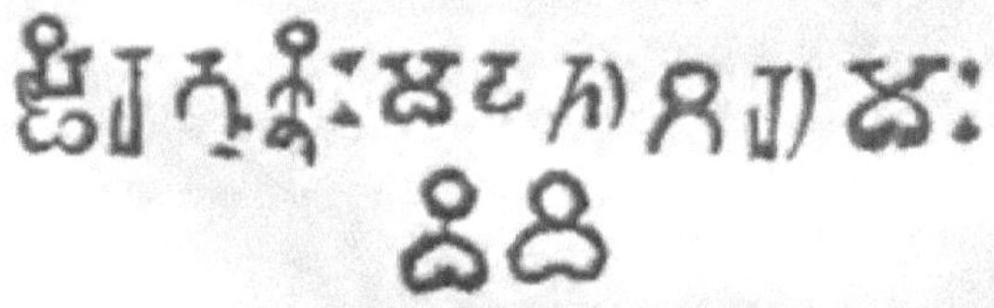

Above a male with four arms, leaning on a bull; the hair plaited, and rolled about the head; a string across the left shoulder, as the Brahmans' string of the present day.

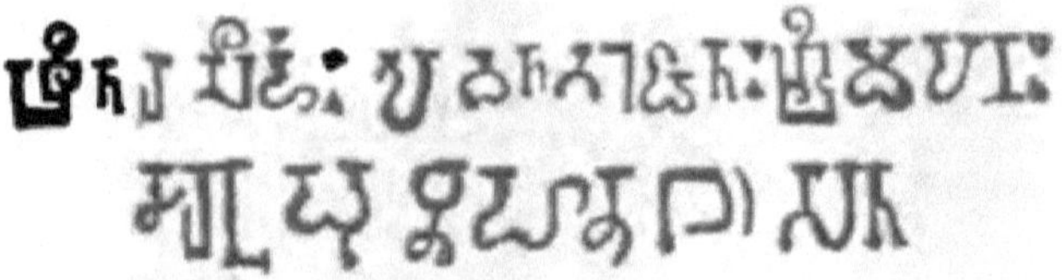

Above two figures, male and female. The former has four arms, and the string as above; is leaning on the latter, who seems to stoop from the weight. The head of the male is covered with a high cap, while the hair of the female is in the same form as that of the female figures at Elephanta.

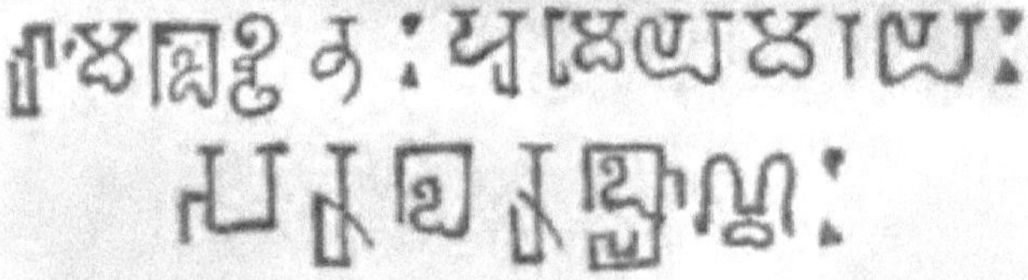

Above two figures, male and female. The former has four arms, and the string.

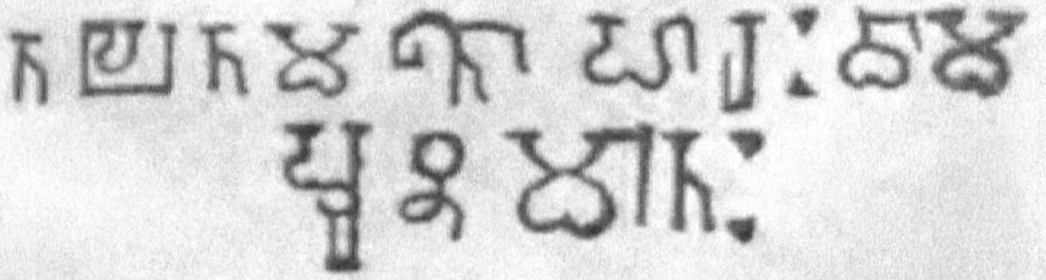

Above a male figure, with four arms, and the Brahmanical string.

Southern Face.

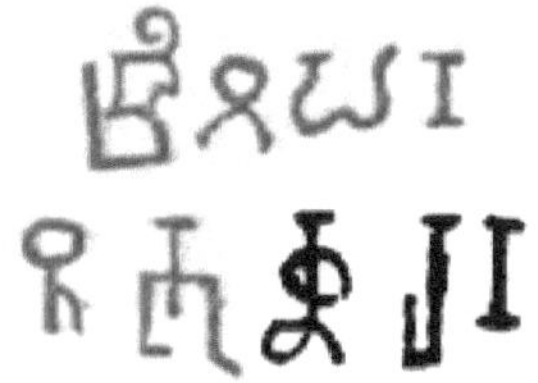

Above a male figure, with four arms.

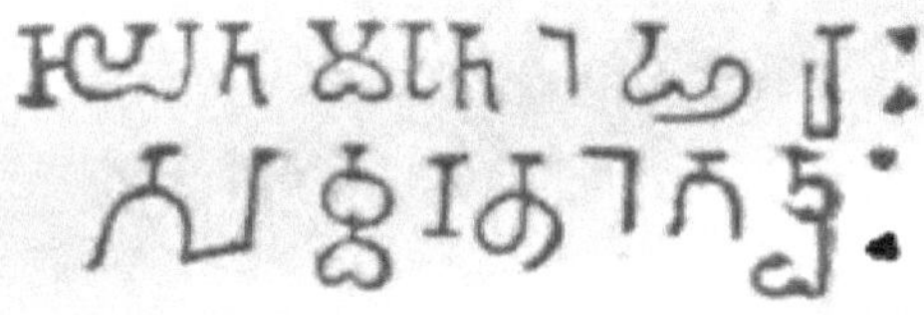

Above a male figure, with four arms, leaning on a female, seeming to stoop under the weight.

Above a male, with four arms. A sceptre appears in one hand. This inscription being very difficult to come at, is perhaps not quite correct.

Above a male figure, with four arms.

West Front.

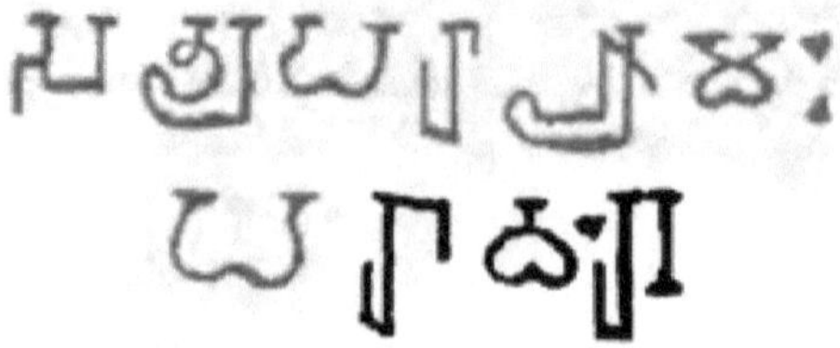

Over a male. The string over the left shoulder, and a warlike weapon on the right.

Another figure on this face, but no inscription above it.

On the Upper Division.

Each front of this division is ornamented with figures, different in some respects from those below: all, however, of the same family.

On the Eastern front is a male figure, (two arms only.) He has two strings or belts; one crossing the other over the shoulder.

Over him is the following inscription, the only one on this division.

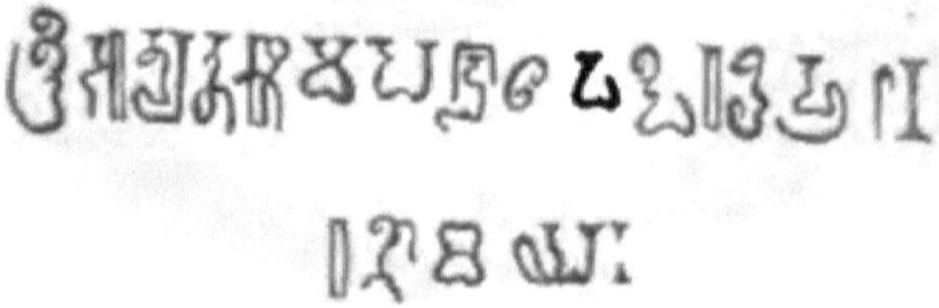

The characters of this inscription bear a strong resemblance to those of the inscription in the stone pagoda, near the village mentioned in the first part of the account of the place.

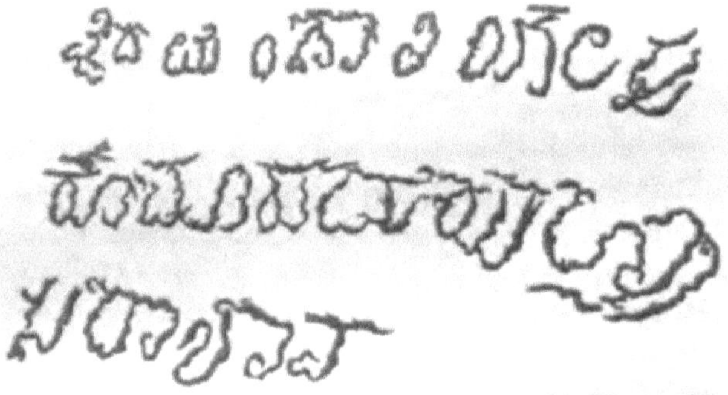

This inscription* is on the pavement of the choultry near the village, very roughly cut, and apparently by different artists from those who cut the former.

[* A scrawl in the modern Telugu character.—Cp. Babington, *infra*.]

III.—*An account of the Sculptures and Inscriptions at Mahâmalaipûr; illustrated by Plates.* By Benjamin Guy Babington, M.B., F.R.S., Sec. R.A.S.

[From Transactions of the Royal Asiatic Society, Vol. II, 1830.]

Read July 12th, 1828.

THE remains of ancient sculpture, called by Europeans the Seven Pagodas, on the Coromandel Coast, thirty-five miles south of Madras, have long attracted the attention of those who feel an interest in Hindu Archæology; and, so long ago as the year 1788, formed the subject of a paper in the first volume of the Asiatic Researches. The author, Mr. William Chambers, wrote from memory, after an interval of twelve years from the period at which he had visited the scene which he described. His account, unaccompanied as it was by drawings or fac-similes of the inscriptions, could therefore scarcely be expected to be sufficiently minute to answer any further purpose than that avowed by himself, of exciting public attention, and "giving rise to more accurate observations, and more complete discoveries on the same subject." In the fifth volume of the Asiatic Researches, published in 1798, there is a more descriptive account of these temples and excavations, written by Mr. Goldingham, a gentleman of well-known talent, on whose observations, as they were recorded on the spot, we may with confidence rely.

Mrs. Graham is indeed a later writer on the subject: but her remarks are desultory, and her information imperfect, as might be expected from the opportunities presenting themselves to a casual and hasty visitor. In Bishop Heber's narrative, three pages are devoted to a notice of Mahábalipúr. (Pages 216—218, vol. iii.) But the author merely follows the legends of the place, and evidently aims at nothing more than a record in his journal of his impressions on a cursory visit. The testimony, however, which this lamented prelate bears to the degree of skill displayed in these sculptures must, from his acknowledged taste, be looked upon as peculiarly valuable; and it is gratifying to one who has taken much interest in them to find, that he considered "some of the porticos, temples and bas-reliefs as very beautifully executed," and pronounced "the general merit of the work as superior to that of Elephanta."*

With these notices already before the public, it would be superfluous to occupy the attention of the Society with another detailed description of these monuments, and I shall therefore content myself with a reference to Mr. Goldingham's paper, as far as may be necessary to accomplish the objects which I have at present in view. These are, first, to convey a just notion of the merits of the principal sculptures, by means of drawings made on the spot by Mr. Andrew Hudleston and myself, several years since; and, secondly, to throw some light upon the inscriptions found among these temples.

To the legendary accounts of the Brahmans at

[* Cp. Fergusson's "Rock-cut Temples of India," London, 1864. Introduction p. xiii.]

Mahâmalaipúr, which are given at such length by Mr. Chambers and Mrs. Graham, I attach little value, because I find that they have not even preserved the memory of the language and character of the inscriptions which here abound; and because this place, in being accounted the work of the five sons of Pându, only shares a tradition common to all the antiquities of unexplained origin in the south of India. So far from believing in the tales of these Brahmans, who are obviously interested in connecting wonderful stories with the remains which they gain a livelihood by shewing to strangers, I even doubt whether Mahâmalaipúr was ever, as asserted by them, the site of a great city, now partly covered by the sea; and still more, whether the gilded summit of one of the five pagodas, said to be so covered, was visible two generations ago. Several circumstances lead me to be sceptical on these points: first, the absence of all remains of buildings,* walls, mounds of rubbish, or broken pottery, such as I have invariably found surrounding the site of other ancient cities; secondly, the fruitless attempts made by the late Mr. Ellis and Colonel Mackenzie to ascertain the existence of sunken buildings by careful soundings made off the shore; thirdly, the silence of tradition on other parts of the Coromandel Coast regarding so vast an encroachment of the sea,† and consequent loss of land, as must necessarily have taken place to effect the submersion of lofty pagodas still remaining erect, and that too since the formation of the present system of

* The small ruined brick edifice on the top of the rock can hardly be considered an exception.

[† Cp. Newbold's Summary of the Geology of Southern India. Journ. R. A. S. Vol. viii. p. 250.]

Hindu mythology, to which the existing sculptures obviously relate; fourthly, the circumstance that the authenticity of the legend must mainly depend on the name of the place as connected with the history of Mahâbali; whereas it will be shewn, when considering the inscriptions, that Mahâbalipûr is not its ancient designation; lastly, the omission of all mention of Mahâbali in the inscriptions, and of any reference to him in the sculptures.*

Although I thus reject the account of the Brahmans on the spot, I have nothing certain to offer in its room. If a conjecture however may be hazarded regarding the origin of this place, I should be inclined to believe that its sequestered situation and the picturesque position of the rocks and caves induced certain Brahmans to obtain royal grants for founding an Agrahârat† here, and that, in order to increase the sanctity of their temples, they from time to time employed stone-masons (several families of whom reside at Mahâmalaipûr, and appear to have worked the quarries of granite time immemorial) to ornament the rocks with the excavations and sculptures which we now find.

Plate I. represents the sculptured rock, which has been described by Mr. Goldingham in his second paragraph, as occupying a surface about ninety feet in extent and thirty in height, and covered with figures in bas-relief. This subject has been represented in Mrs. Graham's Journal by an etching copied from an outline belonging to Colonel Mackenzie, the inaccuracy of which will be sufficiently apparent on

[* The Asura Bali is probably represented by one of the figures in plate VI.]

[† A village granted to Brahmans.]

comparing it with my drawing, which was executed with much care and labour by my companion.

During our visit to the Seven Pagodas, we caused the earth to be removed from the lower part of this rock to its base, and thus exposed to full view some figures (see plate II., No. 1), of which the heads alone were before visible.

Not far from the rock last mentioned is the spacious chamber called the *Krishna Mandapam*, described by Mr. Goldingham in his third paragraph. Of the scene sculptured on the rock facing the entrance, Mr. Hudleston and myself made a joint drawing (see plate II., No. 2); and as this rock is going fast to decay, owing to a spring of water from above, which keeps its surface constantly wet, it is not improbable that in the course of a few years it will be entirely decomposed; it is the more desirable therefore that some record of its subject should be preserved. Several interesting particulars regarding the ancient Hindus may be gathered from this pastoral scene. The dress of the females resembles that now worn by the Neyris* and Tiyyattis† of Malabar, who are uncovered above the waist. The men, it appears, wore turbans, and the women very large ear-rings, with bangles on their hands and feet. The peculiar practice of carrying the infant on the hip, which cannot fail to attract the notice of Europeans at the present day, was then in use; and even the vertical arrangement and method of tying together the three earthen vessels here represented, is recognized by all

[* Nâyar (Nair) women appear to be referred to, but the word is incorrect.]

[† Females of the Tiyyar (Tier) caste.]

Nº1

Nº2

Hindu visitors as being universally adopted by the modern Gopâlas.* The execution of this work is coarse, and the design rude; and though particular parts have much merit, yet the limbs of the principal figures are clumsy and ill-proportioned, the attitudes forced, and the countenances without expression.

Greatly superior is the skill displayed by the artists employed in the excavation described by Mr. Goldingham in his fifth paragraph;† but even here, under the same roof, there is much inequality in the execution of the different subjects. The central compartment (see plate III., No. 1), and that on the left on entrance (see plate III., No. 2) are tame performances, compared with the very spirited representation of Durgâ seated on her lion, and attacking Mahishâsura, which occupies the right compartment.‡ (See plate IV.) I have no hesitation in pronouncing this to be the most animated piece of Hindu sculpture which I have ever seen; and I would venture to recommend that a cast of it should, if possible, be taken for this Society. In the meantime, a tolerably just notion may be formed of its merits from the excellent and accurate delineation of Mr. Hudleston.

The smaller temple, which Mr. Goldingham mentions as placed at a considerable elevation above that just alluded to, and wrought out of a single mass of rock, is so rich in sculpture and ornament, and occupies so picturesque and sequestered a spot, that it is surprising he should have passed it over with so slight a notice. This excavation is in form a parallelogram, open on one of the longer sides, where it is supported on two columns. It contains four large

[* Cowherds.] [† P. 32-33, supra.] [‡ Cp. Braddock, infra.]

compartments or panels of sculpture; namely, one at each end, and one on each side of the central recess opposite the entrance; besides two niches occupied by Dwârapâlas.* The Varâha Avatâra represented in plate V., is placed at the left end of the chamber. Plate VI., the subject of which seems to be some incarnation of Vishnu,† fills the compartment at the opposite end. On the right of the recess a female deity‡ appears, surmounted by an umbrella (see plate VII., No. 1); whilst on the left is a female figure§ seated on a lotus throne, and attended by damsels who bear water-pots, to be discharged in turn over her head by the elephants seen in the background (see plate VIII.) The position of the Dwârapâlas will be seen in plate VIII., No. 2. Of the columns which support the front of the excavation, as well as of the side pilasters, I have thought it worth while, on account of their beauty and singular order, to furnish drawings (plate VII., Nos. 2 and 3); while the general appearance of the cave-temple will be best understood by reference to plate IX.¶

There are several other pieces of sculpture contained in small temples among the rocks, not noticed either by Mr. Chambers or Mr. Goldingham; and of these, plate X., Nos. 1, 2, 3, are examples.

The Dolotsava Ma*nd*apam,‖ seen in the centre of the village, is remarkable for the lightness and elegance of its construction. It is of granite, and is

[* Door-keepers.]

[† The dwarf incarnation, Vâmana Avatâra.]

[‡ Bhadrakâli, a form of Pârvati.]

[§ Pârvati, as Devi.—Cp. plates 30 and 33 in Moor's Hindu Pantheon.—But the Vaishnavas call the figure Gaja Lakshmi.]

[¶ The writer has omitted to mention that the ceiling is painted.]

[‖ See note * p. 34, *supra*.]

SCULPTURES AT MAHÂMALAIPÛR.

PLATE V.

N° 2

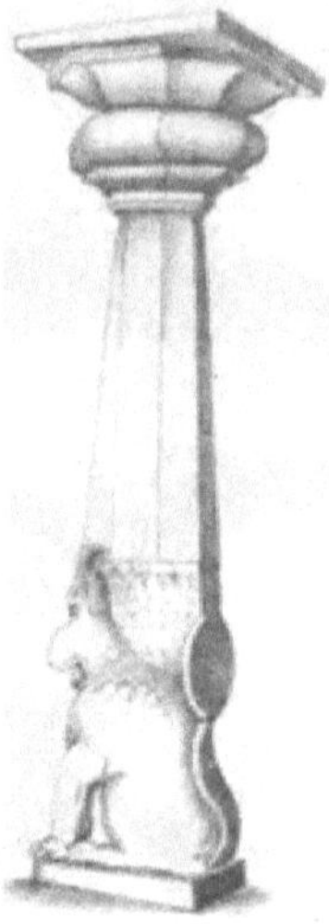

SCULPTURES AT MAHÂMALAIPÛR. PLATE III

No. 1

No. 2

PLATE IX.

No. 1. SCULPTURES AT MAHÂMALAIPÛR PLATE X

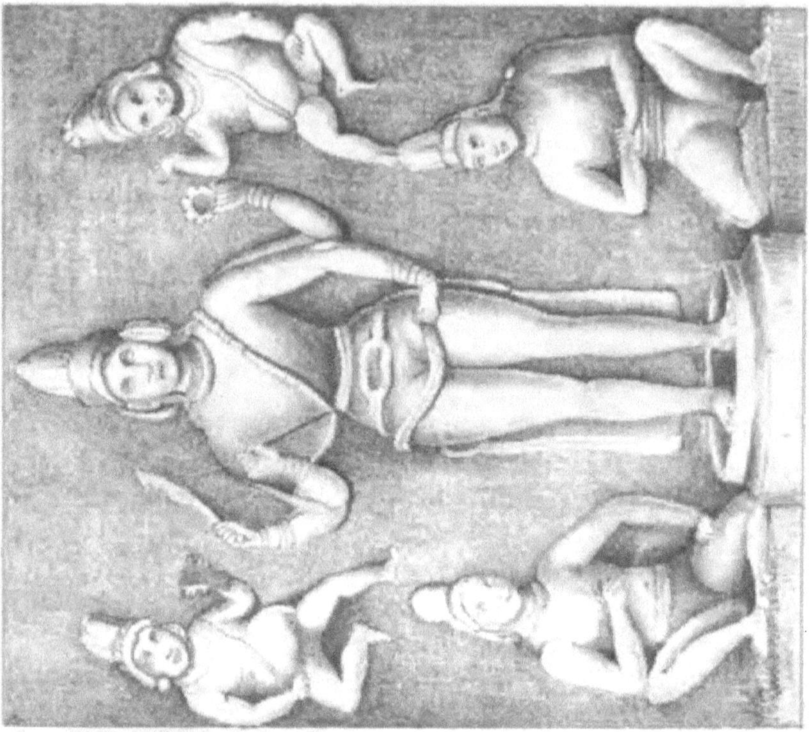

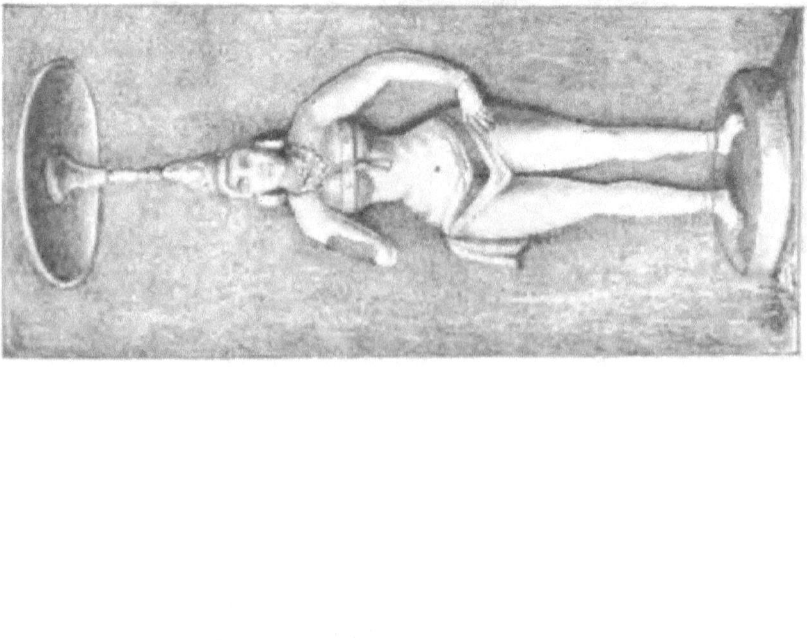

AT MAHAMALAIPUR

No II

No I

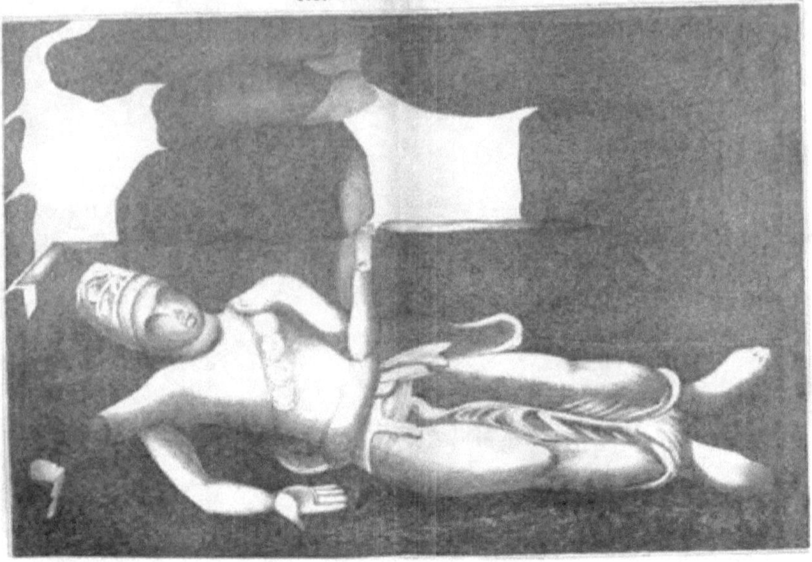

supported on four columns, which rise from a platform elevated by three steps. (See plate XI., No. 1.) The shafts of the columns with the base are hewn from a single stone, and, including the capital, are twenty-seven feet in height.

The stone pagoda on the sea-shore, which serves as a land-mark for shipping, and is erroneously stated by Mr. Chambers to be built of brick,* is delineated in plate XI., No. 2; and the gigantic figure lying stretched on the floor in one of its recesses, in plate XII. At the time when this drawing was made, the figure was enclosed in a small chamber; but on a subsequent visit I found that the walls had given way, thus leaving it exposed to the open air. As a record therefore of the state of this pagoda and figure, I regard these drawings as not without value in the collection now presented to the Society; for such is the dilapidated condition of this structure, that the period cannot be far distant when it will no longer exist. The effects of the salt-water spray add much to those of time in hastening its decay.†

Whether this pagoda was dedicated to Vishnu or to *Siva*, I regard as doubtful: tradition favours the former supposition. At all events, the pillar which stands before it amid the spray of the sea is certainly not a *lingam*, as some suppose, but merely the *stambha* or post, which is found, I believe, fronting all Hindu temples of consideration.‡ That this pillar is now near the high-water mark is by no means a convincing

[* P. 10, *supra*.]

[† The writer greatly under-estimated the strength of this building. There is no probability of its disappearance.]

[‡ See note † p. 11, *supra*.—The Brahmans say it is a lamp-post, *Dîpastambha*.]

proof that the sea has encroached here, for I see no reason why such a spot should not have been originally selected for its erection. If it be a fact, as mentioned by Bishop Heber, that the sea is receding from most other parts of the Coromandel Coast, it is difficult to conceive why it should advance in this place; such a local encroachment could only be effected by a change in the position of the land, and as the primitive rocks here appear on the surface, this cannot be admitted as a probable occurrence, unless under some violent convulsion of nature. Had the coast been of an alluvial formation at this spot, high tides might have advanced upon it with greater facility.

The five monolithic temples, situated about a mile to the southward of the village, have justly attracted the attention of all who have visited Mahámalaipúr. They are called on the spot रथाः *Rathas*, or sacred vehicles: but it is obvious, that they were never meant as imitations of those enormous wooden structures, which are so conspicuous in certain Hindu processions. They were probably intended to serve the purpose of temples; but bear evident marks of having been left in an unfinished state; for though highly ornamented on the outside, they have not been excavated within, being merely solid masses of sculptured granite remaining in their original positions.* For the general view of these Rathas, I would refer to Mrs. Graham's plate, which, together with Mr. Goldingham's description, will serve to

[* "The Brahmans found a group of granite boulders lying on the sea-shore, and have carved them into the form of temples, having all the appearance of structural edifices with the advantage of monolithic durability."—Fergusson, Rock-cut Temples of India. London, 1864. Intro., p. xviii.]

convey a notion of these curious remains of antiquity. Several of the basso relievo figures with which they are ornamented are represented in plate XV., and will be further noticed when I come to speak of the inscriptions which are placed over them.

OF THE INSCRIPTIONS.

Exclusively of a scrap of modern Telugu, very incorrectly designed and rudely sculptured on the floor of the K*ri*sh*n*a Ma*nd*apam, and in consequence erroneously copied as ancient by Mr. Goldingham (see Asiatic Researches, vol. v. page 80),* I noticed three kinds of inscriptions at Mahâmalaipûr, two of which have hitherto remained undeciphered. It is also highly probable that three other kinds, which I shall have occasion to mention, are to be met with in this neighbourhood.

First. An ancient Tamil inscription is seen on a face of rock by the side of the inner entrance to the Varâhasvâmî pagoda, which is still in use. This would be legible throughout, were it not that a wall, which projects from the rock, cuts off a considerable portion of each line; on this account I did not consider it worth while to take a copy.† From what remains visible, it is certain that the inscription records a grant to the Varâhasvâmî pagoda of a quantity of land, the boundaries of which are very minutely defined, both as respects the property of others, and the cardinal points. The act of donation is attested by numerous witnesses, and the name of the donor is also mentioned. A perfect copy of this inscription might easily be made, if the wall which I have noticed were removed; and as the

[* P. 43, *supra*.] [† Cp. Sir Walter Elliot's copy, *infra*.]

date might possibly thus be ascertained, I would suggest that the Madras Literary Society be recommended to take measures for effecting this object. In order to facilitate the task of deciphering this and similar records, I have drawn out an alphabet (see plate XIII.) from a careful collation of several ancient Tamil inscriptions.*

As it seems probable, from a passage in another ancient inscription hereafter noticed, that Mahâmalaipúr was a *Śiva-sthala*, I am inclined to consider the Varàhasvámi pagoda as quite distinct, and probably of a different era from the antiquities,

* The changes which time has produced are in some letters very great; and where characters are so simple as those of the Tamil language, even slight alterations in form give rise to perplexity. I may adduce, as an example, the letter *ka*, the most ancient form of which was a Latin cross . In the course of time a top was added to the left side, and the cross bar was curved thus . The next alteration was in the addition of a perpendicular line falling from the left extremity of the top . The top was then extended to the right , and by prolonging the extremities of the curved line, the modern letter  has at length been formed, or in a still more complicated manner as in the Grantha thus . In its modern form  it might easily be confounded with the  which, though it now has a tail, was anciently written without one, thus . Other examples might be given, but they suggest themselves on an inspection of the alphabet itself.

I cannot touch on the subject of ancient Tamil characters without remarking, that their extreme simplicity seems one among many circumstances, which indicate that the language is of very high antiquity. The Sanscrit of the south of India is written in characters (the Grantha) derived from the Tamil, but they are much more complicated, and therefore probably posterior in point of antiquity. The peculiar structure of the Tamil language, wholly dissimilar from the Sanscrit, its deficiency in aspirated consonants, its

ALPHABET OF ANCIENT TAMIL. PLATE XIII.

properly so called, which belong to this place. The difference of language in the inscription, and the circumstance that the pagoda is a built structure projecting from the face of the rock, and not an excavation, increase the probability of this conclusion. It is not unlikely, however, that there may exist in the sanctuary a subordinate sculpture representing the Varâha Avatâra like that of K*ri*sh*n*a and the Gopâlas in the K*ri*sh*n*a Ma*nd*apam, and of equally ancient date, and that a roof and walls may have been thrown out from this rock, and a temple thus formed.* The Brahmans on the spot did not permit me to enter the sanctuary to ascertain this point.

Throughout this Tamil inscription the place is called Mahâmalaipûr, which signifies the city of the great mountain, evidently with reference to the rocky eminence in the vicinity. This indeed cannot be called a great mountain on account of its size: but the word *mahâ* may refer to greatness of sanctity, or renown, with equal propriety.

To designate the village Mahâbalipuram, the native name at the present day, is therefore an error, which has led to the assumption that this was the capital of that renowned giant Mahâ Bali, whose kingdom, if it ever actually existed, was on the

possession of letters and sounds not found in Sanscrit, its division into dialects, one of which contains but few words of Sanscrit derivation; and lastly, its locality at the southern extremity of India, would seem likewise to indicate an independent origin, and one of at least equal antiquity with the Sanscrit itself; but this is a subject foreign to that now under consideration, and deserving a more lengthened discussion than the limits of a note will allow.

[* This supposition is correct; a temple has been built round an ancient sculpture on the face of the rock, representing the Varâha Avatâra.]

western coast of India, where he is still honoured by an annual festival.

A second kind of character found at Mahâmalaipûr is in a small monolithic pagoda,* now dedicated to Ganesa,† and situated on the north side of the hill. It is contained in an inscription (see plate XIV.) of considerable length, but is so faintly cut, and on such rough granite, that the fac-simile which I have furnished, however imperfect, cost me several days' labour to trace.‡ One of the Jain Brahmans, in the employ of Colonel Mackenzie, had such a knowledge of ancient characters somewhat similar to

* Mrs. Graham gives an engraving of this small pagoda, which she says is called the Tìr of Arjuna, and she explains the word Tìr (properly *Tër*), to mean a place of religious retirement. The explanation is erroneous, as the word Tër signifies, in Tamil, a car or sacred vehicle, corresponding with the Sanscrit *Ratha*.

† When Mr. Goldingham wrote his account, this pagoda contained a *lingam* (see his first paragraph [p. 30 *supra*]), so that it has passed from the *Saivas* into the possession of the Vaishnavas since that period.§ Brahman families of both sects reside on the spot.

‡ In this character there are two forms of affix for long *â*, used indifferently as convenience may suggest. Thus, in the first stanza, we find the syllable (का) *kâ* in the word *kâranam* (कारणं) made thus ; while in the eighth stanza the same syllable in the word *kâma* (काम) is made thus . The letters *p* (प), and *s* (स) seem similar in form; but perhaps some slight difference may have escaped my observation. In modern Grantha, an inflection in the middle of the character makes the difference between *s* and *p*, thus 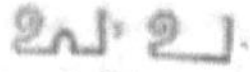. So also in the ancient character, the inflection may have been greater in the *s* than in the *p*, thus 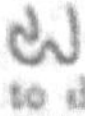 and 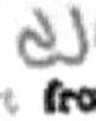; but I have not upon this supposition felt authorised to depart from the copy which I made on the spot.

[§ An old Vaishnava Brahman tells a different tale: he states that the Lingam was taken away, (with an image of Hanumân,) by Lord

[illegible]
[illegible]
[illegible]
[illegible]
[illegible]
[illegible]
[illegible]
[illegible]
[illegible]
[illegible]
[illegible]
[illegible]
[illegible]

this, that on visiting the spot with me, he succeeded in deciphering a great part of this inscription, the language of which is Sanscrit. The following is a translation of the ten slokas which were intelligible, while about two verses at the end were left undeciphered :—

1. May the cause of creation, existence, and destruction, which is itself without cause, the destroyer of Manmatha (desire), be propitious to the desires of the world.
2. May he who is united with Umâ, of many kinds of illusion, without quality, the destroyer of evil dispositions, of incorruptible wealth, the Lord of Kubera, be counted excellent.
3. May that deity (*Siva*) protect us all, who is the seat of prosperity, and by whose means Kailâsa disappeared and descended to Pâtâla, yielding by its weight, which he caused on account of its being with (supported by) the ten-faced (Râvana).
4. May he who bears *Siva* in his mind engrossed by devotion, and the earth on his shoulders, with as much ease as if it were an ornament, long prevail.
5. By that king of satisfied wishes, with crowds of conquered enemies, who is known by the name of Jayarana Stambha, this building was made.

Hobart (?) and sent to England, Lady H. giving 20 pagodas to the villagers as a consideration! Lord Hobart was Governor of Madras from Sept. 1794 to February 1798. Mr. Goldingham's account was *published* in the latter year.]

6. May that fear-inspiring, good-giving, desire-destroying *Siva*, to whom the earth, space, the moon, fire, the sun, &c., are a body, be victorious.

7. The good-faced among nations (the beauty of the world) sprung from a mother bringing forth heroes, remains without doubt in a place of lotuses, full of sacred waters, and is adorned with all sorts of precious stones.

8 and 9. *Siva*, the beautiful, sits in the broad lake Siras which teems with (*lit.* is a mine of) lotuses resembling variegated gems, and is full of water for sprinkling the fortunate and much-loved Kâmarâja, who puts down the pride of his enemies, who is the source (receptacle) of glory, and is earnest in worshipping *Siva*.

10. He (Kâmarâja) who dwells on the heads of kings, caused this temple of *Siva*, which resembles the temple on Kailâsa, to be erected for the happiness of the earth.*

I have lately received from Madras two ancient inscriptions purporting to be from the neighbourhood of Mahâmalaipûr, and two also have been kindly furnished me by Colonel De Havilland. Of these four, two appear to be identical, which reduces the number to three. Their precise localities I have not the means of knowing, with the exception of one, entitled by Colonel De Havilland, "Sanscrit inscription engraven on the north side of the verandah of a pagoda excavated out of the solid granite, two miles north of Mahâbalipuram." All

[* See Appendix.]

[illegible]

[illegible]

[illegible]

[illegible]

[illegible]

these inscriptions differ in character from each other, but agree precisely in matter; and it is remarkable that the slokas of which they are composed are, with the exception of the last, contained, though in different order, in the inscription copied by me from the wall of the Ganesa pagoda and of which a translation has just been furnished. To state this more in detail, my inscription, which, it is to be observed, is in a character differing again from any of the rest, consists of ten slokas deciphered, besides as much as would probably make two slokas more remaining undeciphered. The other inscriptions consist of five slokas only, with some undeciphered portions, with which I have not thought it worth while to encumber the plate; the first four being in the metre called anushtubh, the last in a variety of the metre called vaitáliya.

The first three slokas in my inscription are not found in the others; my fourth sloka is the same as theirs. The fifth, sixth, and seventh slokas of my inscription are wanting in the others. My eighth and ninth slokas are their first and second, and my tenth is their third. Their fifth sloka I have ascertained, after a very careful comparison, to be quite different from the remaining undeciphered portion of my inscription. Its translation is as follows: "Atiranachanda (he who in battle is very furious), Lord of Kings, built this place called Atiranachandesvara. May Siva, the beloved, accompanied by the daughter (Pârvati) of the snowy mountain, by Kârtikeya, and their suite of deities, be present in it for ever."

These inscriptions are peculiarly valuable, as giving us at once four different kinds of Sanscrit writing, whereof two (plate XIV. and plate XV., No. 1.) are, in my opinion, ancient forms of the Grantha, or that character in which Sanscrit is invariably written in the south of India, and in which alone I was able to procure books for study at Madras. The other two will probably be considered as species of ancient Devanâgari. (See plate XV., Nos. 2 and 3.)

This variety of character, with identity of matter, leads me to think it probable that the inscription itself was a kind of general proclamation sculptured in different places, and modified, as in my inscription, to render it applicable to local circumstances. Whether it will throw light upon the history of Mahâmalaipûr, containing as it does the name of the sovereign who founded the temples to which it has been affixed, is a question which I must leave to be examined by those who have studied the ancient dynasties of the south of India.

A third kind of character at Mahâmalaipûr, or a sixth kind, if we reckon those received from Madras and from Colonel De Havilland, is to be found in the inscriptions over the basso-relievo figures which ornament the monolithic pagodas already mentioned as situated to the southward of the village, and of which several are represented in plate XVI. Neither the Jain Brahman employed by Colonel Mackenzie, nor any other native of India who had seen these inscriptions, was able to decipher them, or to offer any conjecture as to the language in which they were written; and even the learned Mr. Ellis, after repeated visits to this place, was equally unsuccessful in his endeavours. Mrs. Graham, indeed, states that Colonel Mackenzie had found a Brah-

ORIGINAL	THE SAME IN DEVANÂGARÎ	ENGLISH TRANSLATION
[illegible]	कामललित: प्रमेयमाय: सकलकल्याण:	Indulging in Kama [illegible] incredible illusion The all-fortunate
[illegible]	श्रीनरसिंह: अप्रतिहतशासन: भुवनभाजन: श्रीमेघ:	The holy Man Lion [illegible] of irresistible authority The [illegible] The [illegible]
[illegible]	स्थिरभक्ति: मदनाभिराम: विधि	The firm in faith. The beautiful as Kama Deva The [illegible] a name of [illegible]
[illegible]	विधाता: विधि:	The [illegible] The [illegible]
[illegible]	श्रीनिधि: निस्तार:	The abode of [illegible] The [illegible]
[illegible]	नयनमनोहर:	The delight of the eye
[illegible]	सर्वतोभद्र:	The universally [illegible]
[illegible]	ललित	The lovely
[illegible]	सत्यपराक्रम:	The truly valorous
[illegible]	श्री नरसिंह:	The holy Man Lion [illegible]
[illegible]	[illegible] भार: श्रीभर:	[illegible]
[illegible]	भुवनभाजन:	The [illegible]
[illegible]	पराचर:	The [illegible] South of India
[illegible]	भयाङ्कुर	The [illegible]
[illegible]	वाम:	The crooked [illegible]
[illegible]	अतिमान:	The [illegible]
[illegible]	श्री [illegible] विहारभोजन:	The happy [illegible] Lord of [illegible]

man who read the character so as to pronounce the sounds, but did not understand the language they express. Whether any person did actually thus impose on that gentleman, or whether Mrs. Graham has confounded these inscriptions with the last, I cannot determine, but it is quite certain that, if any person had been able to decipher the character, he would, without any difficulty, have discovered the language to be Sanscrit. It was by assuming this to be the case, that I succeeded in deciphering these inscriptions.*

I beg now to lay them before the Society, together with a transcript in Devanágari, and a translation. (See plate XVII.)

It is to be regretted that these inscriptions, instead of containing general information respecting the origin or date of the sculptures, are merely epithets applicable to the figures over which they are placed. At the same time we should remember that their brevity and position, having led to the assumption that they were names of deities, thus rendered the task of deciphering them somewhat less difficult. Unimportant as they are in themselves, a knowledge of them may lead to the acquirement of useful or curious information to be drawn from other sources, and I trust that the Society will indulgently consider the utility of this research, not

* There is one instance, as will be seen on a reference to plate XVII., in which the characters are of the same kind as those in the inscription of the Gasem pagoda, a proof that both were in use at the same period. It is probable therefore that one was the round, and the other the square form, analogous to the two varieties of Páli and Ariyam.†

[† Âryam is the round, modern Malayâlam character.]

so much with reference to the information actually obtained, as to its general subserviency to the purposes of history.

There are certainly no historical monuments in India more decidedly authentic than the copper and stone inscriptions found in such abundance in many parts of the country, and it is advancing one step to have determined that these, however different the characters in which they are sculptured from those in use at the present day, are all in the Sanscrit language, in which so little change has taken place in the lapse of ages, that, when once we have succeeded in the task of deciphering, all difficulty is at an end, and the record of a remote antiquity is placed intelligibly before us.

These inscriptions, and those at Kenerah in the island of Salsette, one of which, with the modern Sanscrit, and a translation, I laid before the Society on a late occasion, are perhaps the most ancient, at least the most dissimilar from characters at present in use, which I have met with; and I think myself therefore warranted in concluding that there are no inscriptions of Hindu origin to be found in India which may not, by attentive study, be deciphered, and by the assistance of learned natives, afterwards interpreted.

With a view to rendering the characters of these deciphered inscriptions generally applicable, I have added two tables (plate XVIII.): the one containing all the characters found in the inscription in the Ganesa pagoda; the other, those met with over the basso-relievo figures on the Rathas.

CHARACTERS OF THE ANCIENT INSCRIPTION IN THE GANÉSA PAGODA AT MAHÂMALAIPÛR,
WITH THE CORRESPONDING CHARACTERS IN ROMAN, DEVANÂGARÎ AND GRANTHA.

PLATE XVI

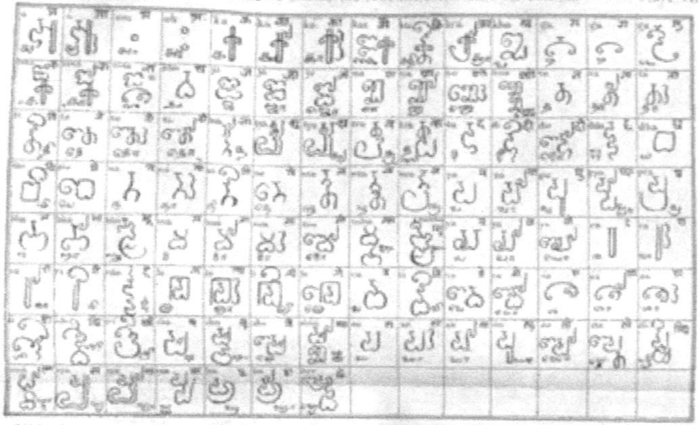

CHARACTERS OF THE ANCIENT INSCRIPTIONS OVER THE BAS-RELIEF FIGURES ON THE RATHAS AT MAHÂMALAIPÛR,
WITH THE CORRESPONDING CHARACTERS IN ROMAN, DEVANÂGARÎ, AND GRANTHA.

IV.—*A Guide to the Sculptures, Excavations, and other remarkable objects at Mâmallaipûr, generally known to Europeans as "the Seven Pagodas," by the late* Lieutenant JOHN BRADDOCK, *of the Madras Establishment. To which are added some Archæological Notes, by the* Reverend WILLIAM TAYLOR, *and a Supplementary account of the remains at Sâluvan Kuppam, by* WALTER ELLIOT, ESQ.,* *of the Madras Civil Service.—Communicated by the* Reverend GEORGE WILLIAM MAHON, A.M., *Garrison Chaplain, Fort St. George.*

[From the Madras Journal of Literature and Science, Vol. XIII. 1844.]

IN the month of June 1840, I accompanied a small party of friends on a visit to the remarkable remains at Mámallaipûr. As our excursion, from its necessary brevity, was likely to prove one of amusement rather than of antiquarian research, and the large quartos of the Asiatic Society are somewhat cumbrous, we borrowed from our friend Mr. Braddock a little pamphlet published by him some years before, which at once served as a guide to what was worth seeing, and explained to such of us as were but slightly acquainted with Hindu Mythology, the subjects and allusions of the various sculptures.

[* Now Sir Walter Elliot, K.C.S.I.]

On our return I expressed to Mr. Braddock a desire that he should undertake a fuller account of the place, and suggested that it should combine the useful and entertaining properties of a Guide Book with the more important lucubrations of the scholar. As topics for the latter I named a more satisfactory account of the Inscriptions, and some information, if obtainable, as to the history of Mâmallaipûr and the origin of the excavations and sculptures. With his habitual modesty he seemed to doubt his competency to deal with the latter subjects, but promised to revise and dilate his former paper. I then suggested that he should solicit the assistance of his old and valued friend, the Rev. W. Taylor, in ascertaining something of the history of the place. This gentleman, so well known as an accomplished oriental linguist, having been recently engaged in the examination of the Mackenzie MSS., might, I thought, have discovered amongst them some information tending to throw light on so interesting a subject. Mr. Taylor, it will be seen, has responded with equal good feeling and ability to the request so made to him; and his notes, appended to Mr. Braddock's paper, must be considered as a most valuable addition to it.

As Mr. Braddock proceeded with his work he forwarded the rough sheets for my perusal, with a request that I should suggest any alterations which my more recent visit to the place might enable me to do. The paper was scarcely completed, no time had been granted for revision, I had not even seen its concluding sheets, when the amiable and talented writer was hurried away by one of those rapid attacks which disease sometimes makes on European constitutions in this climate: and I was called on, all but unexpectedly, to perform the last sad offices for one whom I had so recently seen usefully and actively employed. A marble tablet erected in the Church at Vepery by public subscription, serves to perpetuate the memory of this worthy man; and at the same time to evince the general sense of his Christian virtues, of his scientific acquirements, and of his constant readiness to employ them for the public good.

Some months after Mr. Braddock's death, I was requested by his family to revise and prepare for publication his papers on Mâmallaipûr; a task which I have undertaken not without great diffidence. Had my lamented friend survived, he would, I doubt not, have made many emendations in them, which cannot on many accounts be done by another hand.

It will be seen that neither Mr. Braddock nor Mr. Taylor has treated of the *Inscriptions* at Mâmallaipûr, otherwise than incidentally. Those who wish for some account of them, may be referred to the valuable article by Dr. Babington in the 2nd Volume of the Transactions of the Royal Asiatic Society. He says that he noticed three kinds of inscriptions at "Mâhâmalaipûr," two of which have remained undeciphered, and that it is highly probable that there are other kinds to be met with in the neighbourhood. The first he alludes to is an ancient Tamil inscription on a face of rock, by the side of the inner entrance to the Varáhasvâmi pagoda (No. 29 in the Map.)* He gives no copy of it, but states that "it records

[* Plate XX.]

a grant to the Varâhasvâmi pagoda of a quantity of land."* The language of this inscription renders it doubtful whether it is of earlier or later date than some of the others, which are in Sanscrit. Dr. Babington says that throughout this Tamil inscription the place is called "Mahâmalaipûr," which he translates "city of the great mountain," adding that the word Mahâ may imply "greatness of sanctity or renown." This if correct might be adduced as proof of the more recent age of the inscription; for the hill is by no means remarkable, otherwise than for the "sanctity or renown" which the sculptures may have procured for it. It will be seen, however, that the Rev. W. Taylor speaks of two inscriptions, in which the place is called Mâmallaipûr, with two *l's*, and if this orthography is correct, which he seems to think it is, the translation of Dr. Babington is of course overthrown, since *mallai* does not mean "hill." The present name of the place in common use appears to be Mâvalavaram, and not Mahâbalipuram, as some have stated. The latter mistake can scarcely be regretted, however, by those who have perused the pleasing fiction which the poetical talent of Southey has embodied in his "Curse of Kehama."

The second kind of inscription mentioned by Dr. Babington appears in the temple dedicated to Ganesa, situated near the north end of the hill, and described in its order by Mr. Braddock. By the assistance of his Jain Brahman in deciphering the characters, Dr. Babington was enabled to translate this inscription; and as it appears that much of the substance of it is repeated in some other inscriptions which he

[* Vide Sir Walter Elliot's translation of this inscription, *infra*.]

subsequently examined, it may prove interesting to copy his translation in this place. It consists of ten slokas deciphered, and there remains undeciphered about as much as would make two slokas more.

Translation by Dr. Babington and his Jain Brahman of the ten first slokas in the Sanscrit Inscription found in the Ganesa Pagoda at Mámallaipúr.

"1. May the cause of creation, existence, and destruction, which is "itself without cause, the destroyer of Manmatha *(desire)* be propi-"tious to the desires of the world.

"2. May he who is united with Umá, of many kinds of illusion, "without quality, the destroyer of evil dispositions, of incorruptible "wealth, the Lord of Kubera, be counted excellent.

"3. May that deity (*Siva*) protect us all, who is the seat of pros-"perity, and by whose means Kailása disappeared and descended to "Pátála, yielding by its weight, which he caused on account of its "being with *(supported by)* the ten-faced (Rávana).

"4. May he who bears *Siva* in his mind engrossed by devotion, "and the earth on his shoulders, with as much ease as if it were an "ornament, long prevail.

"5. By that king of satisfied wishes, with crowds of conquered "enemies, who is known by the name of Jayarana Stambha, this "building was made.

"6. May that fear-inspiring, good-giving, desire-destroying *Siva*, "to whom the earth, space, moon, fire, the sun, &c., are a body, be "victorious.

"7. The good-faced among nations *(the beauty of the world)* sprung "from a mother bringing forth heroes, remains without doubt in a "place of lotuses, full of sacred waters, and is adorned with all sorts "of precious stones.

"8 and 9. *Siva* the beautiful, sits in the broad lake Siras, which "teems with *(is a mine of)* lotuses, resembling variegated gems, and "is full of water for sprinkling the fortunate and much-loved "Kámarája, who puts down the pride of his enemies, who is the "source *(receptacle)* of glory, and is earnest in worshipping *Siva*.

"10. He (Kámarája,) who dwells on the heads of Kings, caused "this temple of *Siva*, which resembles the temple on Kailása, to be "erected for the happiness of the earth."

Three additional inscriptions were sent to Dr. Babington by some Madras friends; one by Colonel

De Havilland from the "north side of a verandah of "a pagoda (No. 30 in the Map)* excavated out of the "solid granite, two miles north of the place." Of these Dr. Babington says, "all these inscriptions "differ in character from each other, but agree pre-"cisely in matter; and it is remarkable that the "slokas of which they are composed, are, with the "exception of the last, contained, though in different "order, in the inscription copied by me from the wall "of the Ganesa pagoda. My inscription is in a "character differing again from any of the rest. "The other inscriptions consist of five slokas only, "with some undeciphered portions. The first "three slokas in my inscription are not found in the "others; my fourth sloka is the same as theirs. The "fifth, sixth, and seventh slokas of my inscription are "wanting in the others. My eighth and ninth slokas "are their first and second, and my tenth is their "third. Their fifth sloka I have ascertained after a "very careful comparison, to be quite different from "the undeciphered portion of my inscription. Its "translation is as follows:—

"Atiranachanda (he who in battle is very furious) Lord of Kings "built this place, called Atiranachandesvara. May Siva the beloved, "accompanied by the daughter (Pârvati) of the snowy mountain, by "Kártikeya, and their suite of deities, be present in it for ever."

The third kind of inscription is found over the figures on the monolithic temples to the south of the village. So completely have these characters become obsolete, that none of the learned natives consulted were able to decipher them. After considerable trouble, Dr. Babington himself succeeded in doing so.

It might reasonably have been expected that these

[* Plate XXI.]

inscriptions would have thrown some light on the origin or probable age of the sculptures, excavations, and themselves. They afford no very precise information at all. The appellations given to the prince or princes who "caused the erections," are mere epithets, by which no individual can with certainty be identified, (vide Mr. Taylor's note *d*); and were it possible to do this, the chronology must still be in a very great degree theoretical. I perfectly agree in opinion with Mr. Taylor that there is little in the sculptures themselves, if we except the Rathas, the Varâhasvâmî Pagoda, the Ganesa temple and the temple at *Sâluvan* Kuppam, to justify the supposition of their very great antiquity. Most of them are in the most perfect preservation, and present a freshness of appearance which creates an involuntary idea of their almost recent execution. The subjects of the sculptures too are an evidence that they are not of very remote antiquity. They are representations of various personages and incidents in Hindu mythology, and are chiefly borrowed from the famous poem, the Mahâbhârata. This and the language of the inscriptions which is Sanscrit, or Tamil with Sanscrit derivatives, mark the presence of the Brahmanical faith. Now it appears from Mr. Taylor's researches, that previous to the seventh century of the Christian era, the whole of the district in which Mâmallaipûr stands was occupied by the Kurumbas, a half-civilized people of the Jaina religion; and it was about that period or probably later that, under the auspices of Ado*nd*ai, a prince whose capitals were Conjeveram and Tripati,* the Brahmans were intro-

[* *Prop.* Kâñchîpuram, Tirupati.]

duced into this part of the country. The extent of the works, and the labor and expense bestowed on them seem to indicate a long established Brahmanical influence; and it will be seen from Mr. Taylor's note (c) that an historical paper amongst the Mackenzie MSS. affords grounds for supposing that at least some of these excavations, &c., were executed so lately as the seventeenth century by a prince denominated Siṁhamanâyu*d*u. The supplementary paper by Walter Elliot, Esq., relating to the remains at *Sâl*uvan Kuppam, serves to suggest a much earlier date than the latter for certain of these remarkable productions which he therein specifies.

Works of this nature have been executed in all parts of the world during the earlier stages of civilization. Rocky caves formed by nature offer a congenial shelter for the gloomy rites of a dark superstition, a ready defence from the attacks of enemies or the inclemency of the weather, and supplied appropriate receptacles for the remains of the dead. In the most ancient times the Holy Scriptures speak of caves as places of residence and refuge, as well as of sepulture. Many of these natural recesses were greatly enlarged and rendered more commodious or better adapted for the purposes of shelter and defence by human labor and art. This may still be traced in several countries of the East. Maundrell has described a cave near Sidon, whose sides contain two hundred smaller caverns. Sir R. K. Porter has given an interesting account of a cavern or labyrinth in the mountain of Kerefto, in Eastern Kurdistan. Similar excavations are found according to the same authority at Maraga in Media; in the mountains near the lake Sivan, and near the site of Artaxata, the ancient capital of Armenia. The sepulchral caves of Egypt have been admirably illustrated by Belzoni. Sir Alexander Burnes has given an interesting account of the sculptures and caves at Bameean. Those at Elephanta and Ellora are well known in India; and such as are interested in these remarkable records of past times should not overlook the description and beautiful sketches of Petra by Laborde. Amongst the savages of North-Western Australia, Captain Gray has discovered sculptured rocks and painted caverns. In this way nature appears to have suggested to mankind the earlier efforts of art.

The Rathas, or monolithic temples to the south of the village, are probably the most ancient of the remains at Mâmallaipûr. Their inscriptions are in a character so completely obsolete, that the most learned natives, according to Dr. Babington, are unable to decipher them. This species of sculpture is remarkable, and much more rare than mere excavations. It was, however, practised by the ancient Egyptians, and Herodotus (Lib. ii. cap. 155) has given a short description of a monolithic temple of Latona, which stood at Buto, near the Sebennytic mouth of the Nile. He says it measured 40 cubits or 60 feet in height, breadth, and width: and its roof consisted of a separate stone, four cubits high. This temple, which must have been conveyed to its site, must have weighed on the lowest computation upwards of 5,000 tons. At the 175th chapter of the same book, he describes another monolithic temple at Sais, which had been brought thither by King Amasis from Elephantine, the island opposite Syene, immediately below the first cataract; a distance of twenty days' sail, or of 700 miles by land. The outside measurement of this monolith he states to be—length, 21 cubits; breadth, 14; and height, 8: the inside measurement was—length, 18 cubits and 1 pygon; breadth, 12 cubits; and the height, 5 cubits. Taking the cubit in round numbers at 1 foot 6 inches and the pygon at 1 foot 3 inches, the temple must have been externally 31 feet 6 inches long, 21 feet broad and 12 feet high: and internally 28 feet 3 inches long, 18 feet broad, and 7½ feet high. This monolith then was inferior in point of mere size to the largest of those at Mámallaipûr; the dimensions of which externally, according to Mr. Goldingham, are as follows:—length 49 feet, breadth 25 feet, and height 25 feet. But we must remember that while these are *in loco naturæ*, being cut in fact from large boulders or distinct masses of granite, the monolith of Amasis had to be conveyed to its site by manual labor; and Herodotus affirms that two thousand boatmen were occupied in its removal for a period of upwards of three years. After all indeed it was not placed precisely where the king had proposed; for which two reasons are assigned. First, that the architect, weary of the labor and time expended on the work, heaved a deep sigh as the workmen were dragging it forward, which Amasis interpreted as an unfavorable omen: and secondly, that one of the workmen, having unfortunately fallen under the moving mass, was crushed to death, and on this account it was allowed to remain where it then was. Mr. Burton, in his excerpta (plate 41) gives a representation of a similar monolith said to be of the same king, and found at Tel-et-mai. This measures externally 21 feet 9 inches high, 13 feet broad, and 11 feet 7 inches deep: and internally 19 feet 3 inches high, 8 feet broad, and 8 feet 3 inches deep.

The sculptured rocks at Mâmallaipûr, (on which is represented the penance of Arjuna,) are by no means without their parallel. This primitive application of the art of sculpture seems an obvious mode of perpetuating the memory of events, historical or mythological, and has been adopted from the earliest ages. On the rocks of the river Lycus, near Beirout in Syria, are still to be seen the figure in relief, and the name inscribed, of Remeses the great king of Egypt, who is supposed to have flourished about B. C. 1350, and was therefore contemporary with Ehud and Shamgar mentioned in the book of Judges: but early Egyptian chronology is so exceedingly uncertain, that the era of Remeses must always be conjectural. Not far from this is another sculpture of a Persian king, and an inscription in the arrow-headed character, which not having been yet deciphered affords likewise no conclusive evidence as to its age. Copies of these have been made by Bonomi. No Christian can have forgotten the exclamation of Job, "Oh that my words were now written! Oh "that they were printed in a book! That they were "graven with an iron pen and lead in the rock for "ever!" (Chap. xix., 23, 24.) And from some remains in the wady Mokatteb, and in other valleys near the mountains of Sinai, it would seem that the art of "engraving" on rocks is in those regions of great antiquity. Figures of men and animals accompany those inscriptions; the characters of the latter are for the most part unknown in the present day. These inscribed rocks extend in one place for about three hours march, and are mentioned by Burkhardt, Laborde, and other travellers.

At Be-Sitoon, near Kermansheh in Persia, is a

stream above whose fountain-head is a projecting rock containing the remains of an immense piece of sculpture. The great antiquity of this interesting relic is evidenced by the successive mutilations it has suffered, to afford room for subsequent inscriptions, as well as by the ordinary operations of time upon both it and them. By Mr. Macdonald Kinnier this bas-relief has been supposed identical with one spoken of by Diodorus Siculus, on the authority of Ctesias; who certainly had peculiar advantages for obtaining accurate information connected with Persian tradition and history. He says, "We are informed by Diodorus Siculus that Semiramis, in her march to Ecbatana, encamped near a mountain called Bagistan, in Media. She cut out a piece of the lower part of the rock, and caused her image to be carved upon it, and a hundred of her guards that were lanceteers, standing round her; she wrote likewise in Assyrian letters on the rock, that Semiramis ascended from the plain to the top of the mountain, by laying the packs and fardles of the beasts that followed her one upon another." There are many points of resemblance between the mountain of Be-Sitoon and that of Bagistan described by Diodorus Siculus; and supposing Mr. Kinnier to be right in his conjectures, we have here the remnants, for they are unfortunately no more, of a bas-relief executed at the lowest computation 800 years before the Christian era. Throughout ancient Media and Persia sculptured rocks, of various ages, repeatedly occur: a great many of these bas-reliefs, however, appear to belong to the Sassanian era: (from A. D. 226 to A. D. 632.)

These introductory notes have, I fear, already become too long and tedious; it only remains, therefore, that I acknowledge my obligations to Walter Elliot, Esq., of the Madras Civil Service, to whose friendly kindness I am indebted for the very valuable supplementary paper on the remains at *Sáluvan* Kuppam, as well as for a map of Mâmallaipûr drawn in 1808 by Colonel Mackenzie. The latter I have reduced, and by numbering the several objects both in it and in Mr. Braddock's description, I have endeavoured to render the whole a more useful guide to those who may dedicate a few spare hours to a visit to this interesting spot. The sculptures are for the most part such as do mark no very advanced state of art. They possess none of that finished elegance and refined taste, and but little of that purer poetic spirit which characterize the productions of Europe. Still they are highly deserving attention as the best specimens of native skill to be met with, I believe, in Southern India; and will not be undervalued by those who are capable of comprehending the extent to which art, even in its earliest infancy, has contributed to the civilization of mankind.

G. W. M.

FORT ST. GEORGE.

Lieutenant Braddock's Guide to the Sculptures, Excavations, &c., at Mâmallaipûr.

I shall commence my account of these curious sculptures and ruins with a small dilapidated temple built within fifty yards of the northern termination of the hill. (No. 1.)* It is a rectangular building

[* The Nos. in this paper refer to plates XX. and XXI.]

of plain hewn stone devoid of ornament: 24 feet long, 15 feet broad, and about 12 feet high. It has two apartments, the innermost of which contains a black stone lingam, neatly executed and in good preservation, notwithstanding that from the absence of roofing it is exposed to the weather. This temple is completely overshadowed with trees, which have taken root in the walls, and whose branches forcing their way through the joints of the stones have contributed much to its dilapidation and present ruinous appearance.

At a short distance to the eastward of this pagoda lies the *Group of Monkeys* (No. 2) spoken of in the Asiatic Researches, in an account of this place written in 1784.* The group, now much buried in the sand, consists of a male, a female, and a young one. The male monkey with a laudable love of cleanliness is studying the head of its partner with the most friendly attention, and the young one is satisfying its hunger. At a little distance lies a mutilated figure† of Ganesa or Pillaiyâr, the Hindu God of highways, &c., of whom I shall speak presently.

Looking towards the south, a *loose mass of rock* (No. 3) will be seen resting on a slope of the hill, apparently on so mere a point, that it seems as though a small force would dislodge it and roll it headlong on the plain. Its circumference is 68 feet, and its height about 25.‡ From the eastward it has a circular appearance; from other points of view its figure is irregular.

[* Cp. Chambers, p. 1, supra.]

[† Not found there now (1869).]

‡ Mr. Goldingham gives its diameter as 27 feet.

On the western face of the northern termination of the hill, not far south of the pagoda just described, may be found, after a little search, a circular cistern cut out of a solid stone.* It is 8 feet 6 inches in diameter, and 4 feet deep, but cracked.

Near this cistern the face of the rock is carved and ornamented to the extent of 28 feet in length by 14 feet in height. There are three *large excavated niches* (No. 4) with a flight of four steps leading into each. Figures are sculptured on each side the entrances. The centre or principal niche contains a figure of Mahádeva and four other figures cut on the back wall. The other two niches contain a figure of Vishnu and four others. This rock faces the north-west, and to the right or south of it is an imperfect representation of Durgá, eight-handed, and trampling under foot the head of Mahishásura, whose story will be told presently. On the eastern face of this rock are carvings of a well-proportioned elephant five feet high, and the heads of three smaller elephants; with those of a monkey and of a peacock.† The communication between the eastern and western faces of this rock is through a cleft at the north end of it.

At a short distance in a south-westerly direction from this place is an *excavation* in the solid rock (No. 5) measuring 22 feet long, 9 feet 6 inches deep, and

[* Called the 'Gopis' churn' by the Brahmans, who have also named the boulder on the slope of the rock 'Krishna's butter-ball.'—Cp. Bruce's Scenes and Sights in the East, pp. 130—132.]

[† "The head of the elephant is admirably finished. Perched above the elephant is a monkey, the figure and attitude of which are exquisitely faithful to life. The flow of its tail is full of expression, and is a study in itself. The whole face is marked by the anxious and mischievous spirit so natural to this creature."—Bruce, p. 133.]

8 feet high. The top is supported by two plain, strong, square pillars. It contains a square niche, on each side of which is a figure, probably that of Pârvati, a goddess who will be introduced to the reader presently. This excavation is on the western face of the hill, which is a continuous range of granite masses.

Still keeping on the same side, at 100 or 150 yards southward from the last excavation we come to *another* (No. 6) containing five niches, with steps leading into three of them; and two rows of pillars, four in each. This excavation is 36 feet long, 16 feet deep, and nearly 10 feet high. The niches contain each a kind of recess, (intended probably for a group of figures,) and a circular trench, (intended probably for lingams.) A figure is carved on each side of all the niches at the entrance. Four steps lead into this temple which faces north-west, half-west.

Adjoining is a *rough excavation* 36 feet long, 10 deep, and 10 high. In the middle is a large niche, also rough. About 12 feet of the rock appear to have been cut away before sufficient height was obtained for the front. This occurs in other places also; and a platform or level space is thus formed in the rock in front.

About half a mile westward, at the western extremity of the Palmyra tope which is on the west of the hill, there are three small unfinished temples sculptured out of solid detached masses of stone, (No. 7): but as more elaborately finished and larger temples of the same description will be described hereafter, I shall not dwell on these smaller ones. I would now lead the reader back to the large stone before described as resting on the slope of the rock on the eastern side of the hill, (No. 3.)

Proceeding southerly from this stone, you presently arrive at *a temple* fashioned out of the rock, (No. 8,)* and ornamented according to a style of architecture wholly different from that of this part of India in the present day. The top is elliptical, and bears considerable resemblance to the gothic style. The pillars which support a verandah on the western side are, I think, similar to columns which I have seen in the sketches of Egyptian Ruins by M. Denon. This temple is 28 feet high, 20 feet long, and 11 feet 6 inches broad. On the western face, at what may be called the foundation, there is a rent in the rock, which causes the temple to incline a little out of the perpendicular towards the south-east. This handsome structure (if so it may be termed), has a verandah and a niche, the latter containing an image of Ga*n*esa, which, blackened by smoke and ghee, is still an object of adoration to the people of the village. Their Brahmans, I was told, propitiate the stone deity every Friday with lustrations of ghee and cocoanut oil, and certain rites and prayers. The inner wall of the verandah, south of the niche, bears an inscription in the same kind of character as that hereafter noticed. According to Dr. Babington, (Transactions Royal Asiatic Society, Vol. 2, pp. 265-6,† and plate XIV.) this inscription consists of verses in praise of *Siva*.‡ I have stated that this temple contains an image of Ga*n*esa, and as this is the second time that Ga*n*esa has been mentioned, it may be right to state who and what he is.

[* Called by the Brahmans 'Arjuna's Ratha.'—See note * p. 56, *supra*.]

[† Pp. 56, 57, *supra*.]

‡ See Dr. Babington's translation of this inscription in the introductory notes. [p. 67, *supra*.] M.

Colonel Moor, in his Hindu Pantheon, says—that Ganesa* is the God of prudence and policy, and the reputed eldest son of *Siva* or Mahâdeva and Pârvati. He is represented with an elephant's head; generally with four hands, but sometimes with only two, and sometimes with six or eight. He is said to be propitiated by Hindus of all sects in the outset of any business: if a house is to be built, a book written, or a journey commenced, Ganesa is invoked.

It is very common for Hindu authors to give different versions of the same tale, and there are different accounts of the manner and cause of Ganesa's possession of an elephant's head. One relates that Vishnu and Ganesa fought, and that Ganesa would have been triumphant, but that *Siva* (his father!) cut off his head: whereat his mother Pârvati, being very much distressed and offended, proceeded to revenge the act by performing such austerities as, had they continued, would have deranged the destinies of the universe. This alarmed the whole congregation of the gods, who intreated *Siva* to restore Ganesa to life. He consented to do so, but the severed head could not be found: it was determined therefore to place on the headless trunk the cranium of the first animal they met with, which proved to be an elephant. There is another story to this effect, that Mahâdeva and Pârvati quarrelled; their quarrel was followed by a reconciliation; and their reconciliation by the birth of Ganesa. On this joyful occasion all the gods came to congratulate Pârvati; but one of them,† whose name I have forgotten, kept his eyes cast

[* Lord (isa) of a troop (gana); so called, because he is chief of the subordinate gods attendant upon *Siva*.—Wilson.]

[† *Sani* (Saturn.)]

down and forebore to look up. The goddess observing this asked him the reason of it; when he told her that he was doomed to injure whomsoever he looked upon, and therefore would not venture to look on the child. Pârvati would not believe that any injury could be done, and urged him to admire her beautiful Gaṇesa. But no sooner did he lift up his eyes, than the child's head vanished. This unexpected result astounded Pârvati, who had no sooner recovered from her first surprise, than she gave such passionate vent to her feelings, that Vishṇu, apprehensive of the consequences, flew to the banks of the Ganges, and brought thence the head of an elephant, which he placed on Gaṇesa's shoulders.

Passing the north-western front of the temple just described, and following the foot-path which leads through a narrow acclivity formed by rocks and bushes on either side, we come to an *excavation* with a very pretty frontage, on the left hand. (No. 9.) It is hewn in the side of the hill, is 22 feet long, 11 feet deep, and 10 feet 6 inches high. Of this excavation and of the imagery within it, plates are given in the second Volume of the Royal Asiatic Society's Transactions.*

On the wall, at the right hand or south-west end, there is a group of figures representing the Vâmana Avatâra, or fifth incarnation of Vishṇu, undertaken by him to punish pride and presumption. The story is this:

Mahâbali, a prince who lived in the Treta yuga, or the second age, was so elated by his prosperity, that he omitted to perform the more essential sacrifices to the

[* See plates V.—IX., *supra*.]

gods. This being highly offensive to them, Vishnu, determined to check so bad an example, became incarnate and assumed the form of a wretched Brahman dwarf. Mahâbali was at that time in possession of the whole universe, having previously acquired this dominion in consequence of his signal piety, or punctual performance of certain austerities and rigorous acts of devotion. Vishnu, in the shape just mentioned, appeared before him, and asked as a boon so much of his wide possessions as he could pace in three steps. This the monarch readily undertook to grant, at the same time desiring him to ask something more worthy for a prince to bestow. The pretended Brahman, however, professed his content with what he had already requested, and the king proceeded to ratify his promise by pouring water into the petitioner's hand, which was, it would seem, the most solemn mode of confirming a grant. As he was doing this, the size of the dwarf grew larger and continued to expand until it filled the whole earth. Vishnu then discovering himself, deprived Mahâbali in two steps of earth and heaven; but in consideration of his previous virtue and general good conduct, he deprived him of no more, but left to his government the kingdom of Pâtâla, a lower or inferior world, said to be the abode of serpents. Some say that the water used in this transaction for the purpose of ratification fell from Vishnu's hand on the head of Siva, and flowing thence, formed the origin of the Ganges.

Vishnu in this character is sometimes called "Trivikrama," "the three-step taker." In this sculpture he is represented eight-handed, and in the act of stepping prodigiously: the right foot is on the ground, and the left is raised sideways as high as his head. It looks, therefore, as it is, very unnatural, for the articulation of the head of the thigh bone in its socket would not admit of such a position. The subordinate figures do not appear to illustrate the story, or at least the version above given of it. Perhaps another circumstance should be related, and the imagination may be allowed under some restriction to be the interpreter: but even then only a part of the figures seem to be connected with the tale.

It is said that *S*ukra, regent of the planet Venus and guru of the Asuras, acting as mantri, or minister,* of Mahâbali, faithfully informed the king of the deceit that was being practised upon him. There is a figure with a dog-like head speaking to another, who seems to rest his chin on his right hand in deep reflection. These two figures occupy the upper part of the sculpture on the left of Vishnu. Below them are two figures in human shape represented as falling. Perhaps the former may represent *S*ukra and Mahâbali at the moment when the prince was first made acquainted by his counsellor with the true character of the dwarf, but was too proud to withdraw his royal pledge: and the latter the same after he had fallen from his high estate: or the two falling figures may imply that the two steps of Vish*n*u had deprived him of the dominion of heaven and earth. What the rest of the figures may illustrate, I do not conjecture.†

On the wall of the opposite or north-eastern end is a sculptured delineation in bas-relief of the Varâha

[* Priest and preceptor, not minister.]

[† Cp. the passages descriptive of the dwarf incarnation given in Muir's *S*anscrit texts, Part IV., pp. 114—131.]

Avatâra. Among the legendary stories of the Hindus, several different accounts are given of Vishnu's reasons for taking on himself this incarnation, and particularly why he assumed the shape of a boar. Among others it is said that a Daitya, or evil spirit, named Hiranyâksha, gained from Brahmâ by his scrupulous piety and the performance of penances of very great efficacy, a promise that he should have given to him anything he asked. Accordingly he desired universal dominion, and exemption from being hurt by the bite or power of any living creature. He enumerated all animals and venomous reptiles that bite or sting, except the boar, which was forgotten. His ambitious desires were no sooner obtained than he became exceedingly presumptuous, proud, and wicked; and forgetting the great power of the gods, he ran away with the whole earth, and plunged it and himself into the depths of the sea! This singular exploit made the interposition of the preserving power necessary; and Vishnu changing himself into the form of a boar, plunged into the ocean; fought a dreadful battle which lasted a thousand years; at length slew the impious Daitya; brought back the earth on his tusks, and restored it to its usual good order, peace, and tranquillity.*

The sculptures illustrative of the story appear to refer to a period subsequent to the battle, for the figures supply the imagination with the idea that the boar-headed deity is now solacing himself after the toils and dangers of his thousand years' conflict.

[* There appears to be confusion here between the story of Hiranyakasipu and the legend of the death of his brother Hiranyâksha.—Cp. Vishnupurâna, Book I., chap. 4, Wilson's note (p. 62, Vol. I., 8vo. edn. by Hall) and chap. 17. Also Muir's Sanscrit Texts, Part IV., p. 29 ff.]

The principal figure, Vishnu (four-handed), is executed with considerable spirit. He stands firmly on the left leg. The right leg is raised, and the foot rests on the head of another figure. On the right knee sits a female; Vishnu's left hand grasps the small part of her right leg, and his right hand passes behind her, a little lower than the waist, while he regards her with interesting pig-headed gravity. His two remaining hands hold a conch shell and the chakra.* Below Vishnu's right leg is the upper portion of a figure with the hands raised as in prayer, its lower part being immersed in what may be supposed a representation of the waves of the sea, (the rock being here very rough and unfinished.) Another figure, rising out of this imaginary water, is also in a posture of supplication; and there are other accessories, but they do not appear to explain the story.

From the back wall of this excavated fane is a projection measuring 7 feet 9 inches broad and 3 feet 6 inches deep. It contains an empty niche, in which, however, may be traced the outlines of a deity, which the chisel of the workman has not brought into being. A flight of three small steps leads into the niche, and on either side its entrance, as well as at each end formed by the projection, is a figure in bas-relief, with the name, attributes, or office of which I am unacquainted.

Sculptured on the back wall between this niche and the north-east end of the excavation is a female figure, probably Devî or Pârvati, the consort of *Siva*, bathing. She is attended by her females and two

*The chakra is a circular piece of metal, not unlike our discus or quoit. M.

elephants, one of which is pouring a vessel of water over her, and the other is receiving another vessel from the hands of one of her attendants.*

On a similar space to the south of the niche is another female figure, which I take to be a representation of the same great personage; in this, however, I am not positive.† On each side of the principal figures are two bulky little fellows, and a fourth figure of a more natural size. There are also two heads of animals, one somewhat similar to an antelope's, the other intended perhaps for that of a tiger.

The front of this excavation is supported by two columns and two pilasters of a handsome style of architecture. The ceiling is ornamented with flowery sculpture, but has several cracks in it running lengthways; *i. e.* in a north-east and south-westerly direction.

About eighty yards west of this place, on the top of the hill, may be found, after a little research, the stone bed, with a lion for its pillow, which, in the account published in the Asiatic Researches already alluded to, is called the Dharmarâja's lion-throne, (No. 10); and at a trifling distance S. W. of this, is the bath of Draupadi. The lion and bed measure in length 9 feet 6 inches, and in breadth 3 feet 6 inches; the lion is 18 inches high, and stretching across the south end appears as if intended for a seat or pillow. The bed lies due north and south, and is hewn out and fashioned on the surface of the solid rock. There is not the least appearance of the place having once been an apartment of a palace, as intimated in that account: the top of the hill here-

[* See note § p. 50, *supra.*] [† See note ‡ p. 50, *supra.*]

about is indeed quite uneven and irregular, and abounds with immense blocks and masses of granite.

There is nothing more which merits notice on the surface of the hill, if we except numerous mortice holes, which may be seen running parallel to its western edge, and many small flights of steps cut in several parts of the rocks.

Leaving the top of the hill, and descending by the path in front of the temple last mentioned, at a few feet south-east of the pagoda which contains the image of Ganesa, will be found sculptured in bas-relief, on the eastern faces of two large rocks, the *story of the Tapas* (No. 11) or intense penance of Arjuna. These two rocks adjoin each other, being divided only by a fissure. They measure 84 feet in length, and about 30 feet in height.

In this group of sculptures, the principal figure, that of Arjuna, is not the largest. He is seen on the left of the fissure in the posture of penance; his arms are raised above his head, his right leg is lifted up. He is supposed to stand on the great toe of his left foot. His arms and right leg appear withered, but his left leg is of the natural size. His chest and ribs are prominent, but the stomach and abdomen sunken; the whole figure representing emaciation from long fasting. Besides this figure there is a multitude of others both of men and animals; and among the latter two well-proportioned elephants as large as life. The largest of them measures 17 feet from the proboscis to the tail, and 14 feet in height. The smaller is in height 10 feet, and in length 11. Under the belly of the larger elephant there is a small one, with the heads and trunks of two others, while the head of a fourth is seen between his proboscis and fore feet. These figures of elephants are cut on the right hand rock on a level with the ground. On the rock to the left, near the fissure, and below the figure of Arjuna, is a neat little temple,* with a niche and a figure† in it. Just within the fissure itself is a figure like that of the Mermaid, but in the native languages it has a name purporting half-woman and half-snake.‡ Scattered over the face of both rocks there are many representations of men, ascetics, monkeys, lions (or what are meant for lions), tigers, antelopes, birds, satyrs and monstrous animals which it would puzzle a naturalist of the present age to nomenclate.§ The whole are executed with considerable spirit, and occupy a space of about 2,400 square feet. A plate giving a representation of these sculptures is published in the 2nd Vol. of the Transactions of the Royal Asiatic Society of Great Britain and Ireland.¶

* At the south-east corner of this little fane, in a sitting and stooping posture, and entirely detached from the rock, is an admirable figure of an ascetic, miserably emaciated, which, though somewhat worn by exposure to the weather, bears evidence to the talent, skill, and anatomical knowledge of the artist.‖

[† Said to be Krishna.]

[‡ Nâga, the name of demi-gods inhabiting the lower regions, the upper part of whose bodies is human, and the lower part that of a serpent. There is the figure of a male Nâga as well as that of a female, but the upper part of the body has fallen off and is lying in front of the rock.]

[§ On the north side of the crevice, at the foot of the rock, is the figure of a cat standing on its hind legs, with its fore-paws raised above its head in seeming imitation of Arjuna, performing penance—after eating part of Krishna's butter-ball—in order that the sea may dry up and she be thus able to devour all the fish! Near the cat are rats, enjoying apparently their temporary immunity from persecution.]

[¶ See plate I. and plate II., No. 1, *supra*.]

[‖ Said to be Drona, (see note * p. 31, *supra*,) the figures, now headless, of whose pupils are in front, and somewhat below that of their preceptor.]

The story of the penance of Arjuna may be told as follows:—

The five sons of Pâ*nd*urâja lost their dominions in play with their cousin Duryodhana; who, however, played unfairly and won through "guile and wicked stratagem."* The consequence was that they and their followers were banished for twelve years and upwards, and were doomed to wander in jungles, wilds, and solitudes. During this period the elder brother took counsel with the others, how they might repossess themselves of their patrimony after the term of banishment had expired: and in order to attain this it appeared desirable to gain the mantra Pâsupatâstra.† This mantra, or incantation, was of such wonderful efficacy, that if it was uttered while in the act of shooting an arrow, the arrow became inevitably destructive, and moreover possessed of the power of producing or generating other weapons, which not only scattered death on all sides, but were able to cause the destruction of the whole world.‡ This mantra could be obtained only from the god Ísvara, (a name of *S*iva); and Arjuna, as he was distinguished among his brethren for his prudence, fortitude, and valour, was employed to procure it.§

The hero of this story had to travel far to the north of the Himâlaya mountains, there to perform austere and rigid penance in order to propitiate the

[* See Wheeler's Hist. of India, Vol. I., chap. 7.]

[† The Pâsupata weapon, not mantra.]

[‡ Cp. Muir's Sanscrit Texts, Part IV., p. 196.]

[§ He went first to Indra by the advice of his grandfather Vyâsa, and afterwards, at the suggestion of Indra, to the Himâlaya, to obtain a sight of Mahâdeva.—Cp. Monier Williams' Indian Epic Poetry, pp. 103—104, and Muir's Sanscrit Texts, Part IV., p. 194 ff.]

god and obtain his favor: and as a preparatory measure he was instructed in all requisite mantras and mystic ceremonies. On reaching the appointed place he found a delightful retreat; a grove or forest abounding with streams and fruits and flowers, with whatever could regale the senses or charm the eye. Not only was the earth most bountiful, but the air was filled with the strains of celestial melody. In this place Arjuna commenced and carried on his austerities by meditation, by prayer, and by ceremonial purification.

During the first month he ate but once in four days: during the second month, but once in seven days: during the third month, only once in fourteen days: and during the fourth month he did not eat at all, but completed his penance by standing on the tip of his great toe, the other leg being lifted from the ground, and his hands raised above his head.* This is the period of the penance which the sculptor has selected for illustration, in the curious work now under notice. The figure of Arjuna is exhibited in a posture agreeing exactly with the story, the relation of which, however, it seems necessary to continue a little further, in order to explain the accessories, the figures of men and animals, with which the whole face of the rock is covered.

The nearest *Rishis*, (hermits or ascetics, who by austerities and meditation may attain, as their object is, riches, power, supernatural arms, or beatitude), seeing the intense devotion of Arjuna, went and reported it to the god Îsvara, who was highly gratified: but in order to try the constancy and courage

[* See the passage from the Mahâbhârata given in the Appendix.]

of the hero, the deity assumed the form of a wild hunter.* One of his accompanying attendants was transformed into a wild boar,† and Arjuna preparing to shoot it was interrupted by the unknown deity, who forbade him to strike his game. Arjuna notwithstanding let fly a shaft, and so did the disguised hunter, and the boar fell lifeless. This occasioned an altercation, which brought on a personal combat; and when Arjuna had expended all his arrows on his antagonist without effect, he tore up rocks and mountains to hurl at him, but they too fell harmless at his feet. This so enraged our hero, that he attacked his foe hand to hand. Such was the daring audacity of this act, and the bold and determined courage of Arjuna, that all heaven was filled with surprise, and the beasts of the forest, and the inhabitants of the etherial regions, alike flocked to witness the contest, which was terminated by the god's revealing himself, and bestowing on his votary the boon he wished for, viz., the Pâsupatâstra.‡

This congregating of the inhabitants of the skies and of the forest, this mixture of men and brutes, makes probable the supposition that it is the second point or period of the story that has been selected by the artist for exemplification, as instanced by the particular postures and variety of the figures seen in this curious carving.

[* Kirâta.]

[† A Dânava (demon) in the form of a boar, was about to attack Arjuna.]

[‡ The story is related in the Vanaparva of the Mahâbhârata.—Cp. Muir's Sanscrit Texts, Part IV., pp. 191—196. The combat between Arjuna and Siva, disguised as a Kirâta, is the subject of the poem Kirâtârjunîya, by Bhâravi.]

Adjoining the sculptured imagery of Arjuna, to the south, are the wide beginnings of an excavation (No. 12) having a front of 50 feet, and a depth at the north end of 40 feet, and at the south end of 35 feet. A large portion of the solid rock projects from the back of the excavation 25 feet, with a frontage of 23 feet, leaving deep recesses on either side, in which stone has been left rough cut for three pillars. The front of this excavation is supported by five octagonal columns,* whose bases are formed of figures of a grotesque horned animal: a sixth column originally existed, its base and capital still remain, but its shaft is removed. At a few feet within is a second row of six columns corresponding with those in front. The ground at the entrance is partly overgrown with bushes, and the cave now affords shelter to the village cattle.

A few yards south of this excavation, opposite to a street of the village is an open building, which from the sculptures it contains may very properly be denominated Kr*ish*n*a*'s Choultry (No. 13). These sculptures are executed on the back wall of the building, or rather that part of the solid hill which forms the back wall. They represent the exploit of Kr*ish*n*a* supporting the mountain Govarddhana in order to shelter his followers from the wrath of Indra,†—the god that darts the "swift blue bolt," the

* The capitals of these columns are not unlike those of some of the pillars of the Indra Sabhâ at Ellora, and of the cave temples of Elephanta. M.

[† See the Vishnupurâna, Book V., chap. 11.—"It seems not unlikely that this legend has some reference to the caves or cavern temples in various parts of India. A remarkable representation of it occurs upon the sculptured rocks of Mahâbalipûr." Wilson's note.—

"Sprinkler of genial dews, and fruitful rains
Over hills and thirsty plains."*

This action is fabled to have been performed by *Krishna* with one of his little fingers at the age of seven.

"With one finger raised the vast Goverdhen;
Beneath whose rocky burden,
On pastures dry, the maids and herdmen trod;
The Lord of thunder felt a mightier God."

Sir W. Jones.

In the present sculpture, the attitude of the God corresponds sufficiently with the story. He appears, however, to sustain the mountain with the palm of his left hand, instead of the little finger as in the poetical version.† The only representation of the supported mountain consists of a rough line running above the whole of the figures. This line has been formed by cutting away as much of the rock as would answer the purpose of giving the requisite degree of relief for typifying, in the above manner, the rugged bottom of the mountain, torn up from its foundations, and sustained aloft in the air. The whole group looks clumsy; the proportions are bad; the countenances are destitute of expression; and little praise is due to it either as a work of art or imagination. So singular a deliverance from sudden destruction ought to have supplied the artist with a subject capable of being embodied with great spirit; but here, instead, is an inanimate, meaningless group, which, but for the principal figure, would not at all

The story is also given in the Bhágavatapuráṇa.—See Eastwick's translation of the Prem Ságar, chap. XXVI.]

[* Sir William Jones,—Hymn to Indra.]

[† "With one hand," according to the Vishṇupuráṇa; "on the little finger of his left hand," according to the Prem Ságar.—See plate 61 in Moor's Hindu Pantheon.]

have interpreted the story. There are about twenty figures of men, women, and children, and as many heads of cows or bullocks. There is one tolerable figure of a brahmany bull, and another of a cow licking its calf while in the act of being milked. It may be that the general quietude and repose of the figures are intended to imply their security from the terrible danger so recently, and still but for the god's interposition, impending over them. In another part of the sculpture is a figure playing on a flute or pipe; this may also represent K*ri*shna, in his character of Muralidhara, *the tuneful.** In this form he is called BálaK*ri*shna, and is said to have amused himself by piping to the swains and damsels of Govarddhana.† This figure of K*ri*shna is small, and might be overlooked; it is situated over the hinder part of the cow and calf just mentioned. At the north end of this sculpture, raised 5 or 6 feet from the floor, is a well executed figure of a brahmany bull in full relief; and at the south end are several figures of beasts apparently intended for lions: one of them, however, resembles the Sphynx,‡ having a human face with a body of a quadruped.

K*ri*shna's Choultry extends in front 47 feet; is 26 feet deep and 12 feet high. The roof is made of hewn stone, which is partially covered with earth; and is supported by three rows of columns, 4 in each. The bases of those in the front row consist of grotesque figures of a nondescript animal, sitting on its

[* *Lit.* "the flute-holder."—Cp. plate 60, fig. 8, in Moor's Hindu Pantheon.]

[† See Eastwick's Prem Ságar, chap. XXII.]

‡ A similar figure is met with at Ellora. M.

haunches, having curved horns, and a long tail which is curled upon its back like the figure 8.

On the hill above this choultry is the *foundation of a rectangular building* (No. 14)* measuring 66 feet in length, and 42 in breadth. In the middle of this is a gateway 12 feet wide, running east and west; and in the gateway are two recesses, each 12 feet square, one on each side. Near the corners of these recesses in the gateway there are four large square stone pillars, 16 feet high, 3 broad and 2 thick, with flowery ornaments. This foundation corresponds with *a similar one* (No. 15) about a hundred yards† distant towards the east, in the plain below; and the two form nearly a straight line with a very ancient temple situated on the sea shore.

From the front of Kr*i*shna's Choultry, on looking towards the south-west, may be seen on the top of the hill, a small *dilapidated building* (No. 16) quite in ruins.

Beneath this is an *excavation*‡ in the side of the hill (No. 17) of a rectangular shape, measuring 25 feet long, 18 feet deep, and 10 feet 6 inches high. The front is adorned by two neatly finished pillars and two pilasters. At each end are imperfect traces and outlines of a group of figures; and on each side of the excavation in front is a neatly finished niche, 3 feet high, 3 feet deep, and 2 feet 6 inches wide. In front of the whole is the skeleton of a verandah 48 feet long, 12 feet high, and 12 feet wide. Steps are cut in the side of the hill, at one end of the

[* It is said to be the commencement of a Gopuram.]

[† The distance is more nearly 300 yards.]

[‡ Called Râmânujajiyyar Mandapam. There is a short inscription on the floor.]

verandah, by which there is an easy ascent to the top of it.

At a few yards distance to the eastward, is a stone bed, with an elevation at the north end of it for a seat or pillow. The bed is 7 feet 3 inches long, and 3 feet 9 inches broad, and the pillow is 10 inches high.

On the eastern face of the easternmost of the detached rocks near this place, may be seen another group of sculptures, representing the same story of Arjuna; but the figures are not so distinct as the former, nor equally numerous, and they appear to have suffered much more from the weather.

On the summit of the most southern eminence of the mountain is a *small ruined temple* of sculptured stone (No. 18) 22 feet in length, 16 feet in breadth, and 16 in height.* Its foundation, which is of brick, measures 30 feet by 26. There is no regular access to it: the roof has fallen in, and the temple is partially covered by an old banyan tree. There is a fine open view of the surrounding country from the top of its walls.

Directly beneath, and cut into the same rock on which this little fane is built, is an excavated temple (No. 19) 33 feet long, 13 feet high; and 17 feet deep. In front are four columns, (one of which is broken), and pilasters at each end. The excavation contains three niches, of which the centre one is the principal; it has a sort of portal before it, and contains a group of figures representing Mahâdeva, Pârvati,

[* Called by the Brahmans Arâkkennei ([illegible]) temple, as one ollock (about 1¼ gill) of oil used formerly to be expended daily for lighting it. This temple once, it is said, contained a lingam.]

their infant son Subrahmaṇya, five other figures and a bull, (Nandi).* The bull is in front of the principal figures, and on its back rests one of the feet of Mahâdeva, and one of those of Pârvatî. In the floor of this principal niche is a circular trench, 4 feet 6 inches in diameter, and about 3 inches deep, in the centre of which is a circular hole 16 inches in diameter, intended probably for the reception of a lingam. The other niches contain no sculptures. The portal before the centre niche projects from the back wall 8 feet 6 inches, and has a frontage of 11 feet. The front of this is sustained by two sculptured columns, and it has pilasters where it joins the wall.

This excavation, however, is chiefly remarkable for the sculptures executed on its side walls. These represent, the one, one of Vishṇu's states of existence, and the other a celebrated conflict between Durgâ and Mahishâsura.

I shall first speak of that on the south-western side representing Vishṇu. Previously, however, it will be necessary to observe that considerable uncertainty attaches to Nârâyaṇa,† or the state or mode of being in which Vishṇu here appears. Hindu Mythology sometimes speaks of it as a mode of existence of Brahmâ, sometimes of *Śiva*, and sometimes

[* On Mount Kailâsa, the "residence of Kuvera, and favorite haunt of *Śiva*."—Wilson.]

[† A name of Vishṇu, but especially considered as the deity who was before all worlds. The word has several etymologies. That given by Manu is "he whose resting-place (ayana) was on the primeval waters (nârâ)," so called because they are the offspring of Nara, the embodied deity. See Wilson's Sans. Dict. under Nârâyaṇa, Goldstücker's Dict. under *ayana*, Muir's Sanscrit Texts Part IV., p. 26 ff., and Wilson's Vishṇupurâṇa, 8vo. edn. by Hall, Vol. I. pp. 55—59.]

of Vishnu in the act of willing the creation.* Under this character Vishnu is represented lying on the lotus, as well as on the thousand-headed serpent Sesha.

The sculpture now spoken of is in bas-relief, and measures 13 feet in length and 8 in height. The figure of Vishnu is 9 feet 6 inches long, recumbent on the snake Sesha, which is ingeniously coiled for his support in several convolutions, forming together a couch 3 feet high from the base; while five of its heads, (as many as could well be introduced,) form a kind of canopy over the head of the supposed deity.† Above the god are two small figures, male and female; below him in front in a kneeling posture, three; and at his feet erect, two. All these but the last are diminutive; but the two at his feet are seven feet high, and one of them grasps a club. The village brahmans say that two of the figures in front repre-

[* See passage from the Nāradiyapurāna, translated by Vans Kennedy,—Researches, p. 200.]

† This representation of Vishnu must be very similar to the following. "Hari is one of the titles of Vishnu, the deity in his preserving quality. Nearly opposite Sultan Ganj, a considerable town in the province of Bahar, there stands a rock of granite, forming a small island in the Ganges, known to Europeans by the name of the Rock Jehangiri, which is highly worthy of the traveller's notice for a vast number of images, carved in relief upon every part of its surface. Among the rest there is Hari, of a gigantic size, recumbent on a coiled serpent, whose heads, which are numerous, the artist has contrived to spread into a canopy over the sleeping god: and from each of its mouths issues a forked tongue, seeming to threaten instant death to any whom rashness might prompt to disturb him. The whole lies almost clear of the block on which it is hewn. It is finely imagined and executed with great skill. The Hindoos are taught to believe, that at the end of every Calpa (creation), all things are absorbed into the deity, and that in the interval of another creation, he reposeth himself upon the serpent Sesha (duration)."—*Wilkins' Hitopadesa.* B.

sent cow-keepers, who had been ill-used by Mahishâsura. These cow-keepers (husband and wife) had come to complain to Vishnu. Before they did so, however, they had inquired of the third figure, said to be a "*Sâstrakâran*," or sorcerer, as to the precise time when they might have a propitious opportunity. That while they were making the inquiry, one of the attendants of Mahishâsura, the figure bearing the club, came to carry them to his master, to punish them for daring to appeal to Vishnu. The other figure at the feet of Vishnu hereupon interposed, and being one of Vishnu's attendants, drove from his master's presence the presumptuous servant of the wicked Mahishâsura. The expression and postures of the figures do certainly seem to correspond with the story; but the tale itself suits ill the position and circumstances of Vishnu Nârâyana, which no doubt is represented in this sculpture.

The sculptures on the opposite or north-eastern end of the temple represent the conflict between Durgâ, (a personification* of active, not passive, virtue), and Mahishâsura, (a personification of wickedness.) These figures merit particular description.

The recess in which they are sculptured is 12 feet

* The *Devatâs* are represented as good beings, the *Asuras* as evil ones, in so far only as there is any countenance to the fiction of personified virtue and vice. That fiction is European. All that I have ever read makes the Asuras blameable because of acquired power; and power is subdued by superior skill or force. In some instances the Asuras are described as cheated, injured, oppressed, rebelling in consequence, and then subdued and destroyed. The story of Durgâ and Mahishâsura is the subject of the *Chandipâtha* of the Skândapurâna†; and is the great occasion of celebration at Calcutta in the Durgâpûjâ feast, which is anything but virtuous. W. T.

[† The Chandipâtha is a portion of the Mârkandeyapurâna. See note * p. 101, *infra*. Also Appendix.]

9 inches long and 8 feet high. To the left is seen Durgâ, mounted on what is intended for a fierce lion. To the right is Mahishâsura grasping a short thick club. The figure of Durgâ is 5 feet high and eight-handed: two of her arms have greater relief than the others, a circumstance which imparts to the figure a much greater appearance of truth and nature than would otherwise be the case. The left principal arm is stretched at full length, and the hand grasps a bow: the right arm is drawn back, as if in the act of discharging an arrow: but we see neither the arrow nor the string of the bow. Her six remaining hands hold respectively, on the left, a bell, a saṅkha, and something not easily distinguishable; and on the right, the fatal cord (pâsa,) a chakra (discus), and a sword. Mahishâsura is represented with a buffalo's head and horns and a human body. He stands in a retiring attitude, resting on his left foot, the right being advanced. His figure measures 7 feet 9 inches, not perpendicularly, but according to the posture in which he stands. Above, below, and behind Durgâ, may be seen her attendant warriors, armed with swords and bucklers: and also two domestics, one with a switch of hair* such as horsekeepers use, the other with a kittisal (or umbrella). Mahishâsura has a similar attendant also. Durgâ's attendants are all dwarfish, corpulent figures; those of Mahishâsura seem of more natural proportions. Durgâ appears the assailant, Mahishâsura on the defensive. Of three figures between the two principal personages, two are in active conflict,

[* Châmara (chauri), the tail of the Yak (Bos grunniens or Poëphagus), used to whisk off flies, also as an emblem or insignia of princely rank.—Wilson.]

and the third is falling headlong. One between the legs of Mahishâsura seems to have fallen; and another of the same party supports himself on his left hand, two fingers of the right being held up to indicate discomfiture and alarm. The whole group is executed with much skill and ability, and evinces the talent of the artist. The figure of Durgâ in particular is represented with much spirit, and is graceful and easy. The following from a paper by Mr. Wilkins in the 1st Vol. of the Asiatic Researches, serves to illustrate the story. "The evil "spirit Mahishâsura, in the disguise of a *buffalo* as "the name imports, had fought with Indra and his "celestial bands for a hundred years, defeated him "and usurped his throne: the story is to be found at "length in a little book called *Chandi*.* The van-"quished spirits being banished the heavens, and "doomed to wander the earth, after a while assem-"ble, and resolve to lay their grievances before "Vishnu and Siva. Conducted by Brahmá they "repaired into the presence of those deities, who "heard their complaint with compassion, and their "anger was so violent against Mahishâsura, that a "kind of flame issued from their mouths, and from "the mouths of the rest of the principal gods, of "which was formed a goddess of inexpressible beauty "with ten arms, and each hand holding a different "weapon. This was a transfiguration of Bhavânî,

[* The Chandipâtha, or Devîmâhâtmya, of the Mârkandeyapurâna, "in which the victories of the goddess [Chandî, Devî, Kâlî or Durgâ] over different evil beings or Asuras are detailed with considerable power and spirit. It is daily read in the temple of Durgâ, and furnishes the pomp and circumstance of the great festival of Bengal, the Durgâpûjâ."—Wilson, Preface to the Vishnupúrâna. See also Muir's Sanscrit Texts, Part IV., p. 370 ff.]

"the consort of *Siva*, under which she is generally "called Durgâ.*" She is sent against the usurper. "She mounts her Lion, the gift of the mountain "Himâlaya† (snowy), and attacks the monster, who "shifts his form repeatedly: till at length the god-"dess planteth her foot upon his head, and cuts it off "with a single stroke of her sword. Immediately "the upper part of a human body issues through "the neck of the headless buffalo, and aims a stroke, "which being warded off by the Lion with his right "paw, Durgâ puts an end to the combat, by piercing "him through the heart with a spear." The reader will observe that the latter part of this story does not correspond entirely with the sculpture just described, but this must not surprise us, for the Hindu Poets, Sculptors, and Painters, seem to claim the license of representing the same action in a thousand different ways, and under a thousand different versions.‡

I am tempted here to transcribe the following lines, written by Sir William Jones, in reference to this subject:—

"§ O Durgâ, thou hast deign'd to shield
Man's feeble virtue with celestial might,

[* Bhavâni, wife of Bhava (*Siva*) is the name given to Pârvatî in her pacific and amiable form, she being called Durgâ in her terrific form.—Wilson.]

[† The abode (âlaya) of snow (hima), personified as Himavat the mythical father of Umâ or Durgâ—hence her patronymic Haimavatî, "daughter of Himavat," or Pârvatî, "daughter of the mountain."]

[‡ Cp. plate 33 in Moor's Hindu Pantheon.]

§ It is now almost universally admitted that Sir W. Jones sullied his great talents by writing hymns to Hindu gods. They all borrow scriptural or classical ideas, and paint the personifications of India with colors not their own. The leading idea in these lines is not Hindu, but European. W. T.

Gliding from yon jasper field,
And, on a lión borne, hast brav'd the fight;
For, when the demon Vice thy realms defied,
And arm'd with death each arched horn,
Thy golden lance, O goddess mountain-born,
Touch but the pest—He roar'd and died."

Marks of the workman's chisel may be seen on a large block of granite, opposite the front of this excavation; and also at a few yards to the north-east of it, on a rough hewn stone, intended for a bed, with an elevation at one end for a pillow. The bed measures 10 feet 6 inches by 4 feet 9 inches: the pillow is 2 feet broad and 12 inches high. There are two small steps at the foot of the bed.

On some of the rocks between this place and Krishna's Choultry may be seen the rude commencement of several designs, which have been abandoned. Amongst them, however, is a finished excavation 21 feet long, 17 deep, and 9 high. The roof is sustained by four strong pillars. There are three niches in this excavation, with the outlines of a figure on each side of the centre niche. There is also a long inscription on the south-west end, now almost illegible.

About a mile to the south of the village in a small palmyra tope is a cluster of monolithic temples. It consists of five,* each differing from the rest in shape and dimensions, and each fashioned out of a detached solid mass of rock.

The first I shall notice stands a little to the west of the others, (No. 20), and is in shape similar to a horse-shoe.† It is a neat piece of sculpture 18 feet

* At a second visit to the place I understood that the sculptor's idea was the construction of five dwellings for the five Pândavas. W. T.

[† Called by the Brahmans the Ratha of Nakula and Sahadeva, the youngest two of the five Pândavas.]

in length, 11 feet in width, and about 16 feet in height. At the south end, that which is right-angled, is a roughly hewn niche, and a portal with two pillars.

The four other temples lie nearly in a straight line; but before describing them I would notice an image of a lion* and another of an elephant, both as large as life, which stand between this small temple and the other four. That of the lion is cracked. It measures in length 7 feet, and round the neck 8 feet: it is sunk in the earth about knee deep; nevertheless it has a noble appearance and its body is well proportioned. The elephant measures 14 feet in length and 12 feet in height. Its circumference in the largest part of its body is about 20 feet: round its head and throat, 14 feet; and round the largest part of the proboscis, 7 feet. It appears somewhat unfinished, and is sunk a little in the earth.

On the eastern side of the temples, near the most northern one, is a colossal Brahmany Bull, (Nandî, the vehicle of *Siva*.) Its head and neck only appear above ground: the length of the former being 4 feet, and the distance between the roots of the horns 3 feet 3 inches.

Of the temples, the most northern (No. 21)† is a neat little structure about 16 or 18 feet high and 11 feet square. The top diminishes on all sides by a parabolic curve, till it ends in a ridge 3 or 4 feet long. It has a niche on the western side, in which is a group of figures said to represent Draupadî, the wife of Dharmarâja.‡ My own idea is that it represents one

*Lion, the symbol of kingly power: elephant—that of great prosperity; and in particular the vehicle of Indra, (called Airâvata.) W. T.

[†Called Draupadi's Ratha.] [‡ And of his four brothers.]

of the consorts of Vishnu or Siva. A female figure is also sculptured on each side of the entrance to the niche.

The temple next to this (No. 22)* towards the south is of a pyramidal shape, and covered with ornamental sculpture. It is about 11 feet in front, 16 in depth, and 20 in height. It is much cracked, has a niche on the same face as the last, but there are no figures within.

The largest temple in the group (No. 23)† stands next in order ;‡ it was abandoned before the design was completed and remains in an unfinished state. Across the middle there is a large rent, in some parts 3 or 4 inches wide ; this has divided the body of the temple, and caused the separation of a large piece of the solid stone on the western side about the centre of the verandah. Another large piece has fallen from the south-western corner. Unfinished excavated verandahs exist round the lower part : and above them, on the outside, the body of the temple diminishes in width and length, so as to leave sufficient space to walk round it. The verandah on the south-eastern or sea-face of the temple is almost choked up with sand ; but that on the opposite face retains its original height, and in it a large block of the solid stone projects from the back wall. The roof or top

[* The Brahmans have named this Arjuna's Ratha.]

[† Called Bhîma's Ratha.]

‡ Mr. Braddock has by an oversight omitted to give the measurements of this temple, I therefore supply them from Mr. Goldingham's account ; although I must here observe that in other measurements as given by them respectively I find some trifling discrepancy. Mr. Goldingham's says that the temple measures 42 feet by 25 feet, and 35 feet in height. M.

of this temple is elliptical, and the general design is beautiful and elegant.

The last and most southern temple of the group (No. 24)* is of a pyramidal shape: its base measures 28 feet by 27, and it is 34 feet in height. It is neatly finished and much ornamented. In the two upper stories on the north-western face are niches; and on the ground story of the same face is a portal with four pillars, projecting from the body of the temple 4 feet. Besides the ornaments which it possesses in common with the rest, this temple has a profusion of figures of various sizes, representing Vishnu and Siva, in some of the many different characters which they sustain in the mythology of the natives. These figures are carved in recesses corresponding with their size; and over the majority of them are inscriptions, of which and of the figures, lithographed sketches may be seen in the transactions of the Royal Asiatic Society before alluded to.

About 3 miles to the north of the village, on the sea shore, are several granite rocks, one of which inclining to the eastward projects about 40 feet above the surface like a huge pillar. On another are sculptured various figures representing heads of fierce horned animals, of the precise appearance of which it would be difficult to give a written description. Returning towards the village, about half a mile north of the village choultry, we meet with a small temple built of hewn stone, and resembling in its ornaments those already described.† The entrance is nearly filled with sand, and the walls are much

[* This is called Dharmarâja's Ratha.]

[† Said to be a Jain temple, and called Mukundanâynâr Kôvil.]

dilapidated by trees which grow out of them. There is nothing, I believe, inside.

The last of these ancient remains to be described, are two temples (No. 26) built eastward from the village close to the sea shore. They are indeed so near the sea that the surf dashes against the foundations of them. They occupy a space of about 1,600 square feet and are becoming ruinous. They adjoin each other, being in some sense but one piece of building; but the existence of their two spires impresses one with an idea of their being two separate temples.* The more lofty structure I imagine to be about 60 feet high. This is the most eastern of the two, and has, overlooking the sea, a doorway 7 feet 6 inches high and 6 feet wide. Within this temple will be found a large broken black granite Lingam,† and a group of sculptures representing Mahâdeva, Pârvati, and their son Kârtikeya or Subrahmanya.‡ The smaller temple contains a similar group of figures. The body of the large temple is inclosed with a massive stone wall, which as well as the temple itself bears the appearance of having been decorated with much ornamented sculpture. Small pieces of chunam still adhering to the ornaments give rise to the conjecture that the temples were either originally coated with it, or have been so covered in subsequent repairs. There can,

[* Cp. Gubbins, *infra*.]

[† It is sixteen-sided, with a perimeter of 6 feet 9 inches.]

[‡ The latter name is that generally used in South India. The son of Siva is called Kârtikeya because he was nursed by the Krittikâs, the personified Pleiades, and Subrahmanya because he is the special guardian of the Brahmanical order. For the origin of another of his names, Skanda, see Muir's Sanscrit Texts, Part IV., p. 296.]

I think, be no doubt that they were once elegant specimens of architecture; though they are now too much decayed to retain many traces of their original beauty.* The mineralogist might possibly form some idea of their age from an inspection of the several species of granite of which the walls are composed. Some kinds of this rock, it is known, are much more liable to decomposition than others, (gneiss especially); and the fact is here evident; some of the stones are very much decayed, while others appear as sound as on the day they were hewn. In a kind of passage of the larger temple is a large mutilated statue of Vishnu, now lying supine.†

These temples were formerly surrounded by an outer stone wall, part of which only is now standing. Two pillars also remain shewing the position of the western gateway.

Huge heaps of granite stones, on several of which are sculptured figures, lie in front and on each side of the eastern temple, and have tended greatly to protect it from the hostility of the sea, which has evidently encroached considerably. Many of these stones are of large dimensions, measuring from 6 to 10 feet long, 3 feet wide, and 1 foot thick; and on some of them are appearances of sculptured architectural ornaments, though the injuries of the weather, the action of the water, and the lapse of time have combined to deface them. About 65 feet in front of the eastern temple, and now standing in the sea, is a

[* "Mr. Fergusson, in his 'Ancient Architecture of Hindostan' declares it [the larger temple] to be with the single exception of the Pagoda at Tanjúr, the finest and most important Vimâna in the south of India."—Murray's Hand-Book of India, Part I, p. 31.]

[† See p. 31, *supra*.]

square stone pillar, (a common appendage, I believe, to all the country pagodas), which measures 11 feet in height and is 22 inches square.*

At a few yards north of the temples, on a detached rock (No. 27) close by the sea, may be observed a gigantic figure of Mahishâsura represented with the head of a buffalo. On a similar detached rock to the south are figures of a horse and an elephant's head (No. 28). These sculptures are considerably worn by the continual washing and action of the surf.†

There is no doubt in my mind that the sea has made considerable encroachments since the erection of these temples. I cannot conceive, were it not so, why they should have been built on the shore, so close to the sea that the surf in the calmest weather dashes against the doorway; while some of the well known appendages of such pagodas are actually at some distance in the waters. The large quantities of stones lying about the temple, and others which partially appear buried in the sea, seem even to indicate that other buildings also have existed to the eastward of these, which are now destroyed and overwhelmed by the ocean.

I have now given an account of all the curious sculptures and buildings which came under my observation at three several visits to the Seven Pagodas, and I believe I have omitted nothing which merits notice. I am fully aware that the account is imperfect; indeed, I hold it impossible to convey a correct idea of the remains of former ages by a written description, even if the account be per-

[* See note † p. 11. and note ‡ p. 51, *supra*. Also Gubbins, *infra*.]

[† There are a number of sculptured bulls (Nandi) lying among the rocks close to the temple on the south side.]

fectly accurate. Who could by such means form a just conception of the actual appearance of the ruins of ancient Persepolis, of Tadmor in the desert, of Pompeii, of the various temples in Italy, and the remains of classic elegance in Greece and the Isles of the Ægean Sea? We may indeed read of pillars, colonades, porticoes, rooms, baths, apartments, and a long list of architectural definitions; but after all, the mind possesses but an imperfect image of the originals. Pictures and drawings help the description, but personal inspection is best of all. I therefore advise you, "gentle reader," if you have it in your power, to visit these singular vestiges of antiquity at Mâmallaipur. I can promise you ample recompense for your trouble. If you have antiquarian curiosity, you may here satisfy it. If you have any disposition to moralize,—as a Christian should do,—on the end of human greatness, you will see that though here it has been attempted to "grave it in the rock for ever," it still passes away; and you will turn your thoughts from these, amongst the most durable perhaps of mortal productions, to that heavenly city which is indeed eternal.

Remarks by the Rev. W. Taylor.

The author of the foregoing paper having done me the honor of transmitting it to me for perusal and remark; and the few cursory observations made having called forth a fuller explanation of his wishes, —although I do not think myself fully able to meet them,—I offer the few following observations on the locality which is the subject of his interesting illustrations.

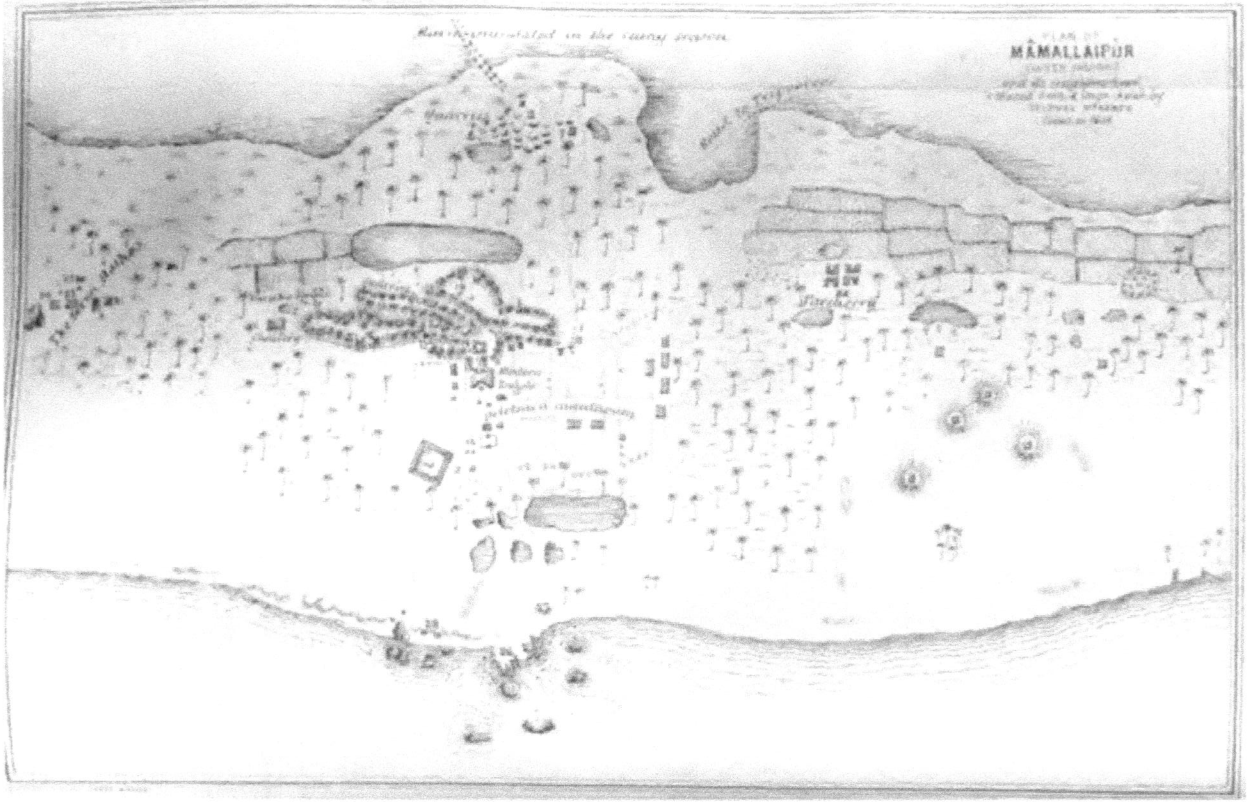
PLAN OF
MÂMALLAIPUR

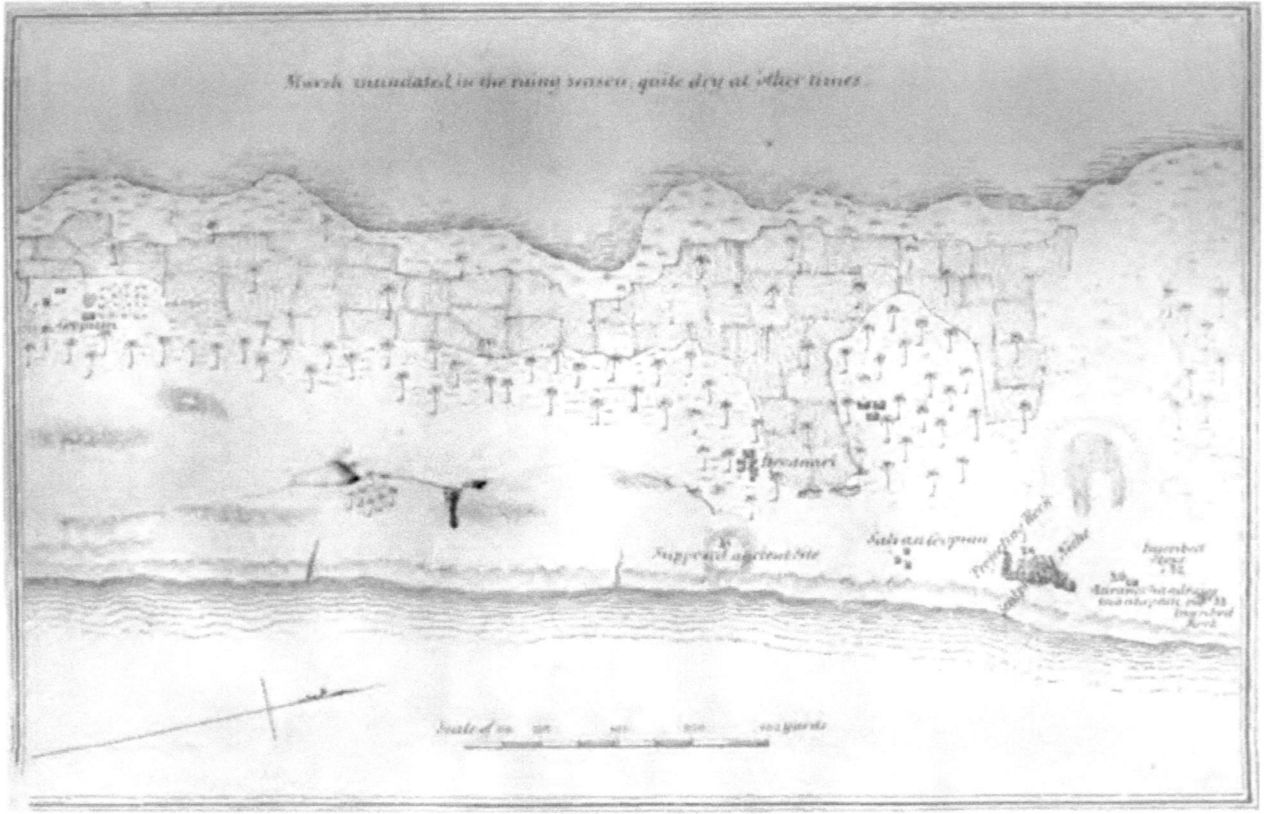
Marsh inundated in the rainy season, quite dry at other times.
Supposed ancient Site

I. THE NAME.* This the people of the neighbourhood colloquially term *Mâvalivaram*. It is also known to natives as *Mâbalipuram*, whence I presume, it became expanded (by Mr. Goldingham if I remember aright) into *Mahâbalipuram*. More recently I observe Dr. Babington has made it *Mahâmalaipûr*, "the town of the great" (or as Dr. Babington understands it, sacred) "hill." If the said reading be actually borne out by the old Tamil inscription near one of the caves, I must submit; but without copy, or fac-simile, the accuracy of the reading may be open to doubt. There is considerable reason[a] to believe that the true reading is *Mâmallapuram*; and the true reading is of consequence.

Malla is a northern patronymic, or rather titular name of a race, like Cæsar, or the Medicis, or the Bourbons. In local papers of the Mackenzie collections, obscure but numerous indications are given of a race of chieftains bearing that surname; of whom Deva-malla-râya is most frequently mentioned. This chieftain was a (Peninsular) highlander in origin; not, properly speaking, Hindu, but of an aboriginal race. Now Deva-malla-râya indicates dignity and lineage: of which title Mâ-malla-râja, would be almost an equivalent; indicating indeed a lower rank, but quite suited as a distinctive epithet of a minor offset from the parent stem. Again in the Mackenzie

[* See Appendix.]

a According to legendary tradition, one named Mallêsndu ruled in early times. He seems not to have been a Hindu, as he mocked a Brahman, and was metamorphosed into an alligator. An appearance of Vishnu is said to have occurred. Before that appearance the place was called *Mallapuri* and *Mallapuri-kshetram*, from the above Mallêsndu. Mackenzie MSS., Book No. 33, C. M. 757, Sect. 9. This paper is in the Telugu language.

local papers, there is abundant evidence of a gradual progress of colonization by Telugu people, from proximity to the Godavery southwards, at least as far as Nellore; and various instances[a] occur in which those who first cleared forest land and began to build a town, gave their own names to the town so formed. I would not assert it as a fact, but I regard it as a probable inference, that the locality, in immediate question, derived its name from its founder, an offset, or junior branch, of the Malla chieftains in the north. I would not leave the name without noticing that in a modern Tamil poem written in the south, mention is made of the king of *Mávalivanam:* but whether this place be designated or not, is doubtful; and I do not think such an authority could be trusted.—Quitting the name of the place we may further advert to

II. The antiquity, or probable antiquity, of the sculptures. That the antiquity is not very great may be concluded by inferential deductions; as 1. The mythology of the figures is Hindu; the general story,

[a] Subsequent to Sál. Sak. 424, or A. D. 502, a person named Mahámalu, or Maválamu, left his native place owing to oppression; emigrated southerly, and built a village of four or five mud huts. It was called after the founder Mavamalúr. It increased; and by a separation of brothers at a later date Nandi-varam was founded, ultimately a town of note. Ibid. Book 49, C. M. 739.

This is merely an illustration. From a yet unpublished abstract of another paper, I find that two persons named Malla-ráya and Annama-deva-ráya, emigrated from Vijayanagaram to the district of Arcot, or neighbourhood of Conjeveram, and obtained some immunities from the wife, or queen, of Deva-ráyar. These people were of the tribe of athletæ, proceeding from the original stock of mountaineers. I cannot identify these persons with Mámalla-puri. At a period later than Krishna-ráyar, there were four avenues leading from Conjeveram to distinguished towns, one of which was Mahábálipuram, then reputed to be of Vaishnava credence.

part of that contained in the Mahâbhârata ; the language of the inscriptions, at least in some places, Sanscrit : therefore Brahmans were some way concerned. But there is much concurring evidence to show that the first immigration of Brahmans to the Peninsula was not of remote antiquity. Besides which consideration, 2. It is beyond doubt that before the time of Kulôttunga Cholan, and his illegitimate son Adon*d*ai, the whole district bounded on the north by the Pennâr, on the south by the Pâlâr, on the east by the sea, and on the west by the ghâ*ts*, was dwelt in by half-civilized people termed Kurumbar, who had embraced the Jaina religion, brought to them from the north. Adon*d*ai chiefly distinguished Kâñchî-puram (Conjeveram) and Tripati, as his places of residence, or capitals. The era of Adon*d*ai is not higher up than the seventh century of our reckoning. He is said to have brought the Brahmans from *S*rî *S*ailam in Telingâna, and certainly attracted a large colony of Sudra *Vellâras*, or agriculturists, from Tuluva or northern Canara. Soon after him the kingdom, which he acquired by the sword, was broken up into petty principalities, and lapsed into a state of partial anarchy. As we can distinctly trace the founding of Vellore to a period later than Adon*d*ai, and to colonization led on by a northern chief, so about the same period, I am inclined to think, the neighbourhood of Mâvalivaram was colonized from the north, by one of the Malla family with his clan. Besides, 3. The Inscriptions are in too perfect a state of preservation to be of remote date. As far as my knowledge extends, inscriptions, with a defined year, have not been met with, in a legible state, higher up than the tenth century. I am aware of one or two *apparent* instances of much higher date, but with the absence of any precise year: hence inconclusive. Fragments of inscriptions in the Pâ*nd*ya kingdom, (the oldest one in the south,) have I believe generally been so worn as to be incapable of connected transcription. But the appearance of the chiselling at Mâvalivaram, (from the distant recollection of about fifteen years), is such that it would tax my credulity greatly to assign them a more distant date than from three to five hundred years.

If then we inquire into

III. The origin, or probable origin, of the place with its sculptures, my own judgment would lead me to fix the possible origin of the settlement at Mâvalivaram to a colonist family of the Malla tribe; subsequent to the rule of Ado*nd*ai, and previous to the ascendancy of the Vijayanagaram ascendancy in the present Carnatic; that is, (loosely stated), between the twelfth and sixteenth centuries of our reckoning. In this opinion I am guided by analogy. The Bhonju family, in that manner, spread itself in a district; afterwards subject to the Gajapati princes of Orissa. The Malla family, from wild mountaineers, became powerful chieftains in Telingâna. Many families, in that way, made subordinate settlements in different village districts of the same country; and, about the period above indicated, some heads of families emigrated from the Kar*nâ*taka-desa proper, and became local chieftains; while many others at a later period, and from different causes, followed a like course. But if I am right in this inference by analogy, it does not follow that a settlement, made in a before pastoral, or waste, country, would at once become a place of power or consequence. The same mode of argument would suggest the need of some centuries, in order to produce such a result; and we know that many mutations occur in such kind of states, when near powerful neighbours. Accordingly though the name of the founder may have continued, yet, the conquest of the South, began by K*r*ish*n*a-râya of Vijayanagaram, and completed by Achyuta-râya, probably* overwhelmed any such principality. Such was the case with the before local powers at Ginjee, and at Tanjore. In those places military commanders became viceroys, and their descendants, kings. And I think it probable that a chief of this latter origin from Karnâ*t*aka proper, (borrowing the idea from Ellora), had the excavations and sculptures made and the inscriptions recorded; especially those in the Ha*l*a Kanna*d*a character and Sanscrit language:

* In my abstract of the Tamil manuscript entitled Karnâ*t*aka-râjâkal, I do not find definite mention of such a supersession: but I think it probable from the general conquest of the neighbourhood; and suppose the district became subject to the local metropolis of Ginjee. In the paper referred to (note *a*) it is stated that Simhama-nâyadu of the Vellugâtivâru race ruled at Mâvalivaram, and employed many artificers, who resorted thither in a time of famine, in making excavations and sculptures on the hill. Following out this indication, I observe that Yachama-nâyadu and Simhama-nâyadu of that race fought a great battle and gained a victory over opposing chiefs in *Sâl. Sak.* 1523 (A. D. 1601). By that time the power of the Vijayanagaram sovereigns was broken; and it said the Mahommedans were concerned in the affair, in connexion with Ginjee and Vellore. The scene of combat was Ootramaloor. This period would mark another change of power superseding the supposed, or rather inferred authority of the viceroys from Vijayanagaram. And if Simhama-nâyadu subsequently employed stone-cutters in the sculptures, then we have the period fixed to the seventeenth century. It is not however absolutely necessary to suppose that all the works were begun by the same chief, or finished (in so far as finished) by the same hands.

of parts of one[d] of which Dr. Babington has given a copy and translation. If this inference approximate to truth, the works alluded to must have been accomplished in the sixteenth or seventeenth century.

These cursory remarks may be concluded with

IV. Miscellaneous observations; chiefly suggested by Dr. Babington's paper in the 2nd volume of Transactions of the Royal Asiatic Society; the latest essay on the subject, of which I have any knowledge. The value of that paper seems principally to be in the plates, from drawings and inscriptions, and especially in the deciphering and translation of the latter. They prove, (as such inscriptions usually prove) very unsatisfying: for this reason perhaps, that the objects in the mind of the recorder, and in that of the archæologist, are entirely different. Of the six inscriptions at this place, to be found in a volume of the Mackenzie MSS., five are of unimportant donations, (including, if I mistake not, the Tamil one mentioned by Dr. Babington;) and one which is of larger import, has only the name of Deva-ráya[e] a clue

[d] In that incomplete inscription on the "small monolithic pagoda," neither date nor proper name of the king or chief appears. *Kámarája* is a mere epithet, and the other name appears to me strange and quite unusual if applied to the ruler. I throw out the conjecture that Jayarana is a Sanscrit word modified into Tamil. *Stambha* is pure Sanscrit for a post, column, or pillar. *Jaya-stambha* is of frequent usage for a triumphal column, or pillar of victory. I would render Jayarana Stambha by "the pillar of the victorious one," without however insisting on being right, because the construction is a little forced; and merely add that possibly Simhama-náyadu may have had the pillar and the inscription cut to commemorate the victory at Ootramaloor: still however preferring the opinion before given.

[e] Connecting this note with note *b*, I think the same Deva-ráya may be meant, but am not certain. There was only one (I believe)

to the date. Now this might be Achyuta-deva-râya, who was very liberal to Conjeveram: or some one later, even a local chieftain; but not, I conceive, any one of the Vijayanagaram dynasty higher up than Achyuta-râya.

The paper by Dr. Babington appears to me to contain some minor inaccuracies,[f] on which it might be trifling, or invidious, to dwell; but the supposition that the place was merely an Agrahâra, and that Brahmans procured the sculptures to be made at their own cost,—with the more astounding denial, that the sea has encroached on the Coast of Coromandel, are not of trifling import. As to the first, it contradicts all known experience, in so far only as relates to Brahmans laying out funds at their own entire control, on such sort of works. The second is a point of greater magnitude. I regard the

of the older Vijayanagaram dynasty that bore that name without any prefix. He ruled about Sâl. Sak. 1334, or A. D. 1412. In these dates I follow one MS. authority, without deciding that it is the best. A list with different dates may be seen in Mr. Campbell's Telugu grammar; in which also instead of simply Deva-râya we read Ganda-Deva-râya. But after Krishna-deva-râya all of the second dynasty bore it, with a distinctive prefix. Probability inclines to the latter period, between S. S. 1451 and 1508, or A. D. 1529 and 1586. Nevertheless it must not be forgotten that about A. D. 1400 the power of the Râyas has been traced at Trichinopoly and Madura, in the person of a general named Companna-udiyâr, who annihilated the remains of the first Mahomedan incursion to the southward. The state of the modern Carnatic was however too unsettled to permit the supposition of the first Deva-râya making grants or donations within its boundaries.

[f] It is not my wish to be very particular: however the statement by Dr. Babington that "the copper and stone inscriptions found……… in many parts of the country, are all in the Sanscrit language," does not agree with the mention made by himself of a Tamil inscription in or near the Varâha-mandapam; nor with the recent discovery of some, as is stated, Pâli inscriptions in the north. But keeping within

few data on which the denial of any encroachment of the sea is founded, as quite inconclusive; though this does not seem to be the place for their discussion, nor yet for the statement of contrary facts and arguments. It is a point on which I apprehend Dr. Babington to be at issue with truth: but beyond this mere expression of an opinion, it does not seem important further to pursue the subject, in these very cursory annotations.

Having had an opportunity of reading over these remarks after an interval of more than a year and a half, and having seen, in the interim, copies of two inscriptions from the neighbourhood of Mâvalivaram, in the Tamil language and old Tamil character, I find that the spelling therein is *Mâmallaipûr*, with two *l's*. The language is not the pure old Tamil; but the orthography is so generally correct, that the two *l's* cannot be an orthographical error; and if not, then the word does not mean *hill*. The language is comparatively modern Tamil; being much mixed with Sanscrit derivatives, which is not the case with very old Tamil. The name of Deva-râya appears; and an opinion seems to have been formed

the limits of the peninsula, the interests of truth require me to state with entire respect, while touching on the subject, that the Mackenzie papers contain many hundred copies of inscriptions in Canarese, Telugu, Malayalam, and Tamil; many of which I have examined, and can attest that, though copies, they are not translations. It is not an unfrequent case to find inscriptions with florid Sanscrit slokas at the beginning or end, with the real matter of fact in plainer prose of the vernacular language. The undeciphered part of the inscription given by Dr. Babington requires further attention, for its present obscurity may involve some such humbler termination.*

[* See Appendix.]

that it meant a Chola king. I cannot positively deny such an inference; nor yet another inference that similarity of character in neighbouring inscriptions, must argue identity of origin. The subject is confessedly open to variation of opinion; and inquiry would seem to be requisite before a decision can be positively made.

Supplement by Walter Elliot, Esq.

Besides the objects of interest usually visited at the Seven Pagodas, there is a spot about two miles north of Mahâmallaipûr, the sculptures and inscriptions at which will be found not unworthy of attention. Proceeding along the sea-shore towards Madras, at the distance above mentioned, a quadrangular space inclosed by mounds of considerable extent, No. 31 in the map, called by the fishermen Devanêri, will be observed. From the appearance of these mounds, added to the fact that numerous copper coins, glass-beads, and bits of iron, copper, &c., are picked up after heavy rain or high winds on their surface, it might be supposed that they indicated the site of some ancient edifice or fortification: but an excavation made in 1840, completely through one side, failed to elicit any discovery in support of such an opinion. The section was carried, through pure sand, to a depth of 20 feet, and the only extraneous substances met with were some pieces of charcoal, at different depths.

About quarter of a mile farther, near a collection of fishermens' huts, called *Sâl*uvan-Kuppam, are some remarkable rocks, standing a considerable height above the beach, and known by the name of I*dai*yan

Pudal. One of these exhibits a niche or panel, surmounted by an arched border composed of the heads of the Simha, or fabulous lion of Hindu mythology, carved in relief; while another has been rough-hewn into the outline of the same animal. Beyond this is a stone Ma*n*dapam, or temple, almost entirely buried in the sand. Within is a Lingam. This is the site of the inscriptions referred to by Dr. Babington, in the 2nd Vol. of the Transactions of the Royal Asiatic Society, as having been sent to him by Colonel De Havilland. Of these Nos. 1 and 2 of plate 15, pronounced by Dr. Babington to be identical, are engraved on the end walls of the Ma*n*dapam on either hand of the entrance. On the frieze above the entrance likewise, occurs the word, in each of the two characters deciphered by Dr. Babington,

"ATIRANACHANDAPALLAVA."

At a little distance to the north-west of this temple, on a flat stone, (No. 32 in the map), level with the surface, occurs the following in old Tamil characters :—

ஸ்வஸ்தி ஸ்ரீ இச்சகதலதமானுர்க்கு மடிதவிட்டாகு மாப்
பட்டியில் திருவமிதிக்கு இருமாவிலமும் திருவிளக்குக்கு
கழஞ்சு பொன்னும் குடுத்தது.

"Salutation! two Más[1] of land in Mápatti[2] for a sufficient daily "meat offering, and a Karanju[3] of gold for maintaining a lamp, are "granted to Ijjagatala[4] Tamánár."

About 100 yards north of the Ma*n*dapam is a mass of natural rock, (No. 33 in the map), one end of

[1] A Má is a 20th part, [here of a Véli = 6·6157 acres.]*

[2] Mápatti is probably the name of a field.

[3] Karanju, an ancient weight [= about 72 grains.]

[4] Ijjagatala Tamánár "the Lord of this world." Tamánár should probably be Tambánár; the title refers to Atiranachandesvara.

which is covered with a long inscription in ancient Tamil. The character, as well as that on the flat stone just mentioned, is quite different from those above alluded to; but corresponds with the one first described in Dr. Babington's paper, as "seen on a face of rock by the side of the inner entrance to the Varâhasvâmi pagoda"[5] on the south side of the hill at Mahâmallaipûr, and of which an alphabet is given in plate 13. The greater portion is buried in the sand; but in 1840 this was cleared away, and a transcript of the whole carefully made, of which the following is a translation. The original in modern characters is given at the end of this article; (marked A.)

"Salutation!

"In the presence of TIRUVÂYKÊRVI.[6]

"In the 37th year (Ându) of the reign of TRIBHUVANACHAKRAVARTI,
"Sovereign of the three worlds,[7] who having taken (or holding)
"Madura, Îram (or Ceylon), and Karuvûr, and the crowned head of
"Pândiyan, made the Virâbhishekam and Vijayâbhishekam, (i. e., the
"lustrations of heroism and victory;...........and, by the grace of
"ADISANDESVARA, in the temple of SUBRAHMANYA DEVAR, in the De-
"vadânam—Brahmadeyam—village[8] of Tiruvirichilûr, in the Âmur
"Kôttam of the victorious Cholamandalam:

"We Ândâr Tillai Nâyakar, the overseer[9] of (the temple of) SRI
"MAHESVARA; Chembiya Mûvênda Vêlâr, the steward[10] of this tem-
"ple; Pan Mahesvara Battan, otherwise called Âfkonda Villi Selvap-

[5] Page 263, [p. 53, supra.]

[6] This is read in two senses. Some explain Tiruvâkêrvi as Sarasvatî, the goddess of learning; while others read the invocation thus, May the Âgamas and Vedas be pre-eminent.

[7] Tribhuvanachakravartigal, a repetition of the King's tirolar name.

[8] Granted for the support of the gods and of Brahmans.

[9] Kangâni, literally a watchman or superintendent.

[10] Srikâryam or chief servant.

"pirân, a Siva Brahman, having proprietary right[11] in this temple "and officiating in it[12]; Nârpattennâyira Battan, also named Âludaiyân "Jñânam Pôttân, a Siva Brahman, having proprietary right in this "temple and officiating in it; and Tiruvirichiludaiyân, the accountant "of this temple; all of us have sold the lands, (herein undermention- "ed), and executed a deed engraved on stone, in favour of Ândâr Ka- "ruppûrudaiyân Nambi Anputa Kûttar,[13] performing his adorations "in this temple. The lands, which we sold to this person because the "revenue[14] in the treasury[15] of the god has proved deficient, on "account of the decrease in the collections (or assessment[16]) of Tiruvi- "richilûr, the property of the sacred name[17] of Pillaiyâr, are as "follows:

"In Peri yêri Karani, Kuri
" { Adaikâdu Tenkûru........................180
" { Attipattam..................................250
"In Ûnal êri Karani,
" { Âdi Mallai Nâtan
" { Rettai Cheruvu
"In Têngam Karavu or Anputa Kûttan,
" { Tâdcheruvu [?]
" { Urâkkundil
" { Pâvasâni
" { In Nîrôdu Karuval
" { Chi*** Karuval
"amounting to Kuris...................2,390

[11] Kâni.

[12] Devarkanmi-kshetra.

[13] Kûttan is still a title of the nobler class of Todavers on the Neilgherry Hills.

[14] இறை. In the Saduragarâdi, the meaning of this word is given as Kadirvâram, the ryot's share.

[15] பண்டாரம், a sacred treasury. Hence, in the Travancore state, the terms employed for that Sircar; to intimate that the Government is under the especial protection of the deity.

[16] இறைத்திரட்டு.

[17] திருநாமக்காணி, a respectful mode of describing the property of the god.

In Talai Sari Pálam.

" Udaiya Nambi

" Kottamânu

" Kuditângi

" Sivadâsa

" Pattavritti

" amounting to Kuris..................1,440

" Total Kuris...4,150

" Being Nilams 2, Mâ 1½.*

" This extent 2 Nilams, 1½ Mâ, and also the building site and " garden containing 400 Kuris situated to the east of Aaputa Kûttan " and Urâkkundil, we have sold to this person (aforesaid), to be his " property, and have received its value, 200 new cash, into the " Pillaiyâr's treasury, and engraved the deed (of sale) on a stone.

" Having consented (to his) irrigating these lands either naturally " or artificially, and also conveying sufficiency of water to the trees, " we engraved this on stone in favor of Karuppûrudaiyân Nambi " Aaputa Kûttar.

" We, the Proprietors of this Temple, have given.

" Thus (Signed) Tillai Nâyaka.

" Thus (,,) Pan Mahesvara Battan, or Âkonda Villi Selvappirân, a Siva Brahman, having hereditary right in this temple and officiating in it.

" Thus (,,) Âludaiyân Jñânam Pettân Nârpattennâyira Battan, a Siva Brahman, having hereditary right in this temple and officiating in it.

" Thus (,,) Siva [? Sri] Kâryam Chembiya Mûvênda Vêlân.

" Thus (,,) Tiruvirichilududaiyân, accountant of this temple.

" I, Nârpattennâyira Pillai, of Tiruppôriyûr, know this.

" I, Munichettu Nârâyana Bhattan, of Chiaudâvûr, know this.

" I, Vêlân, of Chirudâvûr, Âmûr Nâttu, know this.

" I, Periâudân, for Muran Kali Nesi and Nekkunmaravu, [? Kali Nesi, Mananeri, and Marava] of Mâmbâkam, know this.

[* 144 sq. ft. = 1 Kuri, 100 Kuris = 1 Mâ, 20 Mâs = 1 Vêli, or Nilam.—See note 1, p. 120, supra.]

"I, Kurôvi Donnya Battan, of Paiyanûr, know this.

"I, Mayindi Kuri [Nârâyana] Battan, [of Paiyanûr] know this.

"I, Vishamûr Kiravan, know this.

"I, Âmûr Nâttu Vêlân, of Mâmallapuram, know this.

"I, Kuvalaikkanni Maya Kirân Vichan, [? Mâmbâkirân Vichâsiran.] Warden of the Pillaiyâr temple, know this.

The inscription appears to be an ancient deed of sale, and its importance in this place depends on the means it affords of obtaining some clue to the date at which it was made, and which Dr. Babington hopes may yet be obtained from the similar Varâhasvâmi Sâsanam. That however given in the commencement is only the ându, or year of the reign of one of the Chola Princes, the exact chronology of which dynasty is yet to be ascertained. There is, however, another inscription, of an ascertained date, at the neighbouring hamlet of Pavarakkâran's Choultry, engraven on a stone under a large Pipal tree, near the steps on the south side of the tank, the characters of which are precisely the same as those of the Sâluvan Kuppam rock and the temple of Varâhasvâmi; who appears moreover to have been the common divinity of all three villages. It is as follows: (vide the original, in modern characters, marked B.)

"Prosperity! at the holy time of the Makara Saṅkrama, on Wed-
"nesday, the 5th in the constellation of Uttiratâdi, in the Brahma
"yoga, in the Bâlavâkarana, in the light fortnight of the month of
"Makara, in the cycle year Manmatha, and Saka year 1157, when
"Sriman Mahârâjâdhirâja Paramesvara Srî Vîra Pratâpa Vikrama
"Deva Mahârâyar ruled over the earth, (on that occasion,) Tiruven-
"gala Nâyakar gave the piece of land surrounding the Mandapam,
"dedicated by Timmappa, for the halting place at the festivals of
"Pârivêttai of Perumâl Âdivarâha Jñâna Pirân, the deity of [the three
"villages] of Puñjâri, Tiruppârkadal, and Mahâmallaipuram, extend-

"ing over 1,000 Vélis* of land, in the Vadakanâdu,† of the Kôttam of "Âmûr, in the Victorious Chulamandalam.—This piece of land, and "the salt pan in Kûttapâkam, called Vîraya Pâmban, have been "given so long as the moon endures for the Pâdivêttai Tirunâl of "this deity. Additions may be made to this donation. May this "charity be continued so long as the moon endures! Let the "hidden treasures, waters, minerals, and every thing which the "land or the salt pan contain within their limits, become the pro-"perty of this deity. Any person that injures this charity, will incur "the guilt of having killed a cow on the banks of the Ganges. The "Kâniyâlars, (or Proprietors of the land), Sengalangamâr, Nayina Mu-"daliyâr, and Vayirava Nayinâr, have affixed their signatures to this "gift. Thus also Paiyanûrudaiyân Uttamaprâyan Annappan, the "village accountant has signed. May prosperity continue!"

Who Vikrama Deva was, does not appear; but he may have been a local officer, perhaps a feudatory or governor under the Cholas; which dynasty shortly afterwards gave way to that of the Râyas of Vijayanagaram (Bijanagar.) The *Sâlivâhana* year 1157, corresponding with A. D. 1235, however, gives a tolerable approximation to the Era of the Tamil inscriptions; which, as connected with the worship of Vishnu under the form of the Boar incarnation, and the representation of the same subject in one of the caves, (plate 5 of Dr. Babington), affords also some clue to the period at which the sculptures were executed. A further guide to the eras of both the Tamil and Nâgari inscriptions may be obtained by combining and comparing some scattered notices obtained in other inscriptions.

An inscription at Dhâravaram in Rajahmundry shews that a Vira Chola Deva‡ was reigning in *S. S.*

[* See note 1, p. 120, *supra*.] † Northern District.

‡ He also bore the titles of Kulôttunga, which seems to have been adopted by several Chola princes; of the 7th Vishnu Varddhana; and of Tribhuvana Malla in other inscriptions from the same district. See MS. Catalogue of the McKenzie inscriptions.

1001 or A. D. 1079. His name too occurs in the best authenticated lists of the Chola dynasty. I have no doubt that this is the prince above alluded to. The grant would, therefore, be in 1038, or about a century anterior to that of Pavarakkâran's Choultry.

That these Tamil inscriptions were posterior to the formation of the Atichandesvara Mandapam, the *Rathas* and the temple cut out of a single mass of rock, (from which Dr. Babington copied the Kâmarâja inscription,) is established by the invocation of Adisandesvar,* the tutelary deity of Tiruvirichilûr, in the inscription on the rock.

In a copy of a Grant at Pithâpûr, in my possession, Vijayâditya, the founder of the Chalukya dynasty of Kalinga, about the middle of the 6th century,† is described as "destroying the southern "King Trilochana Pallava, and, through the decree of "Fate, losing his life in that country." From the title Pallava it may be inferred that this chief was of the same race and probably the same family as Kâmarâja, surnamed Jayaranastambha (the pillar of successful war), and Atiranachanda Pallava.

Another inscription, engraved on a set of copper plates, (in the possession of Mahendra Shanta, a Jain Guru at Hyderabad,) and of an era 60 or 70 years later, contains the following passage :—

* Adisandesvara must be identical with "Atiranachandesvara," the Lingam set up by Atiranachanda. See Dr. Babington, Trans. Roy. As. Soc., Vol. II., p. 267, [p. 59, *supra*.]

[In Tamil, the ட pronounced "ta" at beginning of a word, and "da" in the middle, is identical with the Grantha and Nâgarî "ta"; and ச is the only Tamil equivalent for the Nâgarî "cha," ["sa," and "sa."]

† About S. S. 475 or A. D. 553.

"Having conquered in battle, the hostile kings in the different "quarters, &c., he acquired the names of Paramesvara and Vikramâ-"ditya.* Moreover, Pallava Mardu was overcome by this Lord *Srî* "Vallabha, who annihilated the renown of Narasimha, surpassed the "valour of Mahendra, and excelled Isvara in affability. He has justly "assumed the title of *Srî* Vallabha, being in the unprecedented pos-"session of Kâñchi, as it were the loosened zone (kâñchî) of the "Nymph of the south. He is also rightly entitled to the name of Râja-"malla, having secured his acquisition by his large and strong arms, "and conquered the chief (Pâlaka) of the Mahâmalla race."

From these facts it may be inferred, that the rulers of Mâmallaipura were in a state of independence in the 6th and beginning of the 7th centuries. We know from other sources that the Chola Kings reduced To*n*da*m*a*nd*alam about the 7th century.† At that time it was parcelled out among a number of petty chiefs of the Kurumbar race,‡ who with their followers were almost entirely extirpated by the Cholas. The family that possessed Mâmallaipura was probably one of the principal of these. The excavations therefore could not well have been made later than the 6th century. Neither could they have been much earlier, for the forms of the letters both Grantha and Nâgarî do not justify the supposition of a higher antiquity.§

Under the Chola dynasty we find Tamil invariably employed as the character of inscriptions.

* This refers to one of the early Chalukya kings of Kalyân, who is described in the beginning of the copper plates as son of *Satya Srîya*, grandson of Kîrti Varma and great grandson of Pulikesi. His era was about *S. Saka* 548, corresponding with A. D. 626. The Kalinga and Kalyân dynasties were collateral branches of the same race.

† Ellis in Trans. Mad. Lit. Soc. p. 19.

‡ 2nd Report on the McKenzie MSS. by the Rev. W. Taylor, p. 86. [Madras] Journal VII., p. 311.

§ See Prinsep's comparative table of Hindu alphabets.

Whether all the temples were excavated by the Pallavas seems questionable. They were evidently worshippers of Siva. Many of the subjects, particularly those in plates 2, 5, 7, 10 of Dr. Babington's paper, belong to the Vaishnava creed, which is more particularly referred to in the inscription at Pavarakkâran's Choultry, and is known to have been of later origin. It is not improbable, therefore, that these may have been the work of more recent devotees, emulous of the fame of Kâmarâja and Atiranachanda Pallava.

In the possession of the Pujâri of the modern temple is a deed in Telugu, engraved on copper plates connected by a ring, with the figure of a boar and a sword on the seal, purporting to be a grant of the village of Nelatûr to Kesavârya Srî Rangâchârya by Venkatapati Srîdevarâya in the Saka year 1532, Plava Samvatsara.

A.

[illegible] முன்பாக [illegible] [illegible] மதுரையும் [illegible] [illegible] கொண்டு [illegible] [illegible] [illegible] [illegible] [illegible] [illegible] வேளாரும் கோயில் [illegible] [illegible] [illegible]

டையபிலவரு ராஜனைவ்தேவர்கன்பிகெடித்திரத்து ஆளுடையா
ன் ஞானம்பெற்றுளுன கற்பத்தென்னுயிரபட்டனும் - கோ
யில் கணக்கு திருவிழிச்சிறுடையானும் - இவ்வனைவோரும் இ
க்கோயிலில் கும்பிட்டிருக்கும் ஆண்டார் கருப்பூருடையா
னம்பி அற்புத கூத்தற்கு விலையிலே ஊரோ ணம் பண்ணி கல்
வெட்டி குடுத்த பரிசாவது பிள்ளையார் **திருகாம** காணியாக
திருவிழிச்சில் உள்ளூரில் இறை **இரப்பு** அமிதாய ஸ்ரீ பண்
டாரத்தில்தட்டிறை இருக்கையால் காங்கள் இவர்க்கு விற்று
குடுத்த நிலமாவது - பெரியேரி கழனியில் அடைகாடுதென்
கூறு - தி ஏஅல ம் - அக்கிப் பட்டன் தி - உஏஇல ம - வை
றன் ஏரிகழனியிலை நிமல்லே காதனும் - செட்டை செறுவும்
தேக்கமகழுவனுமான அற்புதகூத்தனும் - உவாருண்டிறம்-
பாவசாகியும் நீரோகெழுவனும். சீ க க க கழுவனும் - ஆ தி -
உதஉஏஅல - தலைசரிப்பானத்தில் உடைய சம்பியும் - கொற்
றமானும் - குடிதாங்கியுந் - சிவதாசனும் - பட்டவிருத்தி
யும் - ஆ தி - **தசாசாய** - ம - ஆ தி - சதாஇல - னுல் -
நிலம் **- உட்சு - நிக்கிலம் - இரண்டே** ஒருமாவரையும் - அ
ற்புதகூத்தனுக்**கும் - உவாக்குண்டிஇக்குங் கிழக்கு**மனையும்-
உள்படப்படையும் **-** தி **சா ம-இவர்க்கு காணியாக பெறும்**
விலைக்கு விற்று பிள்ளையார் ஸ்ரீ பண்**டாரத்துக்கு கைக்கொட்**
டுதுக்காசு - கூ - இக்காசு மூன்றுற்றுக்கும் - விலைக்குற
விற்று கல்வெட்டிக் குடுத்தோமிக்கிலக்களுக்கு நீர்பாய வே
ண்டுவதும் - இறைக்கக்கடவதும் - ஏரிகளிலே நீர்பாய வே
ண்டின் கொத்த நீர்பாயவும் இப்படிக்குச் சம்மதித்து கருப்பூ
ருடையானம்பி அற்புதகூத்தர்க்கு கல்வெட்டி குடுத்தோம்.
இக்கோயில் ஸ்ரீமாகேதேரம் - இப்படிக்கு இவை தில்லை காய
கன் எழுத்து - இப்படிக்கு இவை இக்கோயில்காணி உடைய
சிவப்பிரானனவ்கெடித்திரத்து ஆட்கொண்ட வில்லிசெல்வ
பிரானுன பன்மாகெஇ மூரபட்டன் எழுத்து - இப்படிக்கு இ
வைகோயில் காணியுடைய சிவப்பிரானைவ் கெடித்திரத்து
ஆளுடையான் ஞானம் பெற்றுளுன கர்ப்பத்தென்னுயிரபட்
டனெழுத்து - இப்படிக்கு இவை சிவகாரியம் செம்பியமூ
வேந்த வேளான் எழுத்து -, இப்படிக்கு இவை கோயில் த

ணக்கு திருவிழிச்சிறுடையான் எழுத்து—இப்படி அறிவேன் திருப்போரியூர் நாற்பத்தெண்ணாயிர பிள்ளையோன் - இப்படி அறிவேன் சிறுதாவூர் மூறிச்செட்டு நாராயண பட்டனேன் - இப்படி அறிவேன் சிறுதாவூர் ஆமூர்நாட்டு வேளானேன் - இப்படி அறிவேன் மாம்பாக்கிழான் கலினெறிக்கு மறனெறிக்குமறவுக்கு பெரியாண்டானேன் - இப்படி அறிவேன் வையனூர் குசோவி டொ னையபட்டனேன் - இப்படி அறிவேன் வையனூர்மலிந்திருதி நாராயண பட்டனேன் - இப்படி அறிவேன் விசலூர்கிழவனேன் - இப்படி அறிவேன் மாமல்ல புரத்தேரில் ஆமூர்காட்டுவேளானேன் - இப்படி அறிவேன் இப்பிள்ளையார் **தேவதருமதுவகைக்** கண்ணிமாம்பாக்கிழான் விச்சாதிரனேன்.

8.

ஸ்வஸ்திஸ்ரீமன் மகாராசாதிராசபரமேஸ்வரஸ்ரீவீரப்பிரதாப விக்கிரம தேவமகாராயர் பிறுதிவிராச்சியம் பண்ணியருளாநின்ற - சகாப்தம் - ஆஉஇலி - மேற்செல்லாநின்ற மன்மதவருஷத்து மகரநாயற்று **பூறுவபக்ஷத்து** பஞ்சமியும் - புதவாரமும் - உத்திரட்டாதியும் - பிறம்மயோகமும் - பாலவகரணமும் **பெற்ற - மகாசங்கிரம** புண்ணியகாலத்திலே - செயங்கொண்டசோழமண்டலத்து - ஆமூர் கோட்டத்து - வடகரட்டு ஆமிரவெளிப்பற்று ஆன பூஞ்சேரி திருப்பார்க்கடல் மகாமல்லைபுரத்து பெருமான் - ஆதிவராகம் - ஞானப்பிரான் பாடிவேட்டை திருநாள் எழுந்தருளுகிற மண்டபம் சூழ்நாற்பாற்கெல்லையும் திம்மப்பனல் சாதனமாகவும் - சுவாமி இறக்குவதற்கு தானமாகவும் - இக்கிலம் கூடநபாக்கத்தில் வீரயப்பாம்பன் - **அனம் - ஒன்றம்** - இந்தப்பெருமாளுக்கு பாடிவேட்டை திருநாள் ஆசந்திரஸூரியராக இந்தத்தற்மம் விருத்தியாய் தானமாகத் திருவேங்கடநாயக்கன் விட்டதன்மம் - ஆசந்திரஸூரியரில் நடக்கக்கடவதாகவும் - இந்த நாற்பாற்கெல்

லையிலும் - இந்த ஒரு அரைத்திலும் - உண்டான இந்தகிகெடி
பாஜலபாஷாண சகலசமுதாயப் பிராப்தியும் - இந்த நூனப்
பிராஜுக்கே செல்லக்கடவதாகவும் - இந்த தன்மத்துக்கு - அ
க்கிரமம்பண்ணினவன் - கெங்கைக்கரையிலே கபிலைப்பசுவை
வதைத்த தோஷத்திலே போகக்கடவராகவும் - இந்த தன்ம
த்துக்கு காணியாளர் - செங்கலங்கமார். கவினமுதலியார்-வ
யிரவகவிஞர் எழுத்து. இப்படிக்கு ஊர்க்கணக்கு பெயலூ
ருடையான் உத்தமபிராயன் அன்னப்பன் எழுத்து - ஸஹஸ
ரீ வடை.

V.—*On the Inscription near the Varâhasvâmi Temple, at Mâmallaipuram or the Seven Pagodas, with a transcript and translation.* [By Sir Walter Elliot, K.C.S.I.]

[From the Madras Journal of Literature and Science, Vol. XIII. 1844.]

THE above-mentioned inscription is cut in a niche, on the face of the rock against which the modern pagoda is built. The eastern side of the building abuts on the niche, about one-fourth of which is in consequence covered by the wall, and a considerable portion of the writing is thereby hidden from view. The circumstances under which the transcript was made, will be found in the Proceedings of the Committee of the Literary Society of the 6th July 1844, at the end of this No. [31]. Three copies of the inscription were made by three different parties, which were collated by Tàndavaràya Mudaliyâr, the learned Principal Sadr Amîn of Chingleput, who also supplied a Telugu paraphrase of the whole, by the aid of which the present translation has been prepared.

Svasti *Sri*!

In the 9th *âṇḍu* of Koppara-kesari-varma, also called Udaiyâr *Sri* Râjendra Devar, who having taken the whole Irattaippâdi seven lakhs and a half, having intimidated Âhava-Malla in battle amid the pitfal (koppam) of his army, seized upon his elephants and horses, and performed lustrations of victory, when he deigned to sit upon his throne;—the citizens of *Jananâthapura*, which is Mâmallapura the chief city of Âmûrnâd in Âmûrkoṭṭa in the prosperous Cholamandalam, (Sôramandalam) and we the inhabitants of Pêrilam, do record that the eastern boundary of the land which we have granted for Âlvâr (Ârvâr)* in the temple of Paramesvara Mâhavarâha Vishnu in our village, inclusive of the land formerly held free of tax, as *Devadânam*, lies west of Sikuṭṭichêri—its southern boundary is the north side of Vayaluṟân kaṇṇâr nilam, belonging to Mahâvishnu in this village,—its western boundary is the vast (shore of the) backwater (or creek)—and its northern boundary (reaches to the) south side of the temple of Mâmallai Perumâl and to the fresh water well on the south-east of the Kônêri—we have granted to the Devar as *Devadânam*, free of tax, all the lands within these four limits, over which the guana has run and the tortoise has crawled, inclusive of *ûr nilams* and *punjey nilams*, setting apart four *kulis*† of land with trees and arable fields within this tract, for the expenses of meat-offerings (*bali*) to the deity, and determining that from the produce of the remaining *ûr nilams*, one *padakku*‡ and four *nâris*§ of paddy, which at the rate of two-fifths are (or yield) one *kuṟuni*¶ of rice, shall be set apart for the offerings of food to the Devar for the two *sandhis* or stated periods of worship at four *nâris* of rice for a *sandhi*—and also one *kuṟuni* of paddy for two *sandhis* at four *nâris* for a *sandhi*—for two sorts of *kaṟis* (or meats) for each *sandhi*, two and a half *sevidas*‖ of ghee, one *nari*** of curds, *adaikkâya* consisting of two areca nuts and eight beetle leaves for a *sandhi*, in all three *kuṟunis*

* This Âlvâr is still worshipped by the Vaishnava sect under the name of Bhûta, in the following invocation:

[illegible]
[illegible]††

"I adore Bhûta who from a portion of Vishnu's Club, was born in a blue lotus at Mallâpuri on the sea-shore, under the sign of the Balance in the constellation of the Dolphin."

[† *Lit.* "rods." 1 square rod = 1 *kuri*.—See note * p. 123, *supra*.]

‡ Two marcals, [*marakkâl*.]

§ A padi or measure, [= in different localities, from 80 to upwards of 100 cubic inches, the present standard Government measure,] the [fourth, fifth, sixth or] eighth part of a marcal.

¶ A marcal.

‖ A sevida is the 120th part of a padi or measure.

** Half padi or measure.

[†† तुलाश्रविष्ठासंभूतं भूतं कल्लोलमालिनः ।
तीरे फुल्लोत्पलान्मल्लापुर्यामीडे गदांशकं ॥]

and four *saris* of paddy for two *sandhis* should be paid, and that the people who cultivate the lands, and the people in the *Madavilâgam** of this Devar shall not be subjected to the payment of any tax.—I wrote at the desire of the citizens of Mâmallapura or Jananâthapura and the people of Périlam—signed: Tiruverichiludaiyâr Tondan Âdavalân—Karnattân of this village; this is my writing.

This is Olinâgan Mâdaiyân Aragiya Chola the Âmûr-nâttu Mûvéndavêlân's writing.

This is Olinâgan Chandrasekara's signature.

This is Olinâgan Nârâyana's signature.

This is Kalatturân Sûtti Araisan's signature.

This is Konandai Sirâlan Setti's signature.

This is Indipuravan Sanganâgan's signature.

This is Mâppûdi Nârâyanan Mâdakkali's signature.

This is Mâppûdi Ammôdi Ârâva Murti's signature.

This is Uchâm[illegible]ravan Mugalinâgan's signature.

This is Vandârañchêri Udaiyân Arayan Pichan's signature.

The person who molests this charity will incur the sins of having committed capital crimes on the banks of the Ganges and at Kumari.

Svasti *Srî*!

In the 9th *ându* of Koppara-kesari-varmar (or) Udaiyâr *Srî* Râjendra Devar when, having taken Irattaipâdi of the whole seven lakhs and a half, having intimidated Âhava Malla midst the pitfal of his troops, having seized upon his elephants and horses, and having performed lustrations of victory,—he deigned to sit on his mighty throne; we the inhabitants of Tiruverichi, the *Devadânam* and *Brahmadeyam* (village) in Âmurnâd of Âmûrkotta in the prosperous Cholamandalam, do write—that the eastern boundary of the lands which we are to grant as *Devadânam* free of rent, for the *Âlvâr* in the temple of *Srî* Paramesvara Mahâvarâha Vishnu, in Mâmallaparam or Jananâthapura the chief city of this *Nâd* lies west of Kommadikundil in the road to the tank Vannakkanêri—the southern boundary (of it) is the north of Pallachezuvu or the land called Kalatturân paramana mugali—the western boundary (of it) is east of the field (called) Sâtturân Chandra Sekara kirama vittan—and the northern boundary (of it) south to the field (called) Kariyan semme mettan konavan. We have granted for this Devar, the three hundred kuris of the land (named) Esamennu within this boundary as *Devadânam* free of rent, together with the water to irrigate this land from the tank Vannakkanêri and also the water channel.—We are to free the cultivators of this land from the payment of the principal

* The establishment or inmates of the temple.

(*peruvari* or *ayin*) and sundry (*silavari* or additional) taxes—and also from forced labour, (*vetti*) and the carrying of burdens and pounding of grain for the food of persons of all descriptions. Thus having agreed, we have granted (this) as *Devadânam* free of rent.

I, Bhâradvaji Âdavalân, a *Siva* Brahman of Kaspâkkam in this Nâd, wrote this at the request of the inhabitants of Tiruverichi. This is my writing.

This is the writing of Pâdâyakkiram vittan.

This is the writing of Devaganâta *pattan* of this *kshetram*.

This: Sâtandai mallan sanagan.

* * * * (effaced.)

* * * * Olinâgan Nârâyanan.

This is my writing. * * * *

This * * * * of this *kshetram*.

* * * * * Pattan.

I know, this is the writing of Arumbakirân Kâri Irâman, Mûvêndavêlân of Âmûrnâd in the prosperous Cholamandalam.

This is the writing of Tonda Âdavalân the Karnattân of this village.

In this *ându*, Olinâgan Mâdaiyân, Mûvêndavelân of Âmûrnâd, granted 90 goats, for a lamp to be kept always burning.

Kâmakôdan selavan, &c.

The remainder is defaced.

Two grants to the same temple are here recorded, both made in the same year but by different parties. The opening sentence of both is word for word the same, and constitutes the most important portion of the deeds; possessing a double value both as affording the means of ascertaining the exact date of the Tamil inscriptions at Mâmallaipuram, and as a historical record confirming in a remarkable manner, a fact of some importance ascertained from totally distinct sources. In a paper on the Chalukya Princes of Kalyân in the Dakhan published in the IVth Vol. of the Journal of the Royal Asiatic Society, and republished in Vol. VII. p. 193 of this Journal, it is stated on the authority of an inscription at Anigiri in the Dhârwâr district, that Somesvara Deva Chalukya I., surnamed Âhava

Malla had been invaded by the Chola Râjâ who had ravaged the southern provinces of Kuntala-desa, and destroyed the city of Pulikara-nagara, the modern Lakshmesvar near Savanûr. The Chalukya inscription asserts that Âhava Malla defeated and slew the invader, and there is no doubt the invasion was ultimately repelled. But enough is admitted to show that it had been in the first instance eminently successful. The present inscription evidently refers to the same fact, and there is no doubt that Vira Râjendra Chola, surnamed Koppara-Kesari-Varma is the Chola Râjâ above referred to. This is further confirmed by other inscriptions of this same prince, on the magnificent temple at Gangondaram, on the north bank of the Cavery, of which he appears to have been the founder. One of these, in the 5th year of his reign, runs thus, "Ko-Virâja-Kesari Varma named Râjendra Deva, wielding the sceptre with valour for a companion and munificence for an ornament, freeing himself from the blackest sins, having intimidated Âhava Malla of Kudala Sangama, having vanquished the Vikkilan and Singalan,* and taken their queens with their effects and carriages, and having a second time terrified Âhava Malla in battle; having also recovered Venginâdu and fulfilled the vows of his elder brothers, &c." In a subsequent grant in the same temple he is described as "having perpetuated his fame in the northern country which he conquered, &c."

The kingdom of Kalyân had not long before been rescued from foreign enemies by the great grand-

* The Singalan must refer to the King of Ceylon.

father of Somesvara Deva I., and may not have been yet fully re-established, thereby inviting the attacks of its southern neighbours, who were then in the height of their power. The inscriptions of the father of Somesvara Deva I. named Jayasimha, show that he also was at war with the Cholas, but their differences must have ceased with the contest recorded in the present inscription, for the youngest son of Somesvara Deva,—Vikramâditya II. was the most powerful sovereign, not only of his race but of his time, and ruled over an enlarged and extensive kingdom for 52 years, in the numerous extant inscriptions of which, no mention occurs of a Chola war. On the other hand, the Cholas had attained their greatest prosperity at the period of the inscription, in the time of Vira Râjendra Chola, whose father Râja Râja Narendra, acquired possession of the whole of Telingâna, by intermarriage with the eastern branch of the Chalukya family, sovereigns of Vegidesam, and left to his son a kingdom, extending along the coast from the mouth of the Godâvari to Râmesvaram, and inland probably over the greatest part of the southern provinces of this Presidency.

The next point is to identify the era of Vira Râjendra Chola with that of Somesvara Deva I, surnamed Âhava Malla. The latter has been ascertained with tolerable precision in the paper above referred to, and is shown from a comparison of several inscriptions, to be from about *S. S.* 962 to 991.* By a valuable inscription recently procured, I find

* Madras Journal, Vol. VII., p. 196.

that Râjendra Chola succeeded his father Râja Râja Chola in *S. S.* 986, and the same authority shows that he still continued reigning in *S. S.* 1001. It is clear therefore that he was not killed in the action with Somesvara Deva. But besides that the metaphorical language of the inscription does not imperatively require such a rendering, it is very possible that Râjendra Chola may not have commanded in person, but may have intrusted the expedition to one of his generals who, as shewn by numerous inscriptions of that age, were in the habit of assuming the family name of the sovereigns under whom they served. The date of the inscription, the 9th of his reign, would therefore be *S. S.* 995 or A. D. 1073. The battle of Lakshmesvar must have occurred very shortly after his accession, for the Gangondaram inscription already quoted is dated in the 5th of his reign. The synchronism therefore of the three records is perfect.

The last object of inquiry is the identity of the places referred to as the scene of the war. The term Ira*tt*aippâ*d*i used in both the Chola grants, does not occur in any of the Dakhan inscriptions that I recollect. It may, however, have been the familiar term for Kuntala-desa in the south. Instances of such diversity of nomenclature are not uncommon. In the Dakhan, at this day the Tamil country and people are invariably called Konga-des and Kongas. At Malacca and by the Malays generally, the people of Southern India pass under the name of Klings, from the ancient Kalinga. Now we know that a powerful race, the Ratta Kula, originally overcome by the Cha*l*ukyas and held in subjection for several centuries, again obtained the ascendancy about the

9th century, and were finally subdued by Tailapa Deva Chalukya, the great grandfather of Âhava Malla in *S. S.* 895 or A. D. 973. Among the titles of Âhava Malla himself, we find an indication of the more recent independence of the Rattas. In an inscription at Nilgund in the Dambal Taluk of the Dhârwâr district, he is described as "possessing the lofty golden parasol and the whole territory that had belonged to the Rattakula chief, *Sri* Vira Mârtanda." A distinguished family of this Rattakula, likewise flourished at Parsghur and Samdatty in the Dhârwâr district under the Chalukya dynasty, and a considerable town yet exists under the name of Rattehalli on the Wardah, about 30 or 40 miles south of Lakshmesvar.

In the Gangondaram inscription, the Chalukya prince is designated as Âhava Malla of the Kadal Sangama. This is the name of the junction of the Tungâ with the Bhadrâ river near Huli Honore, where is situated the Matham of a celebrated Guru of the Smârta sect, usually called the Kudalgi Svâmi.*

There is good reason to believe, therefore, that "Irattaippâdi" was the name applied by the Tamilians to the southern province, at least of the Chalukya empire, and even to suppose that it was used to signify the whole kingdom. This opinion is strengthened by the use of the expression "the whole 7½ lakhs." In the same inscription that gives

* There are two Mathams of the Sankara Bhârati or Smârta sect in this neighbourhood—*Sringeri* and Kudalgi, besides another at *Sankesvar*, near Kolapûr.

the history of the union of the eastern Chaḷukya and Chola families, it is stated that the first founder of the former race, descended from the rulers of Ayodhyâ, "having conquered Kadamba Ganga and other earthly rulers, reigned over the southern country of 7½ lakhs from Narmadâ to Setu" and elsewhere, similar references are made to the 7½ lakhs dominion of the Kalyân kingdom. This evidently refers to the kingdom of Kuntala-desa only, of which Kalyán was the capital; for that of Kalinga or Vegidesam* was the subsequent acquisition of a collateral branch. What the number 7½ lakhs refers to is not clear. In all the inscriptions of that era, territorial divisions are designated by a number unaccompanied by any explanation of the objects to which it refers. Thus the Kadamba family which became a feudatory to the Kalyân Chaḷukyas, are always described as lords of the Banawassi 12,000. It may refer to the number of villages or townships, to their revenue, or to the quota of troops the chief was bound to bring into the field.

The inferences bearing on the local history of the Seven Pagodas to be drawn from the preceding inscription are the following. The era of the oldest Tamil inscription is clearly fixed at the latter part of the 11th century, and that previously assigned to the rock *sâsanam* of Sâḷuvan Kuppam is confirmed. For Vîra Chola Deva surnamed Tribhuvana Malla is shown by the same inscription as that which gives the date of Vîra Râjendra Chola, to have been the second son of that prince, and to have been

* For a notice of Vegidesam or Vengidesam, see Journal Vol. xi, p. 304.

nominated by him viceroy of Telingana in *S. S.* 1001, (A. D. 1079) which would place the execution of the rock inscription stated to have been cut in his 36th year, in the beginning of the 12th century or *S. S.* 1037, corresponding with A. D. 1115. Further, it is evident from the facts of the grant to Âlvâr, in the temple of Paramesvara Mahâ-varâha Vishnu, and the subsequent mention of the temple of Mâmallai Perumâl, that the more modern creed of the Vaishnava sect had been established, and that of the *S*aiva subverted. Lastly, the place appears to have borne the name of Jananâthapuram in addition to that of Mâmallâipuram, which it is remarkable is invariably here written Mâmallapuram. [மாமல்லபுரம்.]

In the Appendix to Mr. Ellis' treatise on Mirâsi rights, a copy and translation of the *S*âluvan Kuppam inscription will be found, which, had it been known at the time, would have rendered the publication of that given in a former part of this volume (p. 47)* unnecessary. The two documents agree pretty nearly, but Mr. Ellis seems to have had a less accurate transcript, than the one prepared for me, which was obtained from two copies made by different individuals acquainted with the ancient character, and these were carefully collated by Tândavarâya Mudaliyâr. Mr. Ellis has also inserted at the same place a version of the few initial half-lines of the Varâhasvâmi inscription, but these were evidently too imperfect to give the true sense. He, however, agrees in referring the local chiefs antecedent to the Cholas to the Kurumbar race, though he

[* P. 121. *supra*.]

errs in supposing (Âhava) Malla to have been one of them.

The Seven Pagodas have received a greater degree of attention from their vicinity to Madras, than they otherwise would have obtained.* The repeated notice that has in consequence been bestowed on them, has thus brought together almost everything of interest connected with them, and the curious visitor is thus furnished with data, from which to form his own opinion of their age, origin, and object.

* Heyne's Tracts XXI. p. 333.

மூலசாஸநம்.

ஸ்வஸ்திஸ்ரீ இரட்டைப்பாடி யேழரை யிலக்கமுங்கொண்டு பொசிற்றக்கைக்கொப்பத்தாஹவமல்லனை யஞ்சுவித்தவனு லையும் குதிரையும் கைக்கொண்டு விஜயாபிஷேகஞ்செய்து வீரஸிம்ஹாஸநத்து வீற்றிருந்தருளிய கோப்பரகேஸரிவர் மரான உடையார் ஸ்ரீராஜேந்த்ரதேவர்க்கு யாண்டு ஒன்பதாவது ஜயங்கொண்டசோழமண்டலத்து ஆமூர்க்கோட்டத்து ஆமூர் நாட்டு நகரம் மாமல்லபுரமான ஜநநாதபுரத்து நகரத்தார் மேம- பெரியனமைபேருமம் எழுத்து எங்களூர் ஸ்ரீவராஹதேவர்மலை வாரக வி... த்தாழ்வார்க்கு தேவதான இறையிலியா கருணையுடைய திருமுட்டப்படக்கொடுத்த நிலத்துக்குக்கீழ்பா

றகெலலை சிகருடடிசசெரிககுமெறகும தெனபாறகெலலை
யாகமுஙடையமலலாவிடை-யககள நிலமானவயலூரான கவை
றாறறுககுவடககும மெலபாறகெலலை கழிககுககிழககும
வடபாறகெலலை மாமலலைபபெருமான கோயிலுககுமகோ
னெரிததெனனிழைததணணீரககிணறறுககுமதெறகுமஆகஇந
நாறபெரெலலைககும ககொபபட்ட நீரநிலமுமபுனசெயநிலமும
உளளிட்டு உடுமபோடி ஆமைதவழநதெலலைகபபட்ட நில
முமஇறையிழிசசி இககிலமிததெவாககு தெவதாக இறையி
லியாகவும இககிலததுளமாமபுல மூளளிடடகணணூறதடிகா
ணம ஸ்ரீபலிபட்டியாகவுமகெகிநினற நீரநிலததுபபொகக
கொணடு இததெவாககுலநதிபொனறுககுததிருவமுது அரிசி
நாழியாகலநதிபிரணடுககரிசி குறுணிககு நீருசிரணடாக
கெலநபதககுநாநாழியுமலநதிபொனறுககுககறிய முதிர
ணடுமசெயயமுதுஇருசெவிடளயுமதயிரமுதுஉரியும அடை
ககாயமுது-வெறறலைகாயிரணடும இலையமுது எட்டுககுமகெல
லுநாநாழியாக லநதிபிரணடுககுகெலலு குறுணியும ஆகவை
ந்திபிரணடுககு கெலலுமுககுறுணிநாழியாக-நிமநதஞசெல
வதாகவும இககிலமுழுஙகுடிகளையும இநதெவர்மடவிளாகநு
திருபபரளையுமளபபொபபட்ட இறையுமகாட்டபபெறுதொ
மாகவும இபபரிசு இசைநது **தெவதாக** இ**றையிலியாககககொ**
டுததொம. மாமலபுரமான ஜனநாதபுர**தது** நகரததொமும
பெரிளமையொமும இவாகளசொலல எழுதினென. இவ
வூர்கரணததான திருவெழிசசிலுடையான தொணடன ஆட
வலானென இவையெனனெழுதது. இவை ஒளிநாகனமா
தையான அழகியசொழ ஆமூரநாடடு மூவெநத வெளா
னெழுதது. இவைஒளிநாகன-சநதிரசெகரனெழுதது. இவை
ஒளிநாகன நாராயணனெழுதது. இவைகளததூரான குறறி
அரைசனெழுதது. இவைகொனநகைசீராளனசெட்டிபெழு
தது. இவையினைடிபுரவனசஙகரசனெழுதது. இவைமாப
பூதி நாராயணன மாதககலியெழுதது. இவை மாயபூதி அம
மொடி ஆராவமுர்தினெழுதது. இவை உசசாஙகிழவன மூக
விநாகனெழுதது. இவை வணடாழஞசெரியுடையான ஆய
னபிசசனெழுதது. ஐ இபபூமிததுககு அழிவுசெயவான கஙகை
யிடைக் குமரியிடைசசெயதார் செயதபாவங்கொளவான.

இரண்டாவது சாஸநம்.

ஸ்வஸ்திஸ்ரீ இரட்டைப்பாடி ஏழரையிலக்கமுங்கொண்டு
பொரிறறை கணககொபபாததாலைவமலலின பருஙகவிததல
ருஙகியுங குதிரையுமனைககொணடு விஜயாபிஷெகஞசெயது
வீரஸிஙகாஸனததுவீறறிருநதருளியகொபபாரகெஸரிவரமா
ன உடையாரஸ்ரீராஜெநதிரதெவாககுயாணடு ஒனபதாவது
ஜயஙகொணட சொழமணடலதது ஆமூரககொடடதது ஆ
மூரநாடடுதெலதாகமலைபபெருமாதெயமதிருவெழிசசிறெலாம எழு
தது இககொடடுகாமாமலலபுரமான ஜனநாதபுரதது ஸ்ரீவா
ஹெரிமமஸ்வாமியெனனுமபெருமதாழவாரககுதெவதான
இறையிலியாக வைககலுஙகில நாயகனகொடுககிற நிலததுககு
கிழபாறகெலலை வணணககனெரிவழிகொமபடிககுணடிலக
குமெறகும தெனபாறகெலலை களததுழான பாமனுழககி
நிலமான பனனசசெறுவுககுவடககுமமெலபாறகெலலைசாத
தழான சகதிரசெகாககிரமவிததன நிலததுககுககிழககுமவட
பாறகெலலை கழியனசெமமெமொடடனகுணவன நிலததுக
குகதெறகும இககாறபெரெலலை உளளுமககுவெடடபபட்ட எற
மெனனுஞசெறுவுகுழிபிருநிககுறைவு உளபடவுகமுனறுமா
அருழியும இறையிழிசசின இநநிலமும இநநிலததுககு வண
ணககனெரிவழிநீரும நீரொடுகாலுமுளபட இததெவாககு
தெவதான இறையிலிககககொடுதத**தொம** இனனிலமுழுககு
டிகளை இனனிலததால வநதபெருவரியுமசிலவரியும வெட்டி
முடடையாளும எசசொறறுக கூறறுசெலவும உளளிட்டுக
குடிதொனறும காட்டக்கடவொமல்லாதொமாகவும. இப்ப
ரிசு இசைநததெவதான இறையிழிசசிககொடுததொம. திருவெ
ழிசசிறெலாமவாகனலெணடொமுதிரென இககொடடுககுறபாக
கதது பல்லவராஜ வணணன மாராயன ஆடவல்லானேன இவை
எனனெழுதது. இவைபாதாயககிரமவிததனெழுதது. இப
படிககுசெததிரதது தெவககனததபட்டனெழுதது. இப்படிக
குச்சாததநலைமலலனசனகனென

இவைகெமட்டடாக்கி

மறிவேன ஒனிஞாகன காரியனனென இவை எனனெழு

தது இபபடிககு செகதிரதது

பட்டனென இபபடிககு அருமபாககிழா
னகாழி இராமகான ஐயனகொண்ட சொழஆழாகாடடு மூ
வெநதவெளானெழுதது. அரிவென இவலூா கா்ணததான
தொணடூடைவளானெழுதது. இவவாணடெ இதெதவாககு
இவலூா ஞனிகாகனெ மாதையான ஆழாகாடடு மூவெநதவெ
ளானவைதத திருநநதாவிளககு ஞனறுககுவைதத ஆடு
தொணணூறு. இதெதவாககுஇடையா

திருவிளககுஞனறுககுவிடடஆடு காமக
கொடனசெலவனைகயுறற காறபததைநது.

VI.—*Notes on the Ruins at Mahâbalipuram on the Coromandel Coast.* By C. Gubbins, Esq., B. C. S.

[From the Journal of the Asiatic Society of Bengal, Vol XXII. 1853.]

THE temples of Mahábalipûr or Màvalipuram are situated in Lat. 12° 36′ 57″ North, and Long. 80° 14′ 1″ East; nearly thirty-five miles south of Madras, and about five north of the little town of Sadras.

They are built and excavated from a low rocky ridge that, rising isolated from the plain, runs slanting towards the shore for about a mile and a half. The highest part, towards the north, is little more than 120 feet in elevation; and perhaps a mile from the sea, into which the southern extremity runs. It appears to have some small spurs, which may be seen cropping out at various points on the beach.

It is chiefly* of a binary granite, that conveys to a casual observer the idea of having been recently half-wetted by a driving pelt of rain; and although extremely hard, splits readily into masses of various but considerable size. I saw a block from forty to fifty feet in length, and twenty-five to thirty feet in width, that had been divided with an apparently† plane surface by a single blast of gunpowder. The hewers of the caves, however, do not seem to have

* As far as I could perceive, it was entirely so; but I had not leisure for an examination sufficiently minute to authorize my speaking positively.

† I say "*apparently*," because, with reference to the known conchoidal fracture of the rock, it is probable that when closely examined the surface would be found somewhat curved.

enjoyed the assistance of this powerful agent: their method was to trace out on the surface of the rock the line in which they required a separation, along which small holes were made with the chisel and wedges introduced with sufficient force to compel cleavage. It would, however, be difficult at the present day to determine whether these wedges were of wood, well dried before insertion, and subsequently swelled by the application of water; or of metal driven in by repeated blows, as appears to have been the custom in ancient Egypt.*

[* "A series of bare granite rocks, naturally of fantastic contour, nearly a mile long and 120 feet high, has afforded the Hindu artist ample scope for the exercise of his chisel, which must have been wrought of the finest tempered steel, for which India, since the dawn of history, has been justly celebrated. The bronze tools of the Egyptians might answer well enough in the limestone quarries around old Cairo, in working the blocks which constitute the great bulk of the pyramid, but would be of little avail in the quarries of Syene—a type of whose granite we find in the redder felspar. Quarternary granites compose the great monolithic *Rathas* of the Seven Pagodas—a mixture of red and white felspar, white quartz, dark mica, and hornblende. It is more than probable that Indian steel found its way into Egypt during the early traffic that is known to have subsisted between India, Judæa, Yemen, and Egypt. It is absurd to suppose, that the sharply-cut and deeply-engraven hieroglyphics which cover the granite obelisks of Egypt, were done with chisels of bronze, even armed with corundum dust. Quintus Curtius informs us, that Porus presented Alexander with a quantity of steel as one of the most acceptable and valuable gifts India could offer. The granite blocks here, as elsewhere in India, are subject to spontaneous concentric exfoliation and splitting. The globular mass, apparently about sixty feet in circumference, which we see nicely poised on a convex mass of granite—the pat of butter petrified by the god of milkmaids, *Krishna*—is ascribable to the first process; and the rents in the sculptured rocks—one of which cleaving the monolith pagodas, was ascribed by Mr. Chambers to a violent earthquake†—have doubtless been caused by the latter process of spontaneous splitting."—Newbold's "Notes on the Coast of Coromandel, from the Pennár to Pondicherry," in Journal, Asiat. Socy. of Bengal, Vol. xv, p. 210.]

[† P. 10, *supra*.]

The rock yields to the weather by conchoidal peelings, which gives to the group the general appearance of a mass of gigantic boulders, or a confused assemblage of ruined domes. Considering its hardness, it seems to be peculiarly affected by the sea air. This was remarked by Mr. Chambers in 1772 and 1776. "All these figures are doubtless much less distinct than they were at first; for on comparing these and the rest of the sculptures that are exposed to the sea air, with others at the same place whose situation has afforded them protection from it, the difference is striking; the former being every where much defaced, while the others are fresh as recently finished;"* and it is necessary to bear in mind this characteristic when discussing the antiquity, either positive or comparative, of any portion of those edifices.

The greater part of these temples are excavations after the fashion of Ellora and Elephanta; superior in taste and symmetry, though far inferior in dimensions to the first-named.† The most perfect and beautiful is in a narrow ravine, towards the northern part of the range, and facing to the West; whereby it has been well protected from the effects of the sea air. Although small in its dimensions, it is remarkable for its artistic merit: the columns in particular are slender and most graceful; the pedestals couchant tigers facing outwards; the capitals elegant and well proportioned, though fashioned in a style unknown among the orders of Grecian architecture. Mr. Chambers remarks on

[* P. 4 f., *supra*.]

[† See note * p. 27, and p. 45, *supra*.]

its sculpture that "the figures of idols in high relief upon its walls are very well finished, and perfectly fresh."* Another appears to have been dedicated to *Siva*, who is represented, in the middle compartment, of large stature and with four arms. A small figure of Brahmâ is on his right: *Siva* with his consort Pârvati on the left; and his left foot rests on a bull couchant. At one end of the temple is a gigantic figure of Vishnu sleeping on a Cobra da capello, with several heads so disposed as to form a canopy above the god. At the opposite end appears *Sivâni*, in the character of Durgâ, with eight arms, mounted on a lion; opposed to her is a gigantic figure with a human body and buffalo's head,† much resembling that which is elsewhere called the Yamarâja; between them is a human figure suspended head downwards, apparently the object of their dispute: and the monster brandishes a club, while the goddess is armed with various weapons and accompanied by some dwarf attendants.

Mr. Goldingham remarks, "The figure and action of the goddess are executed in a masterly and spirited style:"‡ and Lieutenant Newbold observes that "the best executed figure of the king of the beasts is that on which the goddess Durgâ is seen mounted, in the sculptured cave near the summit of the hill."§

[* P. 6, *supra*.]

[† Mahishâsura.—Cp. Babington, p. 49, and Braddock, pp. 90 ff., *supra*.]

[‡ P. 33, *supra*.]

[§ This passage occurs in a description of the Seven Pagodas quoted, (without Author's name,) at pp. 253 ff. of Pharoah's Gazetteer of Southern India. I have not access to the original paper.—Ed.]

Not far off, a large polished slab about ten feet in length, with the figure of a couchant lion at the southern end, is shown as the bed of the Dharmarája: which may probably be understood as the "Lit de justice," or throne, whence some prince of that name was wont to dispense justice to his people.

Of the other caves some were considerably larger, and had more the appearance of being dedicated to Vishnu: all facing the East. But the striking point in which the whole series resembles that of Ellora is their unfinished state. Mr. James Fergusson remarks of them in a paper read to the R. A. Society in 1843:—

"One of the most singular characteristics of this series of caves is that they are all of one age, and probably the work of one prince, who has carried on the works simultaneously, but from some cause or other has been unable to complete even one of them; had one been finished, or had there been any gradation of style or workmanship, some chronological arrangement might easily have been traced; but nothing of the sort exists."*

Another still more remarkable point of similarity is the repetition of the sculptured group, representing a skeleton figure in a suppliant attitude before a personage appearing to possess authority. Mr. Goldingham describes the group at Mahàbalipùr as follows:

"Near this structure, the surface of the rock, about ninety feet in extent, and thirty in height, is covered with figures in bas-relief. A gigantic figure

(* Journal R. A. S., Vol. viii, p. 87.)

of the god Krishna is the most conspicuous; with Arjuna his favourite, in the Hindu attitude of prayer; but so void of flesh, as to present more the appearance of a skeleton than the representation of a living person. Below is a venerable figure, said to be the father of Arjuna;* both figures proving the sculptor possessed no inconsiderable skill."†

It does not appear whether Mr. Goldingham had any authority for this interpretation, beyond that of the attendant Brahmins, who are always ready to affix the names of some Hindu god or hero to every ancient sculpture; but I could not perceive in the standing figure the usual attributes of Krishna; neither can I recal any tale or legend that represents Arjuna and his father Pându as suppliants to that divinity, in a state of starvation.

When I visited the caves of Ellora in 1841, Lieut. Howarth, then engaged in making drawings of the bas-reliefs, informed me that the group was generally considered to pourtray a miser holding a bag of money, while his wife and son, reduced to skeletons, are vainly supplicating for food; but on minute inspection I was not satisfied with this interpretation, and find my notes on the subject as follows.

What is assumed to be a purse tied round the waist of the miser has not the appearance of a sack containing money; but might rather represent a girdle, drawn tight round the body to ease the sensation of hunger, as is the custom with most semi-civilized nations: neither can it be a bag of coins that he holds in his hand, because the thick

[* See note * p. 31, and note || p. 88, *supra*.]

[† P. 30 f., *supra*.]

part is above the hand and terminates in a point at top; but it *might* be an instrument for cutting the rock, which he is holding out to the half-starved figures at his feet. The little fat cherub may as well be supposed to be bringing him a bag of treasure, as to be taking it away; and then the entire group may be imagined to pourtray the cause and mode of construction of these caves, as a work undertaken by some prince or wealthy chief during a time of famine to relieve the wants of his starving people. Admitting this supposition, we shall have no difficulty in accounting for a continuation of the bas-relief which appears appended, not only to this group but also to a similar one in less perfect preservation in another cave: and we shall recognize Gánesa, at the head of a row of females, each carrying a child in her arms as exhibiting the eventual results of the judicious disbursement.

This interpretation is merely a conjecture, but it seems to derive great support from the existence of the same group on the rocks of Mahâbalipuram.* We can hardly imagine sculptors at such very different parts of India happening to invent precisely the same story: though it might easily occur that both had to relate to posterity the same events. It is no very great stretch of credulity to suppose that in both places the works were undertaken by some prince to employ his famishing subjects during a time of great scarcity, and to furnish them with food without supporting them in slothful idleness. This is exactly what was done by Sir Charles Met-

[* The identity of the scenes represented in the sculptures at the two places is not apparent.]

calfe in our Upper Provinces during the famine of 1837-8, and it does not seem impossible that similar events might suggest similar remedies, to beneficent and intelligent minds, even at an interval of many centuries. Nor are we without some indications that such actually *has* been the case: for Mr. Taylor, quoting from the Mackenzie papers, says:

"In the Kali-yuga, Singhama Nâya*d*u the Zemindar of the Vellugo*t*ivâru race, seems to have ruled here. In that time, during a famine, many artificers resorted hither, and wrought on the mountain a variety of works, during two or three years."*

This theory will explain how in both cases, (Ellora and Mahâbalipuram,) a number of works were commenced simultaneously, in order to employ at once a large number of workmen: and how they came to be left unfinished; the people naturally returning to their ordinary occupations, when the pressure of famine was removed.

I must not omit to mention another tradition which attributes the construction of these works to a body of northern artificers, who fled from the tyranny of their own or some conquering prince, and were suddenly recalled to their homes, by proffered favours and concessions on his part; nor the conjecture of Mr. James Fergusson, who, discrediting this story, accepts Singhama Nâya*d*u as the prince

[* Madras Journal, Vol. viii, p. 65. Cp. note *e*, p. 115, *supra*.—"About 500 years ago a Poligar of the name of Balicota Simcomnaidu lived here, and began to build a little fort on the top of the rock, some ruins of which still remain, as bricks, &c. It is also said that Krishnarailu, who lived about 250 years ago, employed some workmen, who had been driven from the north into the Carnatic in search of bread."—Heyne's Tracts on India. London, 1814, p. 335.]

to whom the excavations are due: and tracing him to his death in battle, while besieging the fort of Jalli palli in the thirteenth century, conceives this event to be a more probable cause of the sudden interruption of the works. "It being entirely a fancy of his own, and neither indigenous in the country, nor a part of the religion of the people, it is not probable that his successor would continue the follies of his parent."* Either of these suppositions would certainly account for the non-completion of the works at Mahâbalipûr: but we should then have to seek out some analogous cause for the same circumstance at Ellora: and the remarkable repetition of the significant group of sculpture would remain totally unexplained.

There are a variety of other sculptures both of beasts and human beings; and often presenting a mixture of both. The most conspicuous is the king snake, with the head and body of a man, terminating in extensive serpentine convolutions, often winding round other groups.† They are nearly all on the eastern face of the rock: and mostly close to the principal caves, which are in the northern half of the range. In the same vicinity is a somewhat remarkable monolith; a mass of living rock left isolated, and artificially fashioned outside, as well as inside. It appears to be above twenty-five feet in height, the same in length, and about half in breadth. It has a long roof curved like a gothic-pointed arch, and gabled at each end.

The walls are of great thickness, so that the interior cell is small: it contains a lingam, and

[* Journal R. A. S., Vol. viii. p. 89.] [† See note ‡ p. 88, *supra*.]

among the sculptures on its walls, appears the figure of Ganesa in small dimensions.* Its door faces the west: and close to it the Brahmans are quarrying the rock, to repair and beautify the interior of the brick pagoda; the only one in which the ceremonials of worship are performed at the present day.

At the extreme south of the ridge, and separated from it by a small level space, along which runs the lower road from Madras to Cuddalore, stand a group of monoliths, seven† in number, surrounded by a grove of cocoanut trees.‡ Five of them are pagodas; of which the most southern (measured by Mr. Goldingham forty feet in height) resembles in general outline a Mussulman mausoleum. Another twenty-five feet in height, and perhaps fifty in length, has a long gothic roof as previously described, and is ornamented on the outside: the other three are more like modern pagodas. The two remaining rocks are fashioned to imitate an elephant and a lion, in colossal proportions. All these monoliths, though close to the sea-beach, and perfectly exposed, are comparatively fresh in their outline, and exhibit very little signs of corrosion. They are composed of this same binary granite, and I think we may thence conclude their comparative antiquity not to be very great.

There still remain two§ temples, differing from

[* The Ganesa temple is more correctly described at page 79, *supra*.]

[† There are eight, including the figure of the sacred bull (Nandi) almost buried in the sand.]

‡ [illegible]—palmyras: my recollection on this point is indistinct.‖

§ I have been told of a third farther north, but did not see it. [See note † p. 106, *supra*.]

[‖ They are palmyras (Borassus flabelliformis) and scrub dates (Phœnix farinifera).]

the former in being *built*, instead of hewn in the solid rock. The first, already alluded to, stands near the village on the level ground not far from the principal caves, and is of brick, plastered and coloured in the modern style. It is of considerable size, and is still used for purposes of worship, and for the accommodation of Hindu travellers. The Brahmans enjoy some revenues attached to the building, and are busily engaged ornamenting and improving it: all which circumstances,* combined with its perfectly recent form and appearance, are conclusive in my mind against any claims to great antiquity that may be advanced on its behalf.†

The last remaining is that which has attracted most attention from travellers: it is built of large masses of hewn granite, on one of the granite rocks already mentioned, as protruding at intervals along the sea shore. It is nearly opposite the highest part of the ridge, and has apparently been built *en rapport* with some part of the excavated hill, from which it is a mile distant in an easterly direction. Its dimensions are small: speaking from memory, I should say, under thirty feet square: but its curiously ornamented conical roof rises to an elevation of nearly fifty feet. It is surrounded on three sides by a granite screen of ten or twelve feet high, and about five feet distant from the body of the temple: on the fourth side (the West,) stands a miniature of the temple, opening towards the West,

* It will generally be found that religious edifices, still possessing endowments, belong to the later phases of Hinduism: the more ancient having been lost, in the various *political and religious contests.*

[† It is called the Sthalasayanasvámí (Vishnu) temple, and is said to be about 100 years old.]

PLATE XXII

and bearing every appearance of having originally been its principal* entrance. The walls and roof of a connecting passage still exist, but all access by this route is now barred by a slab of black basaltic rock, fixed in the eastern wall of the portico, opposite its entrance. A similar, rather larger slab occupies a corresponding place on the inner surface of the western wall of the temple; and on both are images of *Siva*, Pârvati, and their child.† I was unable to discover whether the space intervening between these two slabs is vacant, or has been filled up with masonry: but it is my very strong impression, that they and their immediately surrounding blocks of stone are long subsequent in date to the rest of the building, and have been inserted in order to mark the ancient entry. As matters at present stand, it is impossible to assign any reason for the existence of a blind chamber, or other mass of building, between two temples of *Siva* placed *dos à dos*: and there are only two suppositions that will account for the erection of these two buildings, of obviously the same date, with a covered passage of connection. Either the smaller was a sanctuary, to be entered only from the larger; as appears to have been the case in some of the Arian temples still extant in Cashmere: or else it must have been a portico, through which admission

* As is constantly seen at present to the east of Hindu temples.

† The centre is occupied by a large lingam‡ which, from its dark colour, I conclude to be of this basaltic rock, which must have been brought from a considerable distance. The chaityas§ terminating the roofs of both temple and prophyllum are the same. Every other part is granite.

[‡ See note † p. 107, *supra*.] [§ See note * p. 172, *infra*.]

was obtained to the larger or real temple. The first hypothesis is contradicted by the existence of the western entry to the smaller edifice, which is certainly contemporaneous with its construction: and also by the fact that the stone screen, that so carefully encircles the larger building, *ceases* on arriving opposite the smaller. We are therefore thrown back upon the second;* which is supported not only by these circumstances, but also by the extreme simplicity of the present door to the larger temple; a mere plain opening in the wall. I may also mention that while the smaller building (and through it, were the passage still open, the larger one only) is approached from the west with ease and on a level; the only access to the simple opening in the eastern screen now serving as an entry is over a low but steep and rugged rock washed by the breakers below. This rock has certainly the appearance, both here and elsewhere, of having been partly cut into rude steps and partly perforated as if to receive some superstructure that has since disappeared. One solitary column still raises its head above the waves, and is commonly considered to have been a Stambha, to support lamps:† it should, however, be remarked that there is no vestige of any mode of ascent, to place them; neither of niches wherein they might be placed. The top is formed into a kind of peg, as if to receive some capping stone, and I

* The idea of the original entrance having been from the west will appear less strange if it be remembered that the entrance and portico of the Kailás at Ellora actually are from that quarter.

[† See note † p. 11, and note ‡ p. 51, *supra*. The statement that it is a lamp-post (*Dípastambha*) appears, from the height and shape of the pillar, to be *correct*.]

have myself little doubt that it is the sole relic of some terrace or arcade, once extending in this direction: I also traced out faintly the platforms of two collateral buildings; one on each side of that now standing: and among the débris of the southernmost I discovered several images of the kneeling bull generally placed opposite a lingam, so corroded as to be only recognizable on careful examination. A similar image, in a better state of preservation, is to be seen within the granite screen, on one side of the portico; and on the other, in a closet or small chamber of comparatively recent construction, is a large recumbent statue of Vishnu, with the ordinary Sesh-nága* below and above him.

On the shore close by are several rudely sculptured rocks: one representing a monster with human arms and the head of an ox or buffalo,† commonly called the Yama-rája. They have suffered greatly from the action of the sea air, as has also every part of the adjacent temple, except its chaityas of basalt. In this respect there is a great difference between its appearance and that of the caves, or even of the group of monoliths placed in a situation no less exposed: and after close examination of all surrounding circumstances, I am unable to resist the conclusion that this temple is by many degrees the most ancient of the remains at Mahábalipúr: in fact, that it is one of the most ancient in India. I am aware that Mr. James Fergusson considers "that its age does not differ materially from that of the rest;"‡ and it is with the greatest diffidence that I venture

[* See note * p. 33, *supra*.] [† Mahishásura.]
[‡ Journal R. A. S., Vol viii, p. 87.]

to express an opinion differing from that entertained by so competent an authority: but Mr. Fergusson was specially engaged in the examination of the rock-cut temples; remarking the similarities and the differences existing between them and similar works in other parts of India; so that probably he had little leisure for this structure; to which I, on the contrary, devoted much attention. Besides, if I remember right, he decided these caves to be more modern than those of Ellora: at the same time he considered the celebrated Kailâs of that place to have been copied from some earlier edifice of Southern India: and looking to the very great general similarity of style, I am certainly inclined to refer this shore temple of Mahâbalipûr to the *age* of those earlier structures; although the precise model of the Kailâs may not be found here, but at Chellambram* or Tanjore. This would give a considerable difference of date; and the supposition is borne out by the assurances of the Brahmans who attended Mr. Goldingham, that their ancient books "contained no account of any of the structures here described, except *the stone pagodas near the sea* and the pagodas of brick at the village."† The obvious error of the last statement certainly detracts from the value to be assigned to the former; but it should not be forgotten, that these brick pagodas were in their own possession, and in present use; so that they had a motive for assigning to *them* a fabulous degree of antiquity: while they had no such inducement for making an untrue distinction

[* Prop. Chitambaram.] [† P. 36, *supra*.]

between the caves and the other remains, all equally abandoned and valueless to themselves.

But whatever the age either actual or relative of the various temples of Mahâbalipûr, it seems certain, that at some distant period, the place was one of no small importance. The ground immediately inland from the shore temple has obviously been built over to a considerable extent. The extremely well-cemented foundations of ancient walls are now dug out, as required for building materials, by the inhabitants of the neighbouring village; or for the improvement of the brick pagoda. I examined a large mass of concrete, with bricks on the lower surface, and found it extremely solid and in excellent preservation. It consisted of sharp broken fragments of the granite of the place, mixed with unburned shells: the excellent mortar in which they were embedded being probably these same sea shells burned. The bricks were of the large size usual in all old Hindu structures: but not uniform in their shape. Those I measured varied from eleven to thirteen inches in length, from seven to seven and half in breadth, and were pretty regularly two inches thick;* so well laid in the finest mortar,

* I append a memorandum of the dimensions of old bricks I have collected within the limits of the Mahâbhârata, and an average of a much larger number of specimens from the neighbourhood gives 15¼ by 8¾ by 2½.

Paneeput Fort	...15	inch. long,	9	inch. wide,	2½	inch. thick.
Burnawa do.	...17	„	9	„	2½	„
Hustinapoor do.	...14	„	9	„	2¼	„
Average	...15¼	„	9	„	2½	„

It will be observed that here again the most variable dimension is the length: and the average of these north country bricks will be found to be exactly of the same *proportions* as the average of those at

21

that five of them *in situ* barely measured eleven inches. Most of the houses in the village are built of these old bricks; but the ruins are so completely covered with a deposit of soil, and drift sand, that numerous excavations would be necessary to afford even the vaguest idea of their extent. It is however certain that there must have been a wealthy, and therefore in all probability a numerous population, where dwelling-houses were built of burned bricks, cemented with lime mortar; and where masons were sufficiently acquainted with the mysteries of their art, to use foundations of concrete, formed of the most durable materials, and on the most approved principles. It must be remembered that in classical days the extremity of the peninsula was the entrepôt of commerce between the east and the west. Gibbon says, "Every year, about the summer solstice, a fleet of a hundred and twenty vessels sailed from Myas Hormas, a port of Egypt on the Red Sea. The coast of Malabar or the island of Ceylon was the usual term of their navigation, and it was in those markets that the merchants from the more remote parts of Asia expected their arrival. This fleet traversed the ocean in about forty days by the periodical assistance of the monsoons." Whence we gather that the European fleets proceeded to India with the commencement of the S. W. monsoon; and remained there until the beginning of the N. Easterly; which is consonant with all we know of the habits of the seamen of antiquity. But, at that time of year, the ports

Mahâbalipûr, the length 15½ and breadth 9, being pretty nearly to the length 12 and breadth 7½ inches as the thickness 2½ is to the thickness 2.

of the Malabar Coast would have been extremely unsafe; besides that no large city is known to have flourished at that epoch anywhere near Ceylon, with access from that quarter. It is therefore far more probable that the laden ships, favoured by the strong southerly current along the shore, passed *by* the Malabar Coast, and *by* the island of Ceylon, to find harbour on the Coromandel Coast, and await the change that would take them on their return voyage. I have the authority of a commander of approved skill and well acquainted with these seas for saying that there are no physical features to prohibit the idea that Mâvalipûr may have been one of these ports. He answers my enquiries: "There are no reefs off the Seven Pagodas; and the only danger in the vicinity is a small reef nearly abreast of the Collector's house at Tripalore, hence called the Tripalore reef, upon which one of the Company's vessels was wrecked some fifty years ago: but so near shore (half mile) as not to create any alarm at the present day," when its situation is perfectly ascertained. He adds, that even now ships passing along this coast generally make Sadras hills, to get into a good position for reaching more northern parts; and that "there is no reason why the anchorage at the Seven Pagodas should not be as safe as Madras roads." Nor are there wanting indications of the place having formerly possessed far better anchorage than either Madras or Pondicherry could ever boast. Behind and south of the sculptured ridge for some distance inland, runs a salt-marsh, bearing every appearance of having once formed part of the estuary, which debouches about half-way between Sadras and the shore Pagoda. The soil is not at all like once firm ground, overflowed by the ocean, but rather the light pulpy character of silt, deposited by contending currents and streams in some nook, where their forces neutralised one another: an operation well known to be proceeding down to the present day in every quarter of the globe. A corresponding action, minor in degree because only due to rain and atmosphere, has most certainly taken place on the other side of the sculptured ridge: as is shown by the five or six feet of alluvial soil under which the ruins of the city* are now buried: and we can with equal confidence assert, that foreigners were in the habit of visiting the place, as among the coins found in the vicinity have been some of Rome, of China, and other distant lands. No very great increase of depth in the estuary would (I *believe*, but I could not obtain accurate soundings) be necessary to admit vessels of the burthen then usual, and to afford them shelter equal to any on the coast. We have, therefore, I think, good reason to conclude that in the olden days of which so few records have reached us, when the Chinese, the Phœnicians and the men of Tarsis united, as in the present day, the extreme east and west in bonds of amity by the mutual interchange of commodities, Mâvalipûr or Mahâbalipuram was a place of considerable commercial resort; and perhaps one of the chief ports of Southern India: very probably the Malearpha of Ptolemy.† I am far from considering it equally certain that this was the capital city of the mythological hero Bali. We

[* The writer here begs the question.]

[† Heeren's theory.—See his Historical Researches, Asiatic Nations, Vol. ii, pp. 83, 298.]

all know the tendency of the Brahmans to appropriate to their own sect every relic of antiquity they found in the countries over which they extended their influence: and beyond their own assertions I do not know that we have the least evidence to the fact. "The name still surviving" will seem to many a strong argument: only it will not prove a sound one. The name of Mahâbalipuram, "the city of the great Bali," is only known at the present day to the Brahmans, and to Europeans who derived all their information either directly or indirectly from the Brahmans: and as there is no reason to believe that Sanscrit or Hindi was at any epoch the vernacular of that part of the country, we can hardly suppose that such a purely Sanscrit name ever was in common use thereabouts. Had the current name among the people been one that might possibly be considered a Tamil version of this significant epithet, we might certainly give some weight to the fact of such a name lingering about these remarkable antiquities: but on the contrary, the common names* of Mallapûr or Mâvalipûram are said to have no such meaning;† and the similarity of sound would rather favour the idea that the Brahmans, finding these remains with a name firmly annexed, adapted both to their own purposes; by fixing upon that one of their fabulous heroes, to whose title the foreign word could most easily be converted. Their own books do not afford much

[* The common name is Mâvalivaram, apparently a corruption of Mahâbalipuram. The old name given in the Sthalapurâna (see Appendix) is Mallâpuri, but it is now entirely in disuse.]

† I cannot speak positively nor of my own knowledge, not being sufficient of a Tamil scholar.

support to their present claims. The Mahâbhârata describes the city as being

गङ्गायाः दक्षिणे भागे योजनानां शतद्वयं।
पञ्चयोजनमात्रेण पूर्वाब्धेश्चैव पश्चिमे॥*

"South of the Ganges 200 Yojanas, 5 Yojanas westward from the Eastern sea." It must be admitted that we do not know the exact equivalent of the Indian Yojana:† but it has generally been considered between nine and twelve miles, either of which would carry us far south of Ceylon! If therefore this quotation refers to any city on the present continent of India, we must greatly reduce the length of the Yojana: say to five or even four miles, which would about bring us to the latitude of Mâvalipuram. But we must suppose that the proportion of two hundred to five was somewhat near the truth: and this would oblige us to look for Bali's capital not on the sea shore but twenty miles inland, where to the best of my information no vestige of a city remains. If we assume the Yojana five miles instead of four, we shall certainly be able to satisfy both conditions pretty well in Combaconum, the Benares of the south, or in the ancient capital‡ of the Pândya kingdom, but either explanation is equally fatal to the claims of Mâvalipuram.

It is true that it has been generally believed that

[* See Appendix.]

† A Pandit in this neighbourhood (Rohilcund) called it "four kos:" which would be from five to six English miles; as the local kos is seldom as much as 1½ mile: and from a note to Chap. xxii § of Fa Hian's pilgrimage it would seem that farther south the Yojana was only four miles.

[‡ Madura.]

[§ See also Note 1, Chap. xiii.]

the sea had encroached on this shore, and that many pagodas and buildings of this ancient city had been submerged even since the English settlements took place; and it may therefore be said that in all probability the site of this city was actually twenty miles from the sea in the days when the Mahâbhârata was written. This idea is founded partly on the mariner's name of the Seven Pagodas, said to indicate the existence (in the early days of English intercourse with India) of seven Pagodas on the shore where now only one remains. But personal inspection at once shows the fallacy of this derivation of the name: the shore temples being far too low to be perceived at the distance that ships usually pass; more especially as they are backed by the cave-hewn ridge; and it is infinitely more probable that Mr. Chambers was correct in referring the appellation to the peculiar appearance presented by the rounded peaks of this ridge itself, especially as temples were vaguely known to exist in that neighbourhood without their situation being very accurately settled. He says, "The rock, or rather hill of stone, on which great part of these works are executed, is one of the principal marks for mariners as they approach the coast, and to them the place is known by the name of the Seven Pagodas; possibly because the summits of the rock have presented them with that idea as they passed."*

A far stronger evidence however, in the general opinion, was the tradition imparted by the Brahmans, and perhaps other inhabitants, to the earlier European visitors of the place. Mr. Chambers relates:

[* P. 2, *supra*.]

"The natives of the place declared to the writer of this account, that the more aged people among them remembered to have seen the tops of several Pagodas far out in the sea; which being covered with copper (probably gilt) were particularly visible at sunrise, as their shining surface used *then* to reflect the sun's rays, but that now that effect was no longer produced, as the copper had become encrusted with mould and verdigris."* Passing over as a minor objection that "at sunrise" the dark sides of the pagoda tops would alone be visible from the shore, and that they would be best seen when illuminated by the *setting sun*, I would enquire how is it possible that these slender ornaments should shine "far out" in the surf of the Coromandel Coast, where not years or months, but a few hours of the stiff gales, with which it is so constantly visited, would be all-sufficient not only to destroy the lustre of gilt copper, but to dislodge every stone between high and low water mark? It cannot be supposed that any sudden convulsion lowered the whole coast, so that all at once the waves should roll within a few feet of the top instead of below the foundations of the pagodas; for such a convulsion must infallibly have shaken them to pieces, as well as levelled the existing temple, whose still uninjured pinnacles clearly disprove the hypothesis: therefore the subsidence, if ever it took place, must have been extremely gradual, like those of the Swedish and parts of the Italian coast: and recollecting the numerous years, (not to say centuries) that would be required to sink the forty or fifty feet which may

[* P. 11, *supra*.]

reasonably be assumed to have been the height of the vanished structures, I only ask is it credible that the waves should have spared them until only their tops (still bright and glittering notwithstanding the dashing spray ! ! !) remained above the surface.

I am sorry to be obliged thus to demolish the beautiful romance of the "Wave-covered metropolis of Bali;" but it is not the first of the aerial castles of Indian tradition that has faded before the fuller light of modern European investigation. Like Bishop Heber I find it difficult to understand how this particular spot should have sunk so much, if (as other writers aver) the rest of the Coromandel Coast, both north and south, has rather risen within historical times. I have already mentioned the local features leading me to conclude that this immediate vicinity has not suffered any encroachment from the ocean, but has rather gained from, and increased in elevation above it by alluvial deposits from the higher lands :* and if a Brahman legend is required, there happens to exist one in the Mackenzie papers (vide Mr. Taylor's 3rd report, section 9, page 65,†) that comes as near to my view of the formation of the salt-marsh, as these tales generally do to the natural truths they often dimly chronicle.

* The brick foundations I have mentioned as being five or six feet below the present surface of the land, are very considerably more than that amount above high-water mark. I have not noticed Captain Newbold's argument in favour of the submersion of the city, viz., that Chinese and other coins are often washed ashore in storms;‡ because the fact is equally explicable, by the supposition that this was a port frequented by foreign ships, of which some must necessarily, in the course of years, have been wrecked and sunk in the vicinity.

[† Madras Journal, Vol. viii.]

[‡ Notes on the Coast of Coromandel, in Journ. Asiat. Socy. of Bengal, Vol. xv. p. 210.]

In early times one Mallesu*d*u ruled here prosperously; but having refused charity to a Brahman, he was changed into an alligator. A *R*ishi named Pu*nd*arika, going to pluck a lotus flower in the tank where the alligator lay, was seized by it, but had power to drag it out. The king thus obtained release and went to Svarga. The *R*ishi wished to present the lotus flower to Vish*n*u, but the sea barred his way, and would not retreat; so he sat down to bale the sea out! While thus occupied, an ancient Brahman came and asked for boiled rice, offering to do the *R*ishi's work, while the latter should go and cook it. By taking up a single handful of water the sea retreated a whole coss, and when the *R*ishi returned he found the Brahman reposing in the manner in which statues of Vish*n*u are sometimes represented. He now recognized the god, and a fane was built by him over the spot. If this tale have any real foundation, it probably indicates that after a period of abandonment this site was re-occupied, and great increase of land discovered to have taken place about the time when the worship of Vish*n*u was introduced into the southern peninsula; which being a date tolerably ascertained, may possibly guide some future visitor in fixing the age of the various structures; especially if assisted by some translation of the inscriptions which were unfortunately quite unintelligible to me.

It will be observed that I have made the freest use of the accounts of other travellers: partly, in order to present in a general view the remarks now scattered in half a dozen volumes, and partly in order to support by the authority of others the conclusions drawn in my own confessedly hasty visit. Had I only been as well acquainted at that time as I am now with the writings of my predecessors, I should have investigated far more closely several points that I now perceive with regret I almost overlooked. The shore temple alone can be said to have been thoroughly examined: and I suppose it must have been deemed less worthy of notice by former travellers: else I do not understand how it could escape remark that the original entry of the building must have been through the portico, which is in rear at present.* I trust what I have said may draw the attention of men better versed in Indian antiquities to the subject of the direction in which the entrance is placed in Hindu temples: as it may possibly prove characteristic of some particular sect or epoch. At the present day, all temples in these Upper Provinces (and as far as my observation goes, in the other Presidencies also) are turned towards the east: and a Brahman at Huridwar gave me as a reason the rising of the sun in that quarter. I remember to have seen one exception (besides the Kailâs at Ellora already mentioned:) which is on the grand trunk-road on the banks of the Burachur near Taldanga.† In a group of four temples, not differing essentially in style or architecture, and all apparently quite modern, one is turned to the west, while all the others are to the east. I could not discover that

* I have not been able to procure the papers of Mr. Babington or of Mr. Walter Elliot on the subject: but of the four or five I have perused, no one *touches this point.*

† And I *think* that among the Âryan temples of Cashmere, is said to be a group of four facing to all four cardinal points.

they belonged to different divinities, but there was no person near from whom I could positively ascertain that such was not the case.

Another point that strikes me as deserving attention, more particularly from Engineers and persons engaged on public works, is the very great durability of the basaltic rock as compared with the granite of the Coromandel Coast. We have no reason to believe that the umbrella-shaped summits of the temples, which for want of a better term I have called *chaityas,** are otherwise than contemporaneous with the rest of the temple; and they are, of course, equally exposed to the spray and saline atmosphere: yet they appear perfectly fresh and uninjured, while the granite has lost the whole of its outer surface by gradual disintegration and exfoliation.

I append two sketch plans to elucidate the above descriptions of locality: but they have no pretensions to strict accuracy, being done entirely from memory, months after I visited the place.

[* *Kalasa* is the proper name of these pinnacles.]

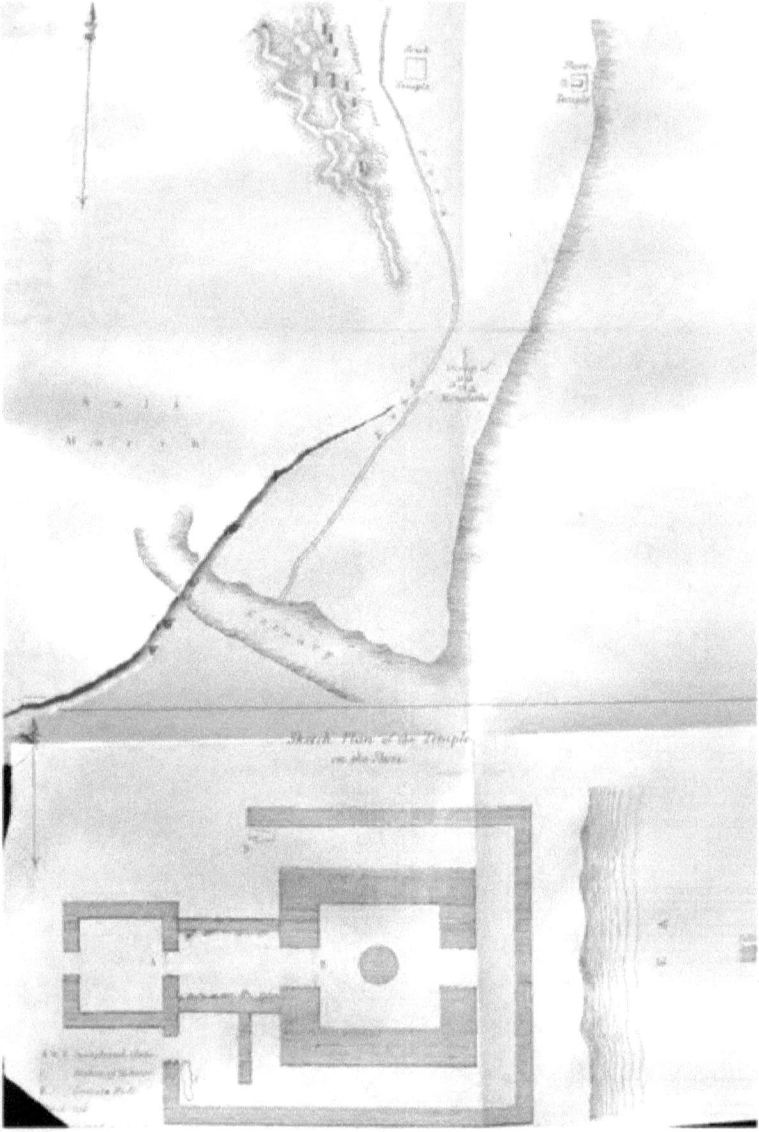
Sketch Plan of the Temple
on the Shore

APPENDIX.

[By the Editor.]

The Sthalapurána.

The Sthalapurána or Local legend of Mallápurí has been examined. It professes to be contained in Adhyâyas 93—100 of the Kshetrakhanda of the Brahmândapurána, and is styled Mallâpurimâhâtmya.

The opening lines are as follows :—

एकदा नारदो **योगी** प्राकृतो बालिशो यथा ।
संक्षुब्धहृदयोभीक्ष्णं नाभूश्चित्ते समाहितः ॥१॥
अथ क्षुब्धाशयो योगी **विचिन्वन् तस्य कारणं** ।
न किंचिन्नाप मतिमान् बहुधापि विचारयन् ॥२॥
अथ चेतस्समाधानं तपसेति विचिंतयन् ।
मतिमांस्तस्य चरणे स्थानवर्यमचिंतयत् ॥३॥
दिक्षु सर्वासु ते मेरौ निश्चयं मे उपेयुषा ।
संतुष्टया यथा तस्य लाभतो मुनिरैधत ॥४॥*
ततस्स नारदो योगी जगाम भ्रमसत्वरः ।

* Three MSS. examined, read as above; the following reading of the 4th sloka has been suggested by a Pandit :—

दिक्षु **सर्वासु** तं मेरौ निश्चयं समुपेयिवान् ।
संतुष्टा **च यथा** तस्या लाभतो मुनिरैधत ॥

मत्यलोकात्सदैकाकी जटामंडलमंडित: ॥५॥
स मुहूर्तेन मतिमान् सुमेरुं रत्नशेखरं ।
क्षणेन तु तटे रम्ये प्राप शीघ्रं मुनीश्वर: ॥६॥
स गत्वा तत्र जटिलान् मुनींद्रिरक्ततासनान् ।
नासाग्रन्यस्तनयनान् माधवार्पितचेतस: ॥७॥
वसमानांश्च दर्भाद्यैर्निश्चलान् नित्यनिर्मदान् ।
ददर्श नारदो हृष्टस्तान्मनाम सहस्रश: ॥८॥
तैरयं कुशलं पृष्टो बहुधा परिभाषित: ।
पृष्टश्चागमनार्थं च बभाषे वचनं मुनि: ॥९॥
मुनयो योगसंसिद्धा: संतुष्टं मानसं मम ।
दर्शनाद्भवतां सद्य: श्रूयतां वचनं मम ॥१०॥
भवतां सन्निधावत्र तपश्चरणनिश्चयात् ।
आगतोहं मनस्तोषात्सत्यलोकान्मुनीश्वरा: ॥११॥
वांछते पुनरप्यस्य मनोनुमतिमत्र व: ।
तस्मान्मयि कृपावस्था नियाम्य: कुत्र योगिभि: ॥१२॥
एतच्छ्रुत्वा वचो रम्यं योगिनो योगिनस्तत: ।
संतुष्टास्तुष्टुवुस्थानं ब्रह्माश्रममुदाहृतं **॥१३॥**
पुरा **किल** मुने तातस्तव लोकपितामह: ।
ऋषिशापाभिभूतस्मन् संक्षुब्धहृदयस्तथा ॥१४॥
माधवेन प्रसन्नेन नियुक्तस्तपसे स्वयं ।
जगत्सृष्टिक्षमो ब्रह्मा तपस्तेपेतिदुष्करं ॥१५॥
अथाष्टशतमब्दांश्च तप्त्वात्युग्रं परं तप: ।
भूय: प्रापातिविमलं मनोनिश्चयमात्मन: ॥१६॥
तत्स्थानं **परमं** दिव्यं तव तातस्य नारद ।
सद्य:सिद्धिकरं पुंसां तदेव तव च **स्वयं** ॥१७॥

अत्रैवाश्रमवर्ये तु परमं तप आचर ।
इति तत्राप्यनुज्ञातस्तपश्चरणलालसः ॥१८॥
आवर्तयन् महामंत्रमतिष्ठत्सुचिरं मुनिः ।
शतं तु देववर्षाणां स चरन् दुश्चरं तपः ॥१८॥

"Once upon a time, Nârada Yogi became, like one of the vulgar and ignorant, much disturbed in mind, and meditation no longer occupied his thoughts. 2. Then the Yogi with mind thus agitated sought for the cause thereof, but the wise man found none, though he searched in many ways. 3. Afterwards, thinking that by penance peace would be restored to his mind, the wise man bethought him of an excellent place for its performance. 4. Out of all places he fixed on Meru, and the Muni greatly rejoiced at the prospect. 5. Then Nârada Yogi, adorned with braided hair, departed speedily and alone from Satyaloka. 6. The sage reached in a Muhûrta the gem-tipped Sumeru; quickly, in a moment, did the great Muni reach the lovely height. 7, 8. He, having gone there, saw the Munis with braided hair, in long continued postures, with eyes fixed on the root of the nose, with minds devoted to Mâdhava, clothed in *darbha*, &c., motionless, ever humble. Nârada rejoiced and saluted them thousands of times. 9. He was enquired of them regarding his health, and conversed with on many matters; asked the reason of his coming, the Muni said—10. 'O perfect Munis! by seeing you my mind is instantly rejoiced, listen ye to my speech: 11. With the resolution of performing penance here, in your presence, O great Munis, have I come with joyful mind from Satyaloka. 12. Now my mind desires to obtain your consent here, and therefore favor must be shown towards me. What place will the Yogîs appoint me?' 13. Then the Yogîs, having heard the sweet speech of [Nârada] Yogî, rejoiced; and praised the place called Brahmâsrama. 14. 'O Muni, was not thy father, the grandfather of the world, formerly humbled in like manner by Atri's curse, and disturbed in his mind? 15. Brahmâ, powerless in creating the world and commanded to do penance by Mâdhava, performed penance the most difficult. 16. Here for eight hundred years having performed penance meritorious and most severe, he obtained again his own very pure and settled mind. 17. O Nârada, that, thy father's excellent and heavenly place which instantly perfects a man, that is thy place also. 18. Here, in the excellent Âsrama, perform the highest penance.' There, thus permitted, he was eagerly desirous of performing penance. 19. That *Rishi* remained for long repeating the Mahâmantra,* and for a hundred divine years performing severe penance."

Nârada however does not experience any benefit from this protracted austerity, and finds his mind remain as disturbed as before. He then goes sorrowing to his father Brahmâ in Brahmaloka, and tells him of his state. Brahmâ bids him recall any probable cause for it, when he recollects having denied Vishnu's accessibility *(saulabhya,)* and maintained his inaccessibility *(paratva)*. (xciii, 20—41.) Brahmâ then relates to him the discussion between Agastya and Sûta on this topic, which again involves Siva's

* The Ashtâkshari.

answers to Pârvatî's questions regarding Vishnu's attributes. (xciii. 42—95). In reply to Pârvatî's question as to how Vishnu became accessible, *S*iva related the story of Pundarika *Ri*shi who went to Yadugiri,* to worship Vishnu, meeting with sundry adventures on the way. The *Rishi* afterwards visited the sacred places on the East Coast, coming to the Varâhakshetra. From thence, going South, he came to a beautiful garden where he saw a *Yogi,* named Vishnusarma, and near that garden he perceived a pond *(pushkarini)* in which were wonderful lotuses. While plucking these, Pundarika heard a voice from heaven, saying, 'Lo! here are large and priceless lotuses of the colour of gold, of delightful perfume, having a thousand petals—these are fit for the worship of the god who dwells on the Sea of milk, but not for that of other deities.' Greatly rejoicing, the Ri*shi* proceeded to pluck the whole of the flowers, when a crocodile came to attack him, but mistook a lotus stalk for the holy man's leg, was pierced in the tongue by the thorns, and from loss of blood lay as dead on the water. (xciv. 1—86.) The Ri*shi* went near, and the crocodile addressed him in a soft voice and told its story, commencing :—

पुरा जन्मन्यहं ब्रह्मन् राजा सर्वमहीपतिः ।
दाता च सर्वकामानां मल्लापुर्यां वसाम्यहं ॥

'In a former birth, O Brahman, I was king of the whole earth, and dwelt at Mallâpuri, granting to all their wishes.' Then the crocodile gave the Ri*shi*

* A sacred hill at Mêlkôta in Mysore.

an elaborate and extravagant description of Mallâpurî, adding :—

मल्लेश्वर इति ख्यातः भुवनत्रयविश्रुतः ।
विष्णुभक्तश्शतानंदः पुत्रो मम महाद्युतिः ॥

'My son *S*atânanda, a votary of Vish*n*u, of exalted mien, and famed in the three worlds, is celebrated as Mallesvara.'

After this follows a description of *S*atânanda's Court, &c. The crocodile then told the *Rishi* how Varâhasvâmi came to Mallâpuri, according to the tradition he had received from his forefathers. Formerly there was a king called Harisekara, endowed with all good qualities. He was in the habit of going daily with his aged and pious mother to worship Vish*n*u at Varâhakshetra,* a *yojana* distant from Mallâpuri, to the North, and feeding Brahmans after coming back to his city. One day, Hari came to Mallâpuri disguised as an old decrepit Brahman, accompanied by his daughter, and asked for food. The king requested him to wait a little until he returned from Varâhakshetra. The old man begged for immediate relief as he was greatly fatigued and his daughter was hungry. The king then suspected that he had been visited by Vish*n*u in disguise, worshipped the old man and gave him food. He then saw Varâhasvâmî in his proper form, with the goddess Earth on his right hip.

The Brahmans who had come as usual for food were suddenly and miraculously filled up to the neck (*âkanthapûrnâ*h) and afterwards besought Varâhasvâmi to remain always at Mallâpuri. The god

* ? The village of Tiruvadandai, near Covelong (Kôvalam.)

consented, and being asked why he looked towards the West replied that he did so because the Punya-kotivimâna* was to come in the East at a distance of five *yojanas.*

The crocodile added that his father Harinandana abdicated the throne in his favor and became an anchorite. His own name he stated to be Haripriya. (xciv. 87—180.)

The crocodile then told the story of his being cursed. One day a Brahman came and asked for food. The king in his pride treated him with contempt. The Brahman enraged cursed him saying "Become thou a crocodile, O king." The people afterwards interceded with the Brahman for their king, and were told that when he met a votary of Vishnu, the curse would be removed. (xcv. 1—20.) The crocodile then was transformed into a youth of 16 years and went to heaven. Pundarika *Rishi* taking with him the lotuses strung in garlands, set out to worship Vishnu on the Sea of Milk and arrived at the shore of the Salt Sea. (xcv. 21—55.) The *Rishi* attempted to bale out the ocean in order to proceed on his journey! This he continued for a year, when he desisted being wearied. At this time an old Brahman approached and questioned him.

The *Rishi* told the Brahman his story and of his wish to visit Vishnu, and the latter recommended him to abandon his attempt to get over the Sea; this enraged Pundarika who requested the Brahman either to help him or to go about his business. The old man then asked for food, girded his loins and commenced to bale. At the first handful thrown out by

* The name of the large Vishnu temple at Conjeveram.

him, the Sea receded a *kôs.* Pu*nd*arika went for food and on returning perceived that his Brahman friend was no other than Vish*n*u, whom he found reclining on the shore, with the lotus garlands round his neck, facing to the East. The Ri*sh*i then worshipped the god, as Sthala*s*ayana, with praises and offerings of lotuses. (xcv. 56—75. xcvi. 1—10.) Vish*n*u then told Pu*nd*arika to ask a boon. The Ri*sh*i replied that having obtained Vish*n*u he sought for nothing else. "Will he who has reached the boundless Sea of nectar care for the water of a small muddy pond?" He begged that the god would always remain in that place, saying he required no other boon. Vish*n*u consented and praised Pu*n*-*d*arika for making this request. Then came Brahmâ to the Sea shore with *Yakshas,** *Gandharvas*† and *Apsarases.*‡ The drums of the gods sounded, flowers rained from heaven, and the sound of "JAYA!" (Victory) was heard like the roaring of the Sea. All worshipped the god and goddess, and praised Vish*n*u for his accessibility *(saulabhya).* Afterwards the Brahmans, and the king Mallâdhipa or *S*atânanda, with the people of the city, came to the Sea shore. All were intoxicated with joy at Vish*n*u's appearance among them, and worshipped him. On being asked under what name he would dwell among them he replied "Know me as Sthalasâyî, who here recline on the ground." The King and people worshipped Vish*n*u and praised Pu*nd*arika. Malle*s*vara then heard the Ri*sh*i's history and was rejoiced to learn that his father had been released

* Demi-gods attendant on Kuvera, the god of wealth.

† See note § p. 204, *infra.* ‡ Nymphs of Svarga, Indra's heaven.

from the Brahman's curse and had gone to heaven. The Brahmans then bathed in the Pundarikasarasu and made offerings. The King, following the counsel of Pundarika, bestowed gifts and lands upon the Brahmans. Afterwards a *Vimâna*, called Ânandanilayam, having 7 pinnacles and containing a shining image, descended from Vaikuntha,* round which the king built a wall with a *Gopura*. *Siva* concluded with praises of Mallâpuri. (xcvi. 11—75, xcvii. 1—78, xcviii. 1—115).

Agastya accepted the arguments of Sûta, (which embodied the story of Pundarika *Rishi* given above), took leave of him and set out for Mallâpuri. He met with favourable omens on his way and came to a great mountain called Samvartana. Hearing a confused noise above him he looked up and perceived some of Yama's† soldiers dragging away a Brahman. He then saw Vishnu's soldiers release the prisoner and heard the dispute between them and the servants of the god of death. The latter described all the great sins which the Brahman had been guilty of, the like of which had never been seen or heard, while the former maintained that having gone to Mallâpuri, and stayed one day at that holy place, all his sins had been washed away and that they who laid hands on him themselves committed sin and rendered themselves liable to be reduced to ashes. (xcix. 1—77).

Agastya was astonished and pressed on towards

*Vishnu's heaven.

† "The Deity of hell; he corresponds with the Grecian god Pluto, and the judge of hell Minos, and in Hindu mythology is often identified with Death and Time."—Wilson.

Mallâpurî. Passing through a dense forest, he saw six virgin devotees performing penance. He approached them, told them he was Agastya and saluted them. They received him with great respect, and told him they were Gangâ, transformed by a curse into the form of six bodies.

The virgins added that formerly when they were performing penance in the forest called Tilavanam all the *Rishis* assembled on the Himavat mountains and discussed the relative merits of the holy waters (*tîrthas*). They praised the Gangâ and Kâverî, but agreed that the Pundarîka pond was the most excellent of all, and that Gangâ and the other rivers should be its slaves!

The Munis having thus decided, went to their respective homes. Gangâ, wandering sorrowfully, met Shanmukha,* while he was performing penance in a certain place, and told him the cause of her grief. He in reply said that she had no ground for complaint, as, great those she was, the Pundarîka pond was yet far superior. Shanmukha then told Gangâ how, after incurring the sin of killing a Brahmin in his fight with the Dânava named Târaka,† he had been cleansed from all guilt by bathing in the Pundarika pond at Mallâpurî. He then told Gangâ that all would approve of her putting aside her jealousy and self-love, and that she would be freed from slavery by bathing in those waters. Shanmukha

* Kartikeya, as the "Six-faced."

† Kartikeya (Skanda) was born to lead the armies of the gods, and to destroy Târaka.—See Coleman's Mythology of the Hindus, p. 74 ff. Wilson's note on v. 297 of the *Meghadûta*, and Muir's *Sanscrit Texts*, Part IV., pp. 292 ff, 398.

then taught Gangâ the Râmatâraka,* and told her to perform penance, repeating with six faces this mantra. This she was doing in the Tila forest. Agastya, leaving the virgins, again hastened on to Mallâpuri. (xcix. 78—134.)

Agastya reached Mallâpuri and met there a crowd of Munis round the temple of Sthalasayanasvâmî, called Ânandanilayam. Some lived on water, some lived on air, some on roots, fruits, and leaves. Emaciated in body, they retained life solely by the power derived from penance. They assumed the *Garuda*-posture, lay like snakes, or sat like fowls. Some stood on the point of the toe, others with upraised arms; some sat self-supported in the air, others between five fires.† They were Brahmins and Kshatriyas. Agastya saluted them and told them his name. They received him with different marks of respect, and he begged to be allowed to live with them without performing penance or repeating prayers, on the ground that Hari would be satisfied with simple worship. To this the Munis agreed, and told him to bathe in the Pundarika pond with a prayerful mind. Agastya did so and then visited the temple. There he saw Sthalasayana, who had graciously descended at the prayer of his worshipper Pundarika, reclining with his head resting on his right hand and with his left inviting his worshippers to approach him.

Agastya was submerged in the ocean of delight, and offered worship and praise to the god. Vishnu received him graciously, commanded the Muni to

* A formula addressed to Râma, as *Râmâya namah.*—Wilson.

† *Pañchâgni*,—four fires and the sun overhead.—See plate 23 in Mrs. Belnos' *Sundhya.*

worship him daily and to perform the five *Dikshas*,* and appointed him an *Asráma* named Asvatha on the North side of the Pundarika pond. Vishnu then, at Agastya's desire, condescended to narrate to him how Tárksha lost and recovered his wings. On one occasion when Vishnu called *Garuda* to carry him on a visit to Svarga, the bird came so fast that the dust he raised fell on a pious worshipper of Vishnu who was engaged in his devotions. Vishnu then in anger caused Tárksha's wings to drop off, and the bird fell into a forest on the shore of the Western Sea. After bathing in vain in many holy waters he at last came to Mallâpurî where his wings began to grow. Vishnu then instructed Agastya in the mode of worship and declared that those were dear to him who loved those that loved him (*matpriyâ matpriya priyâh.*) Agastya took up his abode accordingly at Mallâpurî. (c. 1—113.)

Then Brahmâ concludes:—

तस्मान्नारद जानीहि विष्णुं सौलभ्यसागरं ।
तेनैव निर्मलं चित्तं भवेत्तव न संशयः ॥ ११४ ॥
यो जानातीह सच्चीयं भक्तसौलभ्यसागरं ।
न तस्य क्षुभ्यते बुद्धिः व्यथा न प्रलयेऽपि च ॥ ११५ ॥
तस्मात्त्वं तत्र गत्वा तु सेवित्वा स्थलशायिनं ।
स्नात्वा सरसि पुण्ये च चित्तनैर्मल्यमेष्यसि ॥ ११६ ॥

114. Therefore, O Nârada, know thou Vishnu to be an ocean of accessibility; by him, without doubt, thy mind will become clear. 115. His understanding

* *Diksha* is the ceremony of initiation, the essential part of which is the *Tapta Mudrá* or branding the novice with the conch and discus.—Wilson's *Essays*, Vol. I., p. 56.

will not be confused who in this world knows Lakshmisa,* an ocean of accessibility to his votaries; even at the destruction of the world, [he will suffer] no pain. 116. Therefore having gone there, and bathed in the holy pond and worshipped Sthalasayi, thou shalt obtain purity of mind.

Nârada then goes to Mallâpuri and staying there for "many days," obtains all his desire. (c. 117, 118.)

Note.

It will be observed from the foregoing analysis of the Sthalapurâna that (1) it contains no mention of any of the old rock cut temples or of the shore temple. The Varâhasvamî temple is not an exception, inasmuch as the formation of this temple by enclosing the sculptured representation of the Boar Incarnation on the West face of the hill is of modern date.† And (2) no allusion whatever is made herein to the story of Bali or the submersion of his city.

This legend appears to have been composed for the purpose of attracting pilgrims to the place after the construction of the modern Vishnu temples. The Vaishnava author ingeniously makes Brahmâ, *S*iva, Kârtikeya and all the Saints extol the sin-destroying virtue of Mallâpuri.

The names of kings mentioned in the Mallâpuri Mâhâtmya appear to be fictitious.

* Vishnu, as "Lakshmî's lord."

† See p. 45, *supra.*

Description of the Pagodas, &c., at Mâvalivaram, written in the Telugu language by Kâvali Lakshmayya *in 1803.* [*With a translation.*]

[From the Mackenzie MSS., No. 33. C. M. 787.]

౧. పర్వతానికి వుత్తరభాగమం యీశ్వరునికోవెల. ఇందులో యీశ్వరుడు వున్నాడు. ఈ కోవెలముందరనుండిన లింగ్గం వైపు రెత్తుకొని పోయినారు.

౨. దీనికిముందర రెండు కోతులు పేలుచూచుకొంటూ వున్నవి.

౩. ఆపడమటిపక్కను పాండవులున్నప్పుడు అయిన ద్రౌపది పెనుగుడి కెవత్తొట్టి వకటి గుండుగా వున్నది. మూడుమంటపాలు యేకశిలను చెక్కినముగా తొలిచినవి వున్నవి. మంటపము ౧-కి వున్న చిత్రాలు-ద్వారపాలకులు ౨, లోపల దుర్గ చతుర్భుజాలతోటి వున్నది. పరిచారకవిగ్రహాలు ౪ వున్నవి. తలకిన్నా రెండు ఆరలకు యిరికే ప్రాకారముగా వున్నది. ఈ శిలను దక్షిణపువయిపు పడమటిముఖముచేసుకొని వక దుర్గ అష్టభుజాలతోటి మహిషాసురునిశిరస్సుమీద నిలపాదముజేసి తొక్కి వున్నది.

౪. ఇందుకు సమీపముగా దక్షిణభాగమందు ఘాటుకు పడమటివైపు భీమసేనుడు పాకముచేసిన బాయి వున్నది. దానిమీదికి యెక్కేటందుకు సోపానాలు వున్నవి.

౫. అందుకు సమీపముగా దక్షిణభాగమందు బండమీదను ద్రౌపది చేసిన వెన్నముద్ద వక గొప్పగుండుగా వున్నది. అందులో సగము పిల్లి తినిపోయినది అని చెబ్రిగా అనుపదముగా వున్నది. ఆ పిల్లి అజ్ఞానముకు తపస్సుచేసుకొంటూ వున్న పర్వతానకు కట్టివేసినట్టుగా ముందరికాళ్లు పైకి యెత్తుకొని వున్నది.

౮. ఇందుకు దక్షిణపు వైపు యేకశిలతోటి అజాఘానివరణము వున్నది. ఈశిల తొలిచి కింద మంటపముతొలిచి రెండు స్తంభాలతో అందులో వున్న గర్భగుడి యేర్పరిచి శివప్రతిష్ఠ చేశినారు. ఆ లింగాన్ని యూ** యెత్తుకపోతే యీ స్థలములోవారు దగ్గిర వొక వినాయకుడు వుండగా తీసుకపోయి అందులో వుంచినారు. **ఈ** గర్భగుడికి దక్షిణపు గోడ మీదను శాసనమేమేమో వ్రాసినారు. **అది యే** లిపి **అయినది** తెలిశినది కాదు.

౯. ఇందుకు సమీపముగా దక్షిణభాగమందు వరాహస్వామి వుండే యేక శిలామంటపము వున్నది. ఇందులో స్తంభాలు ౨, గర్భగుడి ౧-యీ గర్భ గుడిలో యేమీ ప్రతిమలు లేవు. ద్వారపాలకులు యిద్దరు. ఈ గర్భగు డికి వుత్తరభాగమందు గోడమీదను వరాహస్వామి వామపాదము భూమి యందు వుంచుకొని, దక్షిణపాదము ఆదిశేషునిశిరస్సుమీద పెట్టి, దక్షిణో రువుమీద లక్ష్మీఅమ్మవారిని అభిముఖముగా వుంచుకొని, దక్షిణహస్తము అమ్మ వారి పిరుదులమీద వుంచుకొని, వామహస్తముచేత దక్షిణపాదము ధరించి తాను పశ్చిమాభిముఖుడై అమ్మవారు పూర్వాభిముఖముతో వుండగా, వరా హస్వామివారు **ఛదము రెండుహస్తాలయందు** శంఖచక్రాలు ధరించి చతు ర్భుజయుక్తుడై ఆనెూగ్యక్య ముఖావలోకన **చేస్తూ శ్రీ**దావిలాపాదశాము అమ్మ వారి దక్షిణస్తనము తనవరాహముఖముతో చుంబనము చేస్తూ వున్నాడు. ఇతి దక్షిణమునకు పూర్వభాగము చతుర్భుజాయుక్తముగా వొక పురుషప్రతిమ వున్నది. ఈ ప్రతిమకు అభిముఖముగా వొక స్త్రీ ప్రతిమ వున్నది. ఈ యిద్దరి మీద వొక భక్తుడు కృతాంజలియుక్తుడై స్తుతిచేస్తూ వున్నాడు. వరాహ స్వామిని ముగ్గురు భక్తులు స్తుతిచేస్తూ వున్నారు. అందు వుత్తరభాగమందు వుండే ప్రతిమలు ౫. పూర్వభాగము గోడమీదను పశ్చిమముఖముగా పద్మా సనముమీద గజలక్ష్మీ వున్నది. ఈమె శిరస్సుమీద గజముఖాలు రెండు వున్నవి. ఈ లక్ష్మీకి వుభయపార్శ్వాలయందు యిద్దరు యిద్దరు స్త్రీలు అభిషేకార్థము పూర్ణకుంభాలు గజలొండాలకు అందిస్తూ వున్నారు. ద్వా రపాలకుడు వొకడు వున్నాడు. అందు స్త్రీలు ౪, పురుషప్రతిమ ౧, గజ ముఖాలు **౨** వున్నవి. దక్షిణభాగమందు యేకచ్ఛత్రము ధరించి చతుర్భుజా యుక్తురాలైన వొక దుర్గ వున్నది. ఈమెకు దక్షిణభాగమందు ముగ్గురు భటులు

ఖడ్గధారులై వున్నారు. వకజంట **వున్నది.** వుత్తరభాగమందు ఖడ్గధారులై ముగ్గురు భటులున్ను వకసింహమున్ను వున్నవి. ద్వారపాలకుడు వకడు వున్నాడు. అంతు ప్రతిమలు ౯, సింహము ౧, జింక ౧. వరాహస్వామికి యెదురుగా దక్షిణపుగోడను త్రివిక్రముడు అష్టభుజాయుక్తుడై శంఖచక్ర గదాది సాధనంబులు ధరించి వున్నాడు. ఇతనికి బలిచక్రవర్తి మూడు పాదాలభూమిదానము యిచ్చె గనుక దక్షిణపాదముచేత భూమి యావత్తు ఆక్రమించి యీపాదము భూమియందు వుంచి వామపాదము వూర్ధ్వలో లోకము ఆక్రమించేనిమిత్తము ఆకాశమందు వుంచుకొని వుండగా యీ **పాదానకు బ్రహ్మ తన** కమండలోదకముచేత అభిషేకము చేసి పూజిస్తూ వున్నాడు. ఇతనికి యెదురుగా జాంబవంతుడు వున్నాడు. బలిచక్రవర్తి దత్తాపహారము చేయరాదని మూడోపాదమునకు భూమిదానము యిచ్చినవె వని స్వామిపాదముదగ్గిర ప్రార్థనచేస్తూ వున్నాడు. ఇతనివెనక శుక్రా చార్యుడు వున్నాడు. ఈ బలిచక్రవర్తిభటులు వూర్ధ్వమందు యిద్దరు పక్క్య మమందు నలుగురు వున్నారు. అంతు ప్రతిమలు ౧౧ వున్నవి. ఇవి వుపప్రతిమలు. ఈ మంటపము పశ్చిమాభిముఖముగా వున్నది.

౭. పర్వతానకు వూర్ధ్వభాగము కొండకింద మెట్లుమీదను కృష్ణస్వామి వారు ఆడుకొని సింహాసనము యెక్కడానకు పదకొండుపడికట్లు. ఆ మెట్లమీదనుంచి ఆటలాడేను జారుతూ వచ్చేవారు. దానియొక్క ఆన వాలు వున్నది.

౮. ఈ **పర్వతానకు పూర్వభాగమందు** అర్జునుడు తపస్సుచేసినట్లు **కిరాతార్జునులవలెనే** పర్వతానికి ప్రతిమలు చెక్కినారు. ఇక్కడ అర్జునుడు బాహుద్వయము శిరస్సునందు వూర్ధ్వముగా వుంచుకొని తపస్సుచేస్తూ వుండగా ఈశ్వరుడు చతుర్భుజాయుక్తుడై పాశుపతాస్త్రము డమరుకము త్రిశూలము మొదలయిన ఆయుధాలు ధరించి ప్రత్యక్షమైనాడు. ఈశ్వరా కారముదగ్గరనుండు వాడికి దక్షిణభుజముమీద వుంచుకొని దక్షిణహస్త ముచేత **పిడి** పట్టుకొని నిశ్చలుడై **వున్నాడు.** ఈశ్వరుని శిరస్సుమీద సూర్యచంద్రాదులు వున్నారు. అర్జునునికి దక్షిణభాగమందు కృష్ణ స్వామి విమానములో శంఖచక్రగదాధరుడై చతుర్భుజాలతో వున్నాడు. ఇతనికి దక్షిణమందు ద్రోణాచార్యుడు తపస్సుచేస్తూ కృశీభూతమైనశరీ

రముకలవారై బత్తాసనాసీనులై వున్నారు. ఈ కృష్ణునికి వామభాగ మందు పర్వతము పగిలినది గనుక పాతాళలోకమునుంచి నాగకన్యకలు వెళ్లివచ్చినట్టుగానే పంచకన్యకలతోకూడా ఆకాశమని వ్రక్షేపించి నాగ కన్యక వచ్చినది. ఇందుకు వుత్తరభాగమందు ఐరావతముతో గజముమీద ఇంద్రుడు భార్యాసమేతముగా శివదర్శనానకు వచ్చినాడు అన్నట్టుగానే వున్నాడు. ఈ ఐరావతానకు వెనుక వక దేవుడు వున్నది. ఐరావతము కింద దేవుడుపిల్లలు మూడు వున్నవి. పెద్ద శివ పిల్లలతోకూడా పూర్వ్వ బాహువులతో పూర్వాభిముఖముగా వున్నది. ఈ దేవేంద్రునికి వలయా కృతిగా గరుడగంధర్వకిన్నరకింపురుషసిద్ధవిద్యాధరులు మొదలైనవారు కొం దరు భార్యాసహితులై కొందరు భార్యారహితులై బహుమార్గులై శివ దర్శనానకు వచ్చినట్టుగానే ప్రతిమలు చెక్కినారు. ఇక్కడ ప్రతిమలు ౩౬ వున్నవి. ఈ దేవతలమధ్యమందు ఊరకలు ౩ వున్నవి. వీటికి వెనుక వుత్తరభాగమున మధ్యమందు సింహాలు ౨ వున్నవి. గొత్రు ౧ వున్నది. ఈశ్వరునికి దక్షిణభాగమందు మహిషాసుర ధర్మరాజు శ్రీమును కలవ్వుచే త్రా చూస్తున్నారు. వీరికి దక్షిణమందు వెండి వ్యాఘ్రము వున్నది. ఈశ్వరునికి దక్షిణభాగమందు ప్రమథగణాలు బుద్ధులు శివదర్శనానకు వచ్చినట్టుగానే చెక్కిఉన్న ప్రతిమలు ౨౮ వున్నవి. సింహాలు ౧౫ వంది ౧౫ జింకలు ౩ వ్యాఘ్రము ౧౬ గోవులు ౨౬ ఈప్రకారము భార్యా సమేత ముగా చిత్రవిచిత్రముగా వున్నారు. అంతప్రతిమలు స్త్రీ పురుషులు వమో ౨౦ వున్నవి.

౧౦. ఇందుకు దక్షిణము రేకశిలామంటపము. పంచపాండవులు చేసు కలిగినది వున్నది. అందుకు స్తంభాలు ౧౮-కి విరిగిపోయినది ౧ గాక తతిమ్మా ౧౭ స్తంభాలు. తతిమ్మా ౧౭ స్తంభాలలోను బాలునీకాళ్లు విరుగు చూచినది. లోతక్కువది బాగా వున్నది. ముందరి స్తంభాలకు సింహము మూరులు వున్నవి. వెనక సింహాలు ఈ మంటపముమధ్యను ఒక వకటి వున్నది. ఇందులో మరేమి లేదు. ఈ అరక బుద్ధిహీనులా అరిలు కట్టుదలవని పొడుచుపెట్టినారుగాని పూరాకాలేదు. అరక యువతల వయుస్సు అవతలవయుస్సు సుమారుగా చేరే కాకుండా మంటపములోనే వున్నవి. మరేమి పొక్కడ చిత్రాలులేవు, పాడావి.

౧౧. ఈ మంటపానకు దక్షిణము రాయలగోపురముయొక్క ఆమీద రాయలుగోపురము మట్టుమాత్రము చేశి నాలుగువయిపులా నాలుగు స్తంభాలుమాత్రము కాటినారు. మట్టా రాతితొన్ని చేశినారుగాని గోపురము కాలేదు.

౧౨. ఇందుకు తూర్పువయిపు ప్రళశేఖరస్వామిగుడి.

౧౩. పర్వతానికి పూర్వభాగమందు కృష్ణుడు గోవర్ధనగిరి యెత్తిన మంటపము ౧. ఇందుకు స్తంభాలు ౧౨. ఈ మంటపము పర్వతముకు అంటుకొని పూర్వాభిముఖముగా వున్నది. ఈ మంటపములో వుండే ప్రతిమలు కృష్ణుడు వామహస్తములో గోవర్ధనగిరి గొడుగుగా యెత్తినాడు. దక్షిణహస్తముచేత గోపికాజనానకు అభయము యిస్తూవున్నాడు. ఈ స్వామికి వామభాగమందు 3 స్త్రీప్రతిమలు వున్నవి. ఇందులో యిద్దరు స్త్రీలు నిలుచుకొని వున్నారు. వకతె తలమీద పెరుగుకుండ వుంచుకొని చిన్నవాణ్ని ముందర పెట్టుకొని వున్నది. దీనివెనుక వకగొల్లవాడు నెత్తిమీద వకపిల్ల చేత వకశిశువును వుంచుకొనివున్నాడు. ఈ నలుగురిమీద గోముఖాలు ౭ వున్నవి. వీరివెనుక వృషభేశ్వరుడు శయనించినాడు. ఇతనికింద సింహాలు ౪ వున్నవి. ఈ కృష్ణునికి దక్షిణభాగమందు బలరాముడు వున్నాడు. ఇతను తన వామహస్తము వకగొల్లవానిమీద వేసుకొని వ్యత్యస్తపాదుడై వున్నాడు. ఈ గొల్లవానికి వామభాగము వక స్త్రీ వున్నది. వీరిమీద గోముఖాలు ౫ వున్నవి. ఈ బలరామునికి దక్షిణమందు, ఆవును పాలు పిదుకుతూ వొక గొల్లవాడు వున్నాడు. ఈ ఆవు ముందర దీనివత్సము వొకటి వున్నది. ఇందుకుమీదను ఆవులు చేసేవానికి వొక గొల్లవాడు పిల్లంగ్రోవి వూదుతూ వున్నాడు. ఇతనిఅందున వక స్త్రీ పిల్లను వుంచుకొని వున్నది. ఈ ఆవు ముందర కోలు మోసుకొని వక స్త్రీ పెరుగుకుండలవుట్టి చేతపట్టుకొని వున్నది. దీనికి దక్షిణము వృషభేశ్వరుడు నిలుచుకొని వున్నాడు. ఈ వృషభమువెనుక వక గొల్లవాడు గొల్లది నిలుచుకొని వున్నారు. ఈ వృషభమువెనుక వక గొల్లవాడు స్త్రీ దక్షిణహస్తము తన వామహస్తముచేత పట్టుకొని వున్నాడు. ఈ వృషభముమీద గోముఖాలు ౧౭, ముందరభాగమందు దూడ ౧, దక్షిణపుగోడకు సింహముఖాలు ౭ వున్నవి. అంతు యీ మంటపములో వుండేటి మూర్తి

దక్షిణపుగోడను సింహాలు ౧౦, స్త్రీ పురుషప్రతిమలు ౧౬, పిల్లలు ౫ వృక్షాలు ౨, ఆవు ౧, దూడలు ౨, గోముఖాలు ౨౬ వున్నవి.

౧౪. ఈ మంటపానకు దక్షిణము రామానుజమంటపమని వున్నది. ఇది కొండను తొలిచి చేసినారు. ఇందుకు మధ్య స్తంభాలు ౨, పూర్వ పశ్చిమము అడుగులు ౨౦, వుత్తర దక్షిణము అడుగులు ౨౬, ఇందులో ప్రతిమలు లేవు. స్తంభాలకు యేక శిలామంటపములో సింహ ముఖాలు ౪ వున్నవి. లోపల వుత్తరదక్షిణము రెండు గోడలకు చిన్న గోపురాలవలె యేర్పరిచి గూళ్లు తవ్వినారు. అందులో ప్రతిమలు వున్నవి. ఈ మంటపముముందర స్తంభాలు రాళ్లతో చేసినిలిపినవి ౬ వున్నవి. ఇందుకు దక్షిణభాగము కొండశిలకే ౧౦ మెట్లు చేసినారు. ఈ మంటపముమీద కెలు గోటి శింగమనాయుడిమంటపము. ఇందుకు స్తంభాలు ౪. ఇది వడ్డెవాండ్ల చేత రాళ్లు తెప్పించి కట్టించినారుగాని, శిల్పప్రకారము కట్టించినది కాదు. ఇప్పుడు అంతా శిథిలమైనది.

౧౫. ఇందుకు దక్షిణభాగమందు పెద్దగుండు వకటి మంటపము చెయ్యవలెనని రెండు స్తంభాలుచేసి యేకశిలామంటపానకు కొంత శిల తొలిచినారు. అది పూరాకాలేదు గనుక అతి గుండుకు గురుతుగా వున్నది.

౧౬. ఈ మంటపానకు దక్షిణము ధర్మరాజావారిమంటపమని యేక శిలామంటపము వున్నది. ఇందుకు స్తంభాలు ౪, గర్భగుళ్లు ౩, ఇందులో మరేమి ప్రతిమలు లేవు. మధ్యవున్న గర్భగుడికి ద్వారపాలకులకు నగను పనిచేసిన ప్రతిమలు ౨ వున్నవి. ఈ మంటపము యిప్పుడు చేసినదానివలెనె శిథిలముకాకుండా వున్నది.

౧౭. ఈ మంటపానకు తూర్పు కొండకిందను పూర్వభాగము రెండు పెద్ద గుండ్లు వుండగా వాటిమీదనున్ను అర్జునుడు తపస్సు చేసినట్టుగా చేసినారు. అక్కడ యీశ్వరుడు చతుర్భుజాకృతిగా వామహస్తమందు పాశుపతము ధరించినాడు. అర్జునుడు వూర్ధ్వబాహువై తపస్సు చేస్తూ వున్నాడు. వీటికి వుత్తరభాగమందు గరుడగంధర్వకిన్నరవిద్యాధరసిద్ధచారణులున్ను మొదలయినవారుగానున్ను స్త్రీలుగానున్ను యేనుగులు సింహాలుగానున్ను ప్రతిమలు చేసినారు. ఇది కొంతపని సాగినది, కొంతపని సాగలేదు.

౧౫. పశ్చిమదక్షిణభాగమందు కొండమీద దేవశిలామంటపము వున్నది. ఇందుకు ప్రామాణము యమపురిమంటపమని అంటారు. ఇందుకు స్తంభాలు ౬, శిథిలమైన స్తంభము ౧ గాక తతిమ్మా ౫ స్తంభాలు బాగా వున్నవి. గర్భగుళ్లు ౨-౩ మధ్యవున్న గర్భాలయమీద కైలాసమనే నామము కలిగినది. ఇందులో చతుర్భుజాకృతితో వామపాదము వృషభముమీద వుంచుకొని పరమేశ్వరుడు వున్నాడు. వీరికి వామభాగమందు పార్వతి కుమారస్వామిని పాదముమీద వుంచుకొని వున్నది. ఈ పార్వతీ పరమేశ్వరులయొక్కమందు రెండువ శ్రీగణాధ్యక్షుడై చతుర్భుజాకృతితో విఘ్నేశ్వరున్నాడు. పరమేశ్వరదక్షిణభాగము బ్రహ్మ చతుర్ముఖాలతో వున్నాడు. పార్వతికింద సేవకజనము స్త్రీ ౧ వున్నది. ఈ పార్వతీపరమేశ్వరులు రెండు సింహాతలాటాలే కాళ్లుగా కలిగిన మంచముమీద కూర్చుండియున్నారు. ఈ మంచముకింద వృషభము ౧ శివునివామపాదము మోసుకొని వున్నది. ద్వారపాలకులు ౨ వున్నారు. ఇందుకు వుభయపార్శ్వములయందువున్న వున్న గర్భగుళ్లలో ప్రతిమలు లేవు. మంటపములో దక్షిణపుగోడను శేషతల్పముమీద రంగనాయకులు పూర్వశిరస్సుతో శయనించినారు. పశ్చిమభాగమందు పాదాలదగ్గిర యిద్దరు భటులు. ఇద్దరిలో రంగనాయకులవారిభటుడు ౧, మహిషాసురుని భటుడు ౧. ఈ భటులు యిద్దరు బాహాబాహి ముష్టాముష్టి దంతాదంతి నఖానఖి కేశాకేశులతో జగడము చేశేటట్లుగా వున్నారు. ఇతనిమీద గంధర్వులు యిద్దరు వున్నారు. ఆమునుప పరిచారకజనులు ముగ్గురు వున్నారు. ఈ వుత్తరపుగోడను మహిషాసురమర్దని అష్టహస్తాలు అష్టాయుధాలతో ఖడ్గధారులై ప్రమథగణాలు అయిన భటులు ౯ మంది, స్త్రీ ప్రతిమ ౧, వెరశి ౧౦ ప్రతిమలుచేసిన యుక్తమైనట్టి సింహవాహనముమీద కూర్చుండి పూర్వాభిముఖముగా ధనుస్సు తన వామహస్తముచేత ధరించి దక్షిణహస్తముతో బాణసంధానముచేసి యుద్ధానకు అభిముఖుడైన మహిషాసురునిమీద వేయ్యవలెనని ఆక్రాంతము యున్నది. కడమ హస్తాలయందు ఖడ్గచాపంటూశంఖచక్రములతో మరిండ్లు మొదలైన ఆయుధంబులు ధరించుండి ఛత్రచామరంబులుపట్టుకొని సేవకజనంబు పరివేష్టించియుండగా కోపాక్రాంతురాలై మహిషాసురుని సంహారముచేయువలెనని బాణసంధానము చేసినది. ఈశక్తికి యెదురుగా మహిషముఖము కలిగి పశ్చిమాభిముఖుడై అష్టహస్తాలతో శక్తికి అభిముఖముగా తన ద్వారపాలకులయందు గదాది

యుంచి వున్నదై అమ్మవారితో యుద్ధముచేయ్యవలెనని మహిషాసురుడు వున్నాడు. ఇతనికి ఛత్రచామరాలుధరించి ఆయుధపాణులై భటులు యుద్ధముచేశేవారివలెనే వున్నారు. ప్రతిమలు ౭ వున్నవి. ఈమంటపానకుయెదురుగా పూర్వభాగమందు గుండు వకటి విమానము చేయవలెనని ఆరంభముచేశినారు. అది పూరా కా లేదు. ఈ గుడికి వుత్తరభాగమందు మహిషాసురునితలగడ వకటి రాతితో **వున్నది.**

౧౯. ఈ మంటపముమీద త్రికక్ష్యగ్నేశ్వరస్వామిగుడి. ఈగుడిలో వున్నస్వామివారికి యూపస్నాము బాగా వున్నప్పుడు అంగడికి వచ్చినవారికి ముత్తిలే కాలుపడిరూకలు వచ్చేవి. అరవ మాటలో కాలుపడిఅనగా కాళప్పు అంటారు. తెనుగున తవ్వెడు అని అంటారు. ఇప్పుడు యీస్వామివారు యెక్కడికో పొలిపోయినారు. అయిది యూనత్తు ఛేదిస్తే అవింగము అగుపడుతుందని అన్నారు.

౨౦. ఈ పర్వతానికి నైర్ఋతిమూలగాను వరాహస్వామివారిగుడి వున్నది. ఇందుకు స్తంభాలు ౪, గర్భగుడి ౧. దీనికి గుహ అనే పంజ్ఞ. ఇది పర్వతానికేతొలిచినారు. దీనికిముందర సరిగా భిక్షాదులు ౬ స్తంభాలతో మంటపముకట్టించినారు. దీనికి ప్రాకారము వున్నది. ప్రాకారమధ్యమందు వకరావిన్ని వేంకాయచెట్లున్ను వున్నవి. ఈదేవస్థానము పశ్చిమాభిముఖముగా వున్నది. గర్భగుడిలో వరాహస్వామి వున్నాడు. ఈ **వరా**హస్వామి వామపాదము భూమియందు వుంచుకొని దక్షిణపాదముదగ్గిర భార్యాయుక్తముగావున్న ఆదిశేషునిశిరసుమీద వుంచుకొని దక్షిణోరువుమీద లక్ష్మిఅమ్మవారిని అభిముఖముగావుంచుకొని వామహస్తముచేత దక్షిణపాదముధరించి దక్షిణహస్తము అమ్మవారి పిరుదులమీద వుంచుకొని తాను పశ్చిమాభిముఖుడై అమ్మవారు పూర్వాభిముఖముతో వుండగా వరాహస్వామివారు కడమ రెండుబాహువులయందు శంఖచక్రాలుధరియించి చతుర్భుజాయుక్తుడై అనోన్యస్యముఖావలోకనచేస్తూ శ్రీవారిలాపార్థము అమ్మవారి దక్షిణస్తనము తనవరాహముఖముతో చుంబనముచేస్తూ వున్నాడు. ఈ స్వామివారికి హరికేశరరాజాకు ప్రత్యక్షమయినారు గనుక అప్పుడు వరాహస్వామివారిని పశ్చిమాభిముఖముగా వున్ననిమిత్తమేమని హరికేశరరాజా అడిగితే అందుకు స్వామివారు ముందర కంచిలో పుణ్యకోటివిమానముతో వరదరాజస్వామివారు అవతారముచేస్తారు గనుక ఈముఖముగా

వున్నాము చెప్పినారు. ఇది పురాణప్రసిద్ధము. ఈస్వామికి పూజాపుర స్కారములు చేటివరకు నడుస్తూ వున్నవి. ఈస్వామికి చిత్తురువు సంబంధ మైనవస్త్రాలు పెట్టినారు. గర్భగుడికి దక్షిణభాగమందు వకశక్తి చతుర్భుజా యుక్తముగా వున్నది. ఈ శక్తికి దక్షిణభాగమందు హరిశేఖరరాజు యిద్దరు భార్యలతో వున్నాడు. ఇతనికి వాము భాగమందు చతుర్భుజాలతో వక పురుషప్రతిమ వున్నది. ఆ గర్భగుడికి వుత్తరభాగమందు గజలక్ష్మి వున్నది. ఉత్తరభాగమున గోడను శ్రీరాములప్రతిమ వున్నది. ఈశ్రీరాములవారికి స్తుతి చేస్తూ అంజనేయుడు వున్నాడు. ఇంకా అక్కడ కొన్ని ప్రతిమలువున్నవి. వాటిపేర్లు తెలియలేదు. ఈదేవస్థానానికి ఉత్తరపుమైపున ప్రాకారములో వల శాసనము వున్నది. ఈ దేవుడు పురాణప్రసిద్ధము.

౨౧. ఈ గుడికి వుత్తరపుమైపు కొండకు వట్టినదుము వకమంటపము వున్నది. శ్రీకల్యాణేశ్వరస్వామిగుడికి దవమాటిపయిన్న అడవిలో వున్నది. అది రాతి శిలామంటపము. ఇందులో రామిని నెమ్మున చిత్రాలు లేవు. అరలు నాలుగు మొదలు పెట్టినారు గాని పూరా కాలేదు. ఇందుకు స్తంభాలు ౮ వున్నవి. ఇదిగాక పర్వతానికి వుత్తరభాగమందు పడికట్లు ౨౬ వున్నవి.

౨౨. కొండమధ్యమందు ద్రౌపదీదేవిపసుపుకోట్టే వకటి. కింద టావిదగ్గిర మహాలక్ష్మీస్థలము. ఇందుకు గుణాలు యిటికెలు మొదలైనవి వున్నవి.

౨౩. ఈ కోట్టికి వుత్తరము ధర్మరాజసింహాసనము అని సింహాతలగవేగా వున్నది. అందుకువుత్తరముగా పాండవులు కొలువనము చేసిన హాలామగుండాలు ౫ వున్నవి.

౨౪. ఈ సింహాసనానకు పూర్వభాగము పాండవులు విద్యనుకదిగిన నీరు పొయ్యేటందుకు కాలువ వకటి వున్నది. ఆ కాలువఅంతమున భవము పెరిగగానే సంధి ఆకృతిగా వున్నది. ఆ నీరు అచేటందుకు దొన వకటి. ఆ దొనకు తూర్పుమైపున దొనలో దిగేటందుకు సోపానాలు వున్నవి. మహాలకు చిన్నగా రాయలగోపురము అని మట్టుచేశేటప్పుడు దగ్గిరకొండను గోపురముదగ్గిర పెద్దరాళ్లకు తూట్లుపెట్టి రాయి భేదించవలెనని తూట్లుపెట్టినారు. ఆ పని పూరా కా లేదు. ఆ తూట్లు కోతితూట్లు అని చెప్పుతారు.

ఈ **పర్వతానకు** పశ్చిమభాగమందు కలిగివున్న యేకశిలామంటపములు ౨-కి కొంచెము కథ వున్నది. ఇందుకు మంటపము దక్షిణభాగమందువున్నదానికి స్తంభాలు ౧౨. ఇందులో గర్భగుళ్లు ౫. ఈ గర్భగుళ్లలోగా దేవుండ్లు ప్రతిమలు లేవు. ఇందుకు గర్భగుడి ౧-కి ద్వారపాలకులు ౨ చొ॥ ౧౦ మంది ద్వారపాలకులు వున్నారు. ఉత్తరపుగోడను **శాసనము** వున్నది. ఇందులో లింగాలను **తిరుకోవిల గుండ నవా** వున్నది. ఈ గుడిముందర నీళ్లునిలిచేమడుగు ౧ వున్నది. అక్కడ శేషుపాదలు వున్నది. వుత్తరభాగమందువున్న మంటపానకు స్తంభాలు ౪, గర్భగుళ్లు లేవు. ప్రతిమలు నాస్తి. ఈ మంటపము పని పూరా కా లేదు. ఈ మంటపానకు వుత్తరభాగము యేకశిలామంటపము ౧-కి స్తంభాలు ౨. మరేమియొక్కనలు లేవు. ద్వారపాలకులు ౨ వున్నారు. అర వకటి వున్నది.

౨౫. పన్నెండు స్తంభాలమంటపము వకటి.

౨౬. నాలుగు స్తంభాలమంటపము వకటి.

౨౭. రెండు స్తంభాలమంటపము వకటి.

౨౮. **ఈ కొండకు పడమటిపార్శ్వము పుష్కర**ణ్య వున్నది.

౨౯. ఈ పుష్కరణ్య పర్వ్యతముసందు మూడు రథాలువున్నవి. రెండు రథాలకు మాత్రము లోపల కొలిచి అరలు చేశినారు. మరివక రథానికి వుత్తరముఖముగా అర మొదలు పెట్టినారుగాని పూరా కా లేదు. దీనివద్ది లింగము పానవట్టమున్న చతుర్భుజాయుక్తమైన గ్రామదేవతగుడివ్క వున్నది. దీనివద్దిరవున్న కొండను రాళ్లుకొట్టే తిరువళిక్కేణి ముదుపిళ్లికట్టడానకు రవానా చేస్తూ వున్నారు.

౩౦. పర్వతానికి దక్షిణభాగము అరగడియదూరము శక్తి చతుర్భుజాయుక్తముగా వున్నది. దక్షిణహస్తమందు చక్రము ధరించినది. ఈమెకు పేరావృత్తికై ధటులు ఖడ్గధారులై వుభయపార్శ్వములయందు అసురులు వున్నారు. ఈమె పశ్చిమాభిముఖముగావున్నది. యెదురుగా పెద్దసింహము వుత్తరాభిముఖముగా వున్నది. ఈశక్తివిమానము యేకశిలతో వున్నది. ద్వారపాలకులు స్త్రీలు యిద్దరు వున్నారు. చతుర్భుజాయుక్తముగా స్త్రీప్రతి

ములు దక్షిణభాగమందు **౧, పూర్వమందు** ౧, వుత్తరమందు ౧, యింగాలో వుండేశక్తిపేరు తెలియలేదు. అందు స్త్రీ ప్రతిమలు ౧౨.

౩౧. ఈ విమానమువెనుక పశ్చిమముఖముగా పెద్ద వృషభేశ్వరప్రతిమ వున్నది. అది భూమిలో పూడి వున్నది. అది చూచవలెనని కొంత యిసుక తీశినారుగనుక నగము అగపడుతూ వున్నది.

౩౨. ఈ విమానము దక్షిణభాగమందు నకులునివిమానము యేకశిలతోటి వున్నది. దానికి అడుగున కొంత మంటపము వున్నది. అందులో ప్రతిమలు **లేవు. ఈ విమానపు** వుత్తరభాగము ప్రతిమలు ౬, పూర్వభాగము ప్రతిమలు ౫, దక్షిణము ౭ వున్నవి.

౩౩. ఈ విమానము పశ్చిమభాగమందు సహదేవునివిమానము యేకశిలతో వున్నది. మంటపము సన్నవి రెండుస్తంభాలతో దక్షిణముఖముగా వున్నది. యిందులో ప్రతిమలు లేవు. ఈ విమానముచుట్టూ చిత్తరుగా వున్నది. దీని అందువల్లే పూర్వభాగమందు యేకశిలతో నకరయేనుగు దక్షిణాభిముఖముగా వున్నది.

౩౪. ఈ విమానానకు పూర్వభాగమందు భీమునివిమానము వున్నది. యేకశిలతో మంటపమువలెనే పశ్చిమముఖముగా వున్నది. ఇందుకు స్తంభాలు పశ్చిమమందు ౬, దక్షిణమందు ౨, పూర్వమందు ౪, వెరశి ౧౨ స్తంభాలచేతను ఈ విమానము బహుంగొప్పది, **దీనిమీద పిడుగు** పడి పడిమికి చీలినది.

౩౫. **ఈ** విమానానికి దక్షిణము ధర్మరాజువిమానము వున్నది. ఇందుకు స్తంభాలు పశ్చిమమందు ౪. ఈ విమానముచుట్టు ప్రతిమలు ౮ వున్నవి. ఈ విమానముమీద ప్రదక్షిణము చెయ్యజానకు రెండు ప్రాకారములు వున్నవి. ఈ ప్రాకారములకు చిత్తరుపు ప్రతిమలు ౨౧. ప్రాకారములలో రెండుఅరలు, స్తంభాలు ౨ వున్నవి. ఈ పయిని వ్రాశిన ౮ ప్రతిమలలో దక్షిణపూర్వోత్తరముపున్న ౫ ప్రతిమల శిరసుమీద అక్షరాలు వ్రాశినారు. అవి తెలియ లేదు.

౩౬. గ్రామములో స్థలశయనస్వామిగుడిరూపుగా ద్వారముగోపురము వాకిళ్లు ౫ వున్నవి. దక్షిణముపయివున ప్రాకారానకులోపల గర్భగుడి

లో స్థలశయనస్వామివారు దక్షిణశిరస్సు పెట్టుకొని శయనించినారు. పాదాలదగ్గిర పుండరీకమహామునిన్ని తామరయున్ను వున్నవి. ఈ మహామునికి యిక్కడనే ముక్తిదొరికినది. ఇందుకు దక్షిణపువయిపు యిలుమంగతాయారుగుడి, వుత్తరపుపైపున మాడెకురుకుంతఅమ్మవారిగుడి, చుట్టూ ఆళ్వార్లగుళ్లు ౭, తిరుమడపల్లి ౧, ధ్వజస్తంభము ౧, తర్వాత పానుగ్రివుండే వుగ్రాణముకొట్టు వకటి. గోపురమువాకిలికి యిరుపార్శ్వములలో బొమ్మలు కోరుటకి లికినచిత్రరుపురాళ్లు వున్నవి. గోపురము వాకిలికియివతల వుత్తరభాగమందు ముప్పైఅరుకాళ్లమంటపము. స్వామివారు వుత్సవదినాలలో అందులోవచ్చివుండేది. ఈగుడికి ప్రాకారము వకటే, చుట్టూవున్నస్తంభాలు ౧౨౨.

౩౭. గోపురమువాకిటికి యెదురుగా తూర్పుభాగాన రాయలుగోపురము అంతా ఛిద్రమైపోయినది. ఇందుచేతను దక్షిణమును ౪౪ అడుగులు కిందముట్టు యివతల వక అరలాగున వుంటుంది. అందులో మరేమి యెక్కువ బింకాలు లేవు. ఇందుకు తూర్పున కృష్ణస్వామివారి పుట్టిన మహాదాదు వుట్లురెక్కమంటపము. అందుకు స్తంభాలు ౪, వయిన గోపురము.

౩౮. ఇందుకుతూర్పున స్థలశయనస్వామివారిపుష్కరిణితోట. అందులో శ్రీహనుమన్తగుడిమంటపము. ఆ లోపల గర్భగుడిలో స్వామి. ఆ స్వామిని అంచిలిను రెత్తుకొనిపోయెను.

౩౯. ఈ హనుమన్తగుడికి పూర్వము పూజత్రాళ్వారు అవతరించినమంటపము. అది శిథిలముయిపోయినది. ఇప్పుడు ౧౬ స్తంభాలు మాత్రము వున్నవి. ఈమంటపమునందర వక మంటపము ఛిద్రముయిపోయినది.

౪౦. ఈమంటపానకు దక్షిణపార్శ్వము వూటికి పూర్వభాగము పుండరీకపుష్కరిణి. ఈపుష్కరిణీమధ్యమందు నాలుగుస్తంభాలమంటపము. దీనికి వుత్తరపుపైపునవున్న చిన్న నాలుగుకాళ్లమంటపము. ఈ వుత్సవదినాలయందు స్థలశయనస్వామివారికి యీ మంటపముదగ్గిర పందిళ్లువేసి అభిషేకోత్సవముచేస్తారట. ఇందుకు సోపానాలు అడుగునుమట్టు అంతవున్న మెట్లు ౧౬. ఇందుకు తుల అడుగులు ౩౦౦, అజా అడుగులు ౩౦౦.

౮౧. ఈవృక్ష్యానికి వుత్తరపువయిపు యిప్పతోట. ఈవృక్ష్యానికి దక్షిణపువయిపు జీడిమామిడిచెట్లు.

౮౨. గ్రామానికి తూర్పుసముద్రతీరమందు సప్తప్రాకారములున్న శివాలయము. ఈస్వామి పేరు స్థలపురాణముతోటి పోయినది. ఈ తర్వాత యెవరికిన్ని తెలియ లేదు. సప్తప్రాకారములకు యిప్పుడు రెండుప్రాకారములుమాత్రము అనుభవముతూవున్నవి. మూడుప్రాకారములకు అడియాళము వున్నది. తక్కిన్నప్రాకారములకు అడియాళము వున్నదిలేనిది అగపడకుండా సముద్రములో మునిగిపోయెను. గర్భగుళ్లు ౨, అందులో వక గర్భగుళ్లో శివలింగము వున్నది. దానివున్నతము రొమ్ముపొడుగువున్నది. పానవట్టము కనపడ లేదు. ఆ లింగము కింద యెంతవున్నదో తెలియ లేదు. ఈ గర్భగుడి * ప్పైకానికి కింద స్వామికి మీదనుంచి ఆరు గంధపుమానులు వేశి కట్టినారు. అందులో రెండుమానులు దొరలో పాటకస్తులు తీసుక పోయినారు. ఇప్పుడు నాలుగుచెక్కలు వున్నవి. పడమటిగోడను పార్వతిపరమేశ్వర్లు యిద్దరూ బాలసుబ్రహ్మణ్యస్వామిని యిద్దరియుందున్న కూర్చుండపెట్టుకొని వున్నారు. యిరుపార్శ్వాలలో బ్రహ్మ విష్ణువు యిద్దరు వున్నారు. స్వామికి తలమీద దెబ్బ తగిలినది. కొంచెము ఛిన్నముగా వున్నది. ఇరుపార్శ్వాలా ద్వారపాలకులు రెండు ప్రతిమలున్న రెండు గోడలు వున్నవి. సింహాలమీదయున్న ప్రతిమలుమాత్రము అలుకొట్టి అరిగిపోయినవి. ఇప్పుడు యిరుపై ముప్పై సింహాలు మొదలయినవి కనుపడుతూవున్నవి. ప్రాకారములయందువున్న **నందులు** కిందపడి మూతులు పగిలినవి. **కొన్నిటికి** కాళ్లుపోయినవి. రెండో ప్రాకారములో శ్రీమహావిష్ణువు దక్షిణము తలపెట్టుకొని పరుండున్నాడు. స్వామిగుడికి యెదట ధ్వజస్తంభము నాటినారు. ఆస్తంభము యిప్పుడు సముద్రములోవున్నది. అక్కడ మోకాలిబంటినీళ్లు.

౮౩. పడమటిపక్కను చిన్నగోపురము. గర్భగుడివున్నది. అందులో పార్వతీ **పరమేశ్వరులూ** యిద్దరు బాలసుబ్రహ్మణ్యేశ్వరస్వామిని యెత్తుకొన్నారు. **యిరుపార్శ్వాలను బ్రహ్మ విష్ణువు** యిద్దరూవున్నారు. ద్వారాల ముందర విజయశీలము **చెక్కినాడు.** నాలుగువయిపులా నాలుగుసింహాలు బహు భీకరముగా వున్నవి. తక్కిన్న విగ్రహాలు ఛిద్రముఅయిపోయి

నది. ఈగర్భగుడిమీదను గోపురముగావున్నది. ఈరెండుగుళ్లమీదనైన కల శాలు పెట్టివున్నవి.

౭౭. ఈదేవస్థానానికి వుత్తరపు వయిపు యేకశిలతో వరాహదేవుడిగుడి తొలిపించినారు. అందులో రాజప్రతిమ చెక్కినారు. ఆశిలలో వుత్తరపు వయిపు మహిషాసురుడు పడుకొనివున్నాడు. ఈశిలకు సముద్రములో అలలుతగులుతగా వున్నది. చంద్రోదయము అయినప్పుడు తరంగాలు కొట్టితే చుట్టూ నీరు వస్తుంది.

౭౮. శివాలయానికి దిబ్బ పదిబారలు మాత్రము సముద్రము వుంది. వుత్తరదక్షిణాలు ఎర బారలు పడమటికి తోసుకవచ్చినాడు.

౭౯. ఈ శివాలయానికి దక్షిణభాగమున మూడుశిలలు వున్నవి. అందులో వకశిలమీదను తూర్పువయిపున చిన్నఅరతొలిచి ప్రతిమను వుంచినారు. అరకు వుత్తరవయిపు యేనుగుమూతి దక్షిణము వక గుర్రము వున్నది. వుత్తరవయిపున యేనుగుపాదము కనపడుతూవున్నది. పడమట వక అర తొలిచినారు. అందులో వక స్త్రీ ప్రతిమ వ్రాశినారు. ఆ క్రింద చిన్న ప్రతిమలు మూడు **వున్నవి.**

౮౦. **రెండోశిలను సింహముఖముగా కనపడుతుంది.** ఇదివకశిల. ఇందుకు యిదే చిత్రముగాని మరియేమి **యెక్కువ లేదు.**

౮౧. ఈ మూడోశిలమీదను పెద్దశిలాసున్న కడుపు చిన్నఅరానున్న ఒకటి విక్కృతాకారముగా వున్నది.

Translation.

1. On the North side of the hill, is an Îsvara temple. In this is Îsvara. Lord Clive took away the Nandî in front of this temple.

2. In front of this are two monkeys, freeing themselves from vermin.

3. On the West side of those figures is a round churn used by Draupadî, the lawful wife of the Pândavas. There are three *Mantapas*,* hollowed slenderly out of the solid rock. The sculptures in the first *Mantapa* are two Doorkeepers, a four-armed Durgâ inside, and four figures of attendants. The other two excavations have the same figures. On the South side of this rock, and facing to the West, is an eight-armed Durgâ, treading with her foot the head of Mahishâsura.

4. Near this, to the South, on the West side of the road, is the fireplace in which Bhîmasena† cooked. There are steps to get up to the top of this.

5. Not far from this, to the South, on the face of the rock, is a large round butter ball made by Draupadî. Half of this is said to have been eaten by a cat, which gives the ball a chipped appearance. The cat is seen, with its fore paws upraised, tied to the hill on which Arjuna is performing penance.

6. On the South side of this is Arjuna's *Ratha*,‡ cut out of a single stone. The stone has been cut

* An open temple building. Also written *Mandapa*.

† The third of the five *Pându* princes, commonly called Bhîma.

‡ See note * p. 213, *infra*.

into the shape of a *Mantapa*, with two pillars and a *Garbhagriha*,* in which was placed *Siva*. When that *Linga* was carried off by Bu * * [*sic*], the people of this place took an image of Vinâyaka† which was near and put it in the *Garbhagriha*. On the wall to the South of the *Garbhagriha*, is some inscription written, the character of which is unknown.

7. Near to this, on the South, is hollowed out of the solid rock, a *Mantapa* containing Varâhasvâmi. In this are two pillars and a *Garbhagriha*. In the *Garbhagriha* are no figures. There are two Door-keepers. On the wall to the North of the *Garbha-griha* is Varâhasvâmi; his left foot is placed on the ground; his right foot rests on the head of Âdisesha;‡ on his right thigh is seated, facing him, Lakshmi; his right hand is on her hinder parts, his left hand holds her right leg; he faces to the West, and the goddess to the East. The four-armed Varâhasvâmi's two other hands hold the *Sankha* and the *Chakra*.§ The god and goddess are regarding each other, and he with his boar-mouth is, in playful dalliance, kissing her right breast. Behind him, to the East, is a four-armed male figure. Facing this figure, is that of a woman. Above these two is a votary with joined hands, uttering praises. Three votaries are praising Varâhasvâmi. Altogether, there are nine figures at the

* The sanctuary or adytum of a Hindu temple.

† Ganesa. ‡ The thousand headed serpent.

§ See note † p. 202, *infra*.

North end. On the East wall and facing to the West is Gaja Lakshmî, on her lotus throne. Above her head are the heads of two Elephants. On either side of Lakshmî, stand two women reaching pots full of water to the Elephants' trunks, for bathing the goddess. There is one Doorkeeper. Altogether, there are figures of five women, one man, and two elephants' heads. On the South side [of the *Garbha-griha*] is a four-armed Durgâ, holding an umbrella. To the South side of the goddess are three attendants, carrying swords. There is also a deer. On the North side, are three more armed attendants, and a lion. There is one Doorkeeper. Altogether eight [human] figures, a lion, and a deer.

Facing Varâhasvâmi, on the South wall, is eight-armed Trivikrama* holding the *Sankha, Chakra, Gadâ*,† &c. Bali Chakravartî had given him three paces of land, whereupon the god usurping the whole earth by placing on it his right foot, stretched his left foot to the sky for the purpose of seizing the upper world. Brahmâ is bathing this foot with water from his sacred water pot and worshipping it. In front of Vishnu is Jâmbavat.‡

Bali Chakravartî, thinking it wrong to withdraw a gift, is praying to the god, near his [right] foot, wishing to give him ground for his third pace.§

* Vishnu, as the "Three-Stepper."

† Vishnu's conch, discus, and mace. ‡ King of the bears.

§ Bali when reproached by Vishnu for failing to give him all he had promised, besought the god to place his third step on his head.—See Muir's *Sanscrit Texts*, Part IV., p. 127 f.

Behind him is *Sukrâchârya*.* Two of Bali Chakravarti's soldiers are on the East side, and four on the West side [of Trivikrama]. Altogether, there are 11 male figures. This *Mantapa* faces to the West.

8. On the East side of the hill, on a rock at the foot, are 11 steps on which Krishnasvâmi used to play at Mounting the Throne. There is also a slide on which he used to amuse himself.

9. On the East side of the hill, the rock has been fashioned into figures representing Arjuna's Penance, as [in the story of] Kirâta and Arjuna.† Here is Arjuna, his two arms extended over his head, performing penance; and here is four-armed Îsvara, as he appeared [to Arjuna,] holding the *Pâsupatâstra*,‡ *Damaruka*,§ *Trisûla*,¶ &c. Between Îsvara and Arjuna stands Visvakarma,‖ with an adze on his right shoulder, the handle of which he holds in his right hand. Above Îsvara's head are Sûrya, Chandra, &c. Below Arjuna, is Krishnasvâmi in a fane, four-armed and holding the *Sankha*, *Chakra*, *Gadâ*, &c. To his right, is Dronâchârya,** seated in the lotus-posture,†† with emaciated body, performing

* See note * p. 83, *supra*.

† See p. 89 ff., *supra*.

‡ A fabulous weapon.

§ A sort of small drum.

¶ *Siva's* trident.

‖ The son of Brahmâ and architect of the gods.—Wilson.

** See note * p. 21, *supra*.

†† "The thighs crossed, one hand resting on the left thigh, the other held up with the thumb upon the heart; the eyes directed to the tip of the nose."—Wilson.

penance. On Krishna's left, the rock is fissured, so Nága-maids* appear issuing from Pâtâlaloka, and with the five virgins comes a Nága-maid for Arjuna. On the North side of these appears Indra, accompanied by his wife, mounted on the elephant called Airâvata, coming to visit *Siva*. Behind Airâvata is another elephant. Below Airâvata are three elephant cubs. And there is a cat, with her kittens, facing to the East, with upstretched paws.†

Round the god Indra, in the form of a ring, are figures of *Garudas*,‡ *Gandharvas*,§ *Kinnaras*,¶ *Kimpurushas*,¶ *Siddhas*,‖ *Vidyâdharas*,‖ &c., some with wives, some without wives, coming, as ascetics, to visit *Siva*. There are here 36 figures. Amongst these demi-gods are three deer. Behind them, to the North, in the middle [of the rock] are seven lions and one sheep. To Îsvara's right, and above, are Dharmarâja and Bhîma sitting, performing penance. On their right are a hog and a tiger. On Îsvara's right are 24 figures of troops of *Pramathas*,** and Rishis,†† coming to visit *Siva*. Also a lion, a hog, three deers, a tiger, and two monkeys. They are thus represented accompanied by their wives [?]. Altogether there are 80 male and female figures.

* See note ‡ p. 88, *supra*. † Cp. note § p. 88, *supra*.

‡ The bird and vehicle of Vishnu. § Celestial musicians. ¶ Demigods or musicians in the service of Kuvera. ‖ Demigods of undefined attributes, inhabiting the middle air.—Wilson.

** Attendants upon *Siva*.

†† Saints or sanctified sages, of whom there are seven orders.

10. To the right of the above is a *Mantapa* [excavated out] of the solid rock. It is called "The five Pâṇḍavas." It has 18 pillars, of which one is broken, leaving 17 pillars. The shafts of four of the 17 pillars are broken; the rest are perfect. The front pillars rest on lions' heads. The total number of lions is eight. In the middle of this *Mantapa* there is a chamber, which contains nothing. On either side of this chamber, the commencement of other chambers, which have not been completed, is visible. There is nothing but a sort of cave on each side of the chamber, with no sculptures; all is plain.

11. To the right of this *Mantapa* you ascend to the *Râyala Gopura*,* the foundation only of which has been built, and four pillars set up on the four sides. Round this the rock has been shaped into a seat but the *Gopura* has not been constructed.

12. On the East side of this is the Sthalasekharasvâmî temple.

13. On the East side of the hill is a *Mantapa* containing Krishṇa lifting the mountain Govardhana.† In this are 12 pillars. The *Mantapa* joins the hill and faces to the East. The figures in this *Mantapa* are as follows: Krishṇa holds up the

* I. e. the *Gopura* of the *Râyals*, the title of the princes of Vijayanagara. A *Gopura* is the pyramidical tower over the gate-way of a Hindu temple.

† See p. 92 *l.*, *supra*,

mountain Govarddhana with his left hand like an umbrella; with his right hand he is giving the sign *Abhaya** to the Gopikás. On the left of the god, are three female figures. Of these, two are in a standing posture. One has a pot of curds on her head, and a little boy before her. Behind her is a cowherd with a child on his head and an infant in his arms. Above these four are the heads of six cows. Behind them lies V*r*ishabhesvara.† Beneath him are four lions. On K*r*ishna's right, is Balarâma.‡ His left hand is on a cowherd, and he is standing with one foot advanced. On the left of the cowherd is a woman. Above them are the heads of five cows. To the right of Balarâma is a cowherd milking a cow. In front of this cow is her calf. Above this, is a cowherd playing on a fife to collect the cows. Near him is a woman with a child. In front of the cow is a woman carrying a mortar and holding in her hand a net containing pots of curds. On her right stands V*r*ishabhesvara. Behind the bull stand a cowherd and cowherdess. Behind [? on the right of] the bull is a cowherd, holding with his left hand the right hand of a woman. Above the bull are the heads of 16 cows; in the front there is a calf. On the South wall there

* Holding up the right hand, with the palm to the front, as an assurance of safety. This however is not the attitude of the god, whose right hand points to the ground, a sign, probably, to the people that they should take refuge at his feet. See plate II., *supra*.

† Nandi, the sacred bull of *Siva*. ‡ The half brother of Krishna.

are 6 lions' heads. Altogether, in this *Mantapa*, there are 10 lions (on the North and South walls,) 16 figures of men and women, 5 children, 2 bulls, 1 cow, 2 calves, and 27 cows' heads.

14. To the South of this *Mantapa* is the Râmânuja *Mantapa*. This is excavated out of the hill. In the middle are two pillars. East and West [it measures] 20 feet, North and South 26 feet. There are no figures in it. [At the bases] of the pillars in this solid rock *Mantapa* are 4 lions' heads. Inside, the North and South walls are formed like small *Gopuras*, with niches. In those niches there are figures. In the front of this *Mantapa* are 6 stone pillars. On the South side of it are 13 steps cut out of the rocky hill. Above this *Mantapa* is the *Mantapa* of Velugôti Singama Nâyadu. This has 4 pillars. It is not built with stones brought by workmen, nor is it built artistically. It is now all in ruins.

15. On the South side of this, two pillars have been made and the rock a little hollowed out, with the intention of forming a large boulder into a monolithic *Mantapa*. The work is unfinished and serves only as a mark for the boulder.

16. To the South of this *Mantapa* is another, cut out of the solid rock, called Dharmarâja's *Mantapa*. It has 4 pillars and 3 *Garbhagrihas*. There are no figures in it. The centre *Garbhagriha* has 2 half finished figures of door-keepers. This *Mantapa* is in as good preservation as if just made.

17. To the East of this *Mantapa*, at the foot of the East side of the hill, are two large boulders on which is figured the Penance of Arjuna. There is Îsvara, in his four-armed form, holding in his left hand the *Pâsupata*.* Arjuna, with upraised arms (*ûrdhvabâhu*) is performing penance. On the North side of these are figures of *Garudas*, *Gandharvas*, *Kinnaras*, *Vidyâdharas*, *Siddhas*, *Châranas*,† *Rishis*, &c., and of women; also of elephants and lions. This is partly finished, partly unfinished.

18. On the South end of the hill, on an elevation, is a solid rock *Mantapa*. The name given to this in the village is Yamapuri‡ *Mantapa*. This has 6 pillars of which one is broken, and the remaining five are in good order. Of the 3 *Garbhagrihas*, the centre one is called Kailâsa. In this, in his four-armed form, with his left foot on a bull, is Paramesvara.§ On his left is Pârvati, with Kumârasvâmi¶ on her thigh. Between Pârvati and Paramesvara is Vishnu in his four-armed form holding the *Sankha*, *Chakra*, and *Gadâ*. On the right side of Paramesvara is Brahmâ with four faces. Below Pârvati is a female attendant. Pârvati and Paramesvara are sitting on a couch, the legs of which are lions' heads. Below this couch is a bull, bearing *Siva's* left foot. There are 2 Doorkeepers. In the *Garbhagrihas* on

* See p. 89, *supra*. † Bards, panegyrists of the gods.

‡ "City of Yama," the god of death. The confusion between Yama and Mahishâsura is probably the origin of this name.

§ Siva. ¶ The son of Siva and Pârvatî.—Cp. note ‡ p. 107, *supra*.

either side of the centre one there are no figures. On the South wall of the *Mantapa* is Raṅganâyaka,* reclining, with his head towards the East, on his *Sesha* bed.† At the West end [of this figure], near the feet, are 2 soldiers. Of these two, one is the soldier of Raṅganâyaka, and one of Mahishâsura. These two soldiers appear fighting, arm to arm, fist to fist, tooth to tooth, nail to nail, hair to hair. Above Vishnu are 2 *Gandharvas.* Below are 3 attendants. On the North wall is the goddess Mahishamardini‡ with eight arms, surrounded by 8 soldiers armed with swords, representing troops of Pramathas, and 1 female figure—altogether 9 figures—mounted on a lion, facing the East, holding a bow in her left hand, an arrow strung with her right hand and stretched back to her ear against Mahishâsura, who is confronting her for the battle. In her other hands she holds a *Khadga,*§ *Gadâ, Ghantâ,*¶ *Sankha, Parasu,*‖ *Tomara,*** and other weapons, also a *Chhatra,*†† and *Châmara,*‡‡ and surrounded by attendants, she, inflamed with anger, has strung an arrow to slay Mahishâsura. In front of the *Sakti*§§ and facing the goddess, is the buffalo-headed Mahishâsura, holding a club in his two hands and furiously intent on doing battle with the goddess.¶¶

* Vishnu, as the 'Lord of Raṅga' (*Srîraṅgam,* near Trichinopoly.)

† See note * p. 33, *supra.*

‡ Pârvatî, as "Slayer of Mahisha."

§ A sword. ¶ A gong. ‖ An axe. ** An iron club. †† An umbrella. ‡‡ See note * p. 100, *supra.* §§ The energy or active power of a deity, personified as his wife.—Wilson. ¶¶ See p. 99 ff., *supra.*

Soldiers, equipped for war, appear also as engaged in the battle, and holding over Mahishásura the *Chhatra* and *Châmara*. There are 7 figures. In front of this *Mantapa*, to the East, the commencement of forming a boulder into a *Vimâna** has been made, but the work is unfinished. On the North side of this temple is the stone bed and pillow of Mahishásura.

19. Above this *Mantapa*, is the temple of Olakkannesvarasvâmi. When this city flourished, a small fanam used to be collected from each shop, making a quarter measureful *(kâlupadi)* of fanams, for the god in this temple. In the Tamil language they call a quarter measure *olakku*.† In Telugu it is called *tavvedu*. The god has rolled away some where. They say that if all the jungle is cut down, that *Linga* will be found.

20. At the South-west corner of the hill is the Varâhasvâmi temple. In this are 4 pillars and 1 *Garbhagriha*. It is called "The Cave." This is excavated out of the hill itself. Exactly in front of it, the votaries and others have erected a *Mantapa* having 6 pillars. There is a wall round this. In the middle of the walled enclosure are a well and cocoanut trees. This temple faces to the West. In the *Garbhagriha* is Varâhasvâmi. This Varáhasvámi has his left foot on the ground; his right foot is placed on

* A pyramidical temple in the form of a god's chariot.

† *Prop.* Urakku (உழக்கு.)

the head of Âdisesha, who is near him with his wife; on his right thigh, and facing him, is the goddess Lakshmî; his left hand holds her right foot, and his right hand is on her hinder parts; he faces to the West, the goddess to the East. The other two hands of the four-armed Varâhasvâmî hold the *Sankha*, *Chakra*, &c. The two are looking into each other's face, and Varâhasvâmî in playful dalliance is, with his boar-mouth, kissing the right breast of the goddess.

This very god appeared to King Harisekhara, and when asked by him the reason of his facing to the West, the god replied that Varadarâjasvâmî* would thereafter appear as an incarnation in the Punyakotivimâna at Kanchi† and that therefore he faced in that direction. This is celebrated in the Purâna.‡ The worship of this god continues to this day. The god has been painted in colours, as in pictures. On the South side of the *Garbhagriha* is a *Sakti* with four arms. To the South of the *Sakti* is Harisekhara and his two wives. On his left is a four-armed male figure. On the North side of the *Garbhagriha* is Gaja Lakshmî. On the wall at the North end is a figure of *Sri* Râma. Âñjaneya§ is praising *Sri* Râma. There are also some other figures there, the names of which are unknown. On the North side of this temple,

* Vishnu, as "The boon-conferring god."

† *Prop.* Kâñchî (Conjeveram).

‡ See p. 178 f., *supra*.

§ Hanumân, the monkey chief; so called from his mother Añjanâ.

within the enclosure, is an inscription. This god is celebrated in the *Purána*.

21. To the North of this temple, on the middle of the hill is a *Mantapa*. It is in the jungle, on the West side of the *Olakkannesvarasvâmi* temple. It is cut out of the solid rock. In it are no particular figures. Four niches have been commenced, but are unfinished. There are 4 pillars. Besides this, there are 24 steps on the hill, on the North side.

22. In the middle of the hill is Draupadi's turmeric vat.* Near this, is the place where the palace was recently built. There are signs of this, viz., bricks, &c.

23. To the North of this vat is the lion-pillowed couch called Dharmarâja's throne (*simhâsana*). To the North of this are 5 pits used by the *Pândavas* for burnt offerings.

24. On the East side of this throne is a channel which carried away the water used by the *Pândavas* for washing rice. On the edge of that channel is [a stone] in the form of a bag, just like a treasure pack. To hold the water there is a reservoir. On the East side of the reservoir there are steps to descend into it. When the foundation of what is called the *Râyala Gopura*, was laid in a line with the Palace, holes were made in the large rocks on the hill near the *Gopura*, with the intention of splitting the stone.

* I. e. bath. Turmeric (Curcuma longa) is smeared over the body by Hindu females after bathing.

That work is unfinished. The rocks are called the "Monkeys' Rocks." There is a story connected with the two solid rock *Mantapas* adjoining each other, on the West side of the hill. Of these, the *Mantapa* on the South side has 12 pillars, and 5 *Garbhagrihas*. There are no gods or figures inside these *Garbhagrihas*. To each *Garbhagriha* there are two Doorkeepers, making 10 Doorkeepers in all. On the North wall there is a *Saukha*. In these [*Garbhagrihas*] there are holes from which *Lingas* have been taken out. In front of this temple the water collects and forms a pond. In this are reeds. The *Mantapa* on the North side has 4 pillars—no *Garbhagrihas*. Figures *nil*. The work is unfinished. To the North of this *Mantapa* is a solid rock *Mantapa*, having 2 pillars. There is nothing else particular about it. There are 2 Doorkeepers and one chamber.

[The above 3 *Mantapas* may be enumerated as:—]

25. A twelve pillared *Mantapa*.
26. A four pillared *Mantapa*.
27. A two pillared *Mantapa*.

28. On the West side of the hill is a salt-marsh.

29. Between this salt-marsh and the hill are three *Rathas*.* In two only of these is the rock hollowed out and formed into chambers. In the third the commencement of a chamber has been

* Chariots, or chariot-shaped temples, otherwise called *Vimánas*.

made on the North side, but it is unfinished. Near this are a *Linga* and *Yoni** and a temple with a four-armed village goddess. Stones are being cut from the hill near this and sent to Tiruvalikkêni† to build a [temple] kitchen.

30. At a half *gadiya's*‡ distance from the hill to the South is a *Sakti* with four arms. In her right hand she holds a *Chakra*. In attendance on the goddess, on both sides of her, are 6 soldiers armed with swords. The *Sakti* faces to the West. In front is a large lion facing to the North. The *Vimâna*§ of this *Sakti* is monolithic. There are 2 female Doorkeepers. There are figures of four-armed females—1 on the South, 1 on the East, and

* The *Linga* is the phallic emblem of *Siva*, symbolic of the attributes ascribed to him by his worshippers, as the supreme lord, the beginning of all existences, the cause of causes. The Telugu word (*Pânavattamu*) above translated "*Yoni*," properly signifies the pedestal *Lingavedi* (or *Argha*—Coleman), on which the *Linga* stands. The raised edge of this represents the *Yoni* (vulva), an emblem of Pârvatî as the female energy of the deity. For a discussion of the question as to whether the phallic emblem was derived from the religion of the aboriginal or non-Arian Indians, see Muir's *Sanscrit Texts*, part IV., p. 344 ff. For Mythological accounts of the origin of Linga-worship, see the same work, p. 325 ff. Also Vans Kennedy's Researches, p. 298 ff.—Twelve great Lingas were set up in different parts of India, several of which were destroyed by the early Mahomedan conquerors. See H. H. Wilson's *Essays*, Vol. I., p. 221 ff. where the names and localities are given.—A miniature Linga is worn on his person by every Lingâyat, generally round the neck in a silver casket.

† Triplicane, the Musulman quarter of the town of Madras.

‡ The Indian hour of 24 English minutes, (Sans. *Ghatikâ*,) into sixty of which the Hindus divide the day. An "hour's [walking] distance" is considered to be 1½ mile.

§ The five *Rathas* are here called *Vimânas*—See note * p. 213, *supra*.

1 on the North side. The name of the *Sakti* in this temple is unknown. Altogether there are 12 female figures.

31. Behind this *Vimâna* is the figure of a large sacred bull facing to the West. It is buried in the ground. Some of the sand has been removed for the purpose of seeing this figure, so half of it is visible.

32. To the South of this *Vimâna* is Nakula's* *Vimâna* formed of a single stone. At the bottom of this is something of a *Mantapa*. There are no figures in it. On the North side of this *Vimâna* are 6 figures, on the East side 5 figures, and on the South side 7.

33. On the West side of this *Vimâna* is Sahadeva's *Vimâna* formed out of a single stone. The *Mantapa* has 2 slender pillars and faces to the South. There are no figures in it. This *Vimâna* is carved all round. Near it, on the East side, is a monolithic elephant facing to the South.

34. To the East of this *Vimâna* is Bhima's *Vimâna*. It is of one stone, like a *Mantapa*, and faces to the West. It has 6 pillars on the West side, 2 on the South, and 4 on the East—with 12 pillars in all. This *Vimâna* is a very large one. It has been struck by a thunder bolt and split in the middle.

35. To the South of this *Vimâna* is Dharma-

* Cp. note † p. 103, *supra*.

rája's *Vimána*. It has 4 pillars on the West side. Round this *Vimána* are 8 figures. On this *Vimána* are 2 parapets for the performance of *Pradakshina*.* On the parapet walls are 21 carved figures. There are 2 chambers on the parapets, with 2 pillars. Of the above mentioned 8 figures, there are letters engraven over the heads of 5 facing to the South, East, and North. These are not understood.

36. In the village is the Sthalasayanasvámi temple with the entrance to the East, a *Gopura*, and 5 doorways. At the South end, within the enclosure, in the *Garbhagriha* reclines Sthalasayanasvámi with his head to the South—near his feet are Pundarika Mahámuni and a lotus. This *Mahámuni* here obtained final emancipation (*mukti*). On the South side of this is Yalamanganáñcháru's† temple. On the North side is the goddess Cûdikoduta's‡ temple; around are 8 Árvárs' temples, 1 sacred kitchen, 1 flagstaff and 1 store room containing utensils.

In the doorway of the *Gopura*, on either side, are paintings of groups of figures and monkeys.

* "Reverential salutation by circumambulating a person or object, keeping the right side towards them."—Wilson.

† *Prop.* Nilammágainácchiyár, the goddess Earth, Bhúdevi.

‡ So called because she, when a girl, took the flowers kept for offerings to the deity, and wore them in her hair. She is said to have sprung from the earth, and to have been found by Peria Árvár in his *Tulasi* (Ocymum sacrum) garden. The Árvár called her Kódai, brought her up as his own daughter, and offered her, at her own desire, in marriage to Vishnu, at *Srirangam*.—See *Guruparamparáprabhávam*, p. 17 ff.

On this side of the doorway at the North end is a *Mantapa* of 36 pillars. The god comes into this on festival days. This temple is enclosed by a wall and round it are 122 pillars.

37. Straight in a line with the *Gopura* doorway, to the East, is the *Ráyala Gopura*, all in ruins. The foundation is 44 feet square and on this side there is a sort of chamber. In that there is nothing very extraordinary. To the East of this is the *Mantapa* in which Krishnasvámi is swung the day after his birth-day. This has 4 pillars and a *Gopura* (?) on the top.*

38. To the East of this is Sthalasayana's flower garden. In that is a temple of *Srí* Hanumân. The god was inside, in the *Garbhagriha*. He was taken away by Andilin (?).

39. To the East of this Hanumân temple is the *Mantapa* into which Pûdattâ*l*vârt descended. It is in ruins. Now only 16 pillars remain. In front of this is a ruined *Mantapa*.

40. On the South side of this *Mantapa*, to the East of the village, is the Pu*nd*arikapushkari*n*i. In the middle of this tank is a four pillared *Mantapa*. On the North bank of it is a small *Mantapa* with 4 pillars. On festival days, they say, sheds are erected near this *Mantapa* for Sthalasayanasvâmi, and the anointing-feast *(abhishekotsava)* is celebrated. This tank has 16 steps to the bottom of it. It is 300 feet square.

41. On the North side of the Pushkari*n*i is a date garden. On the South side are cashew nut trees.‡

* See note * p. 34, *supra*, and plate XI., No. 1.

† The third of the 12 Â*r*vâr or apostles of Vishnu.—See Ziegenbalg's *South-Indian gods*, p. 71 f. Also note * p. 133, *supra*.

‡ Anacardium occidentale.

42. On the Sea shore to the East of the village is the seven-walled *Siva* temple. The [local] name of the god went with the Sthalapurâna, and has since become known to none. Of the seven walls *(prâkâra)* only two now appear. There are signs of three [more] walls; whether traces remain of the other walls cannot be ascertained as [their supposed site] is buried in the sea. There are two *Garbhagrihas,* in one of which is the *Linga* of *Siva*. Its height is that of a man's chest. The *Yoni* is not visible. How deep the *Linga* is below is not known. This *Garbhagriha* had been built with six sandal wood beams above the god. Of these, some sinners have taken away two. Four beams now remain. On the western wall are Pârvati and Paramesvara with the young Subrahmanyasvâmi seated between them. On the two sides are Brahmâ and Vishnu. The god has had a blow on his head, and is somewhat cracked. On the two sides are figures of two Doorkeepers and two monkeys. The figures of lions, &c., only have become effaced by the action of the waves. The figures of twenty or thirty lions, &c., are now visible. The Nandis which were on the walls have fallen down and had their faces broken—some have lost their legs. Within the second wall lies Sri Mahâ Vishnu with his head to the South. In front of the temple is placed a pillar. That pillar is now in the Sea. The water there is knee deep.

43. On the West side is a small *Gopura.* There is a *Garbhagriha.* In that are Pârvati and Paramesvara carrying the young Subrahmanyasvâmi. On the two sides are Brahmâ and Vishnu. In front of the doorways Vinâyakas have been carved. On the four sides are four lions, very terrible. The

rest of the idols are defaced. There is [as before stated] a *Gopura* over* this *Garbhagriha*. *Kalasas** have been placed on both these temples.

44. On the North side of this temple, a temple of the god Varuna† has been cut out of a single stone. In that is sculptured a figure of a King. On the North side of that rock lies Mahishâsura. The waves of the sea reach this rock. At moonrise‡ when the waves beat, it is surrounded by water.

45. The sea has kept himself only 10 fathoms away from the mound on which is the *Siva* temple. On the North and South sides of it, he has receded 24 fathoms to the West.

46. To the South of this *Siva* temple are three rocks. On the East side of one of these rocks a small chamber has been hollowed out and a figure placed in it. On the North side of the chamber is an elephant's head; and on the South, a horse. On the North side [of the rock] appears an elephant's foot. On the West side, a chamber has been hollowed out. In that is sculptured a female figure. Below that are three small figures.

47. On the second rock appears a lion's face. This is one stone. On it there is only this carving, nothing more.

48. On the third rock are a large head, a belly, and a small chamber, of very misshapen form.

* See note * p. 172, *supra*.

† The deity of the waters and regent of the West.—Wilson.

‡ The popular notion is that the Sea boils with delight at the sight of his offspring Chandra, who was produced at the Churning of the Ocean. The phenomenon of the moon's influence on the tides doubtless underlies this fiction.

Sanscrit sloka—pp. 13, 166.

The statement that this couplet is a quotation from the Mahâbhârata appears to be inaccurate. It would seem to have been borrowed from Conjeveram (Kâñchipura) whose Mâhâtmya contains the following lines* :—(*Seshadharma* xlix, 10, 11.)

गंगाया दक्षिणे भागे योजनानां शतद्वये ।
पंचयोजनमात्रेण पूर्वांभोधेस्तु पश्चिमे ॥
वेगवत्युत्तरे तीरे पुण्यकोट्यां हरिः स्वयं ।
वरदस्सर्वभूतानामद्यापि परिदृश्यते ॥

South of the Ganges two hundred *yojanas*, five *yojanas* westward from the Eastern sea; on the north bank of the Vegavati,† in the Puṇyakoṭi[-*vimâna*], Hari himself, the giver of boons to all living beings, is even at this day present.

* Alluded to in Heyne's *Tracts on India*, p. 334 n.

† The stream here called Vegavatî is not to be confounded with the river in Madura which formerly bore that name and is now called the Vaigai. The Nipavana Mâhâtmya tells us of a great *Linga* situated on the North bank of this river, and half a *yojana* west of the "famous city" (? Kalyâṇapura.—Cp. Nelson's *The Madura Country*, part iii, pp. 6 f., 44.)

तपश्चचार परमं शतसंवत्सरावधि ।
वेगवत्युत्तरे तीरे महालिंगस्य चोत्तरे ॥
पश्चिमे श्रीपुरस्यापि योजनार्धे तपस्थलं ।
तत्र लिंगं प्रतिष्ठाप्य ब्रह्मेश्वरसमाह्वयं ॥
अर्चयन्नामसाहस्रैस्त्रिकालं कमलैश्शुभैः ।
जपन् श्रीरुद्रमंत्रेण शतरुद्रीयमेव च ॥

The Inscriptions—p. 53 ff.

Mr. Arthur Burnell of the Madras Civil Service has been good enough to place at the Editor's disposal copies of the inscriptions on the Ganesa temple and Ratha at Mâvalivaram, and the buried *S*iva temple at *Sâ*luvan Kuppam, made (so far as the inscriptions were legible,) by that gentleman in 1867. They are here given in the modern Devanâgari character :—

Inscription on the Ganesa temple—p. 57 and plate XIV.

सम्भवस्थितिसंहारकारणं वीतकारण: भूयादत्यन्तकामाय जगतां काममर्द्दन: ॥।

श्रमायश्चित्रमायोसावगुणो गुणभाजन: स्वा — [जीयात्]

यस्याङ्गुष्ठभराक्रान्त: कैलास: सदशानन: पातालमगमद् * श्रीनिधिस्ता —

भक्तिप्रह्वेण मनसा भवभूषणलीलया दोष्णा च यो म * भारञ्जीयात् स श्रीभरश्चिरं ॥।

अत्यन्तकामो नृपतिर्निर्ज्जितारातिमण्डल: ख्यातो रणजय: शम्भोस्तेनेदं वेश्म कारितं ॥।

* * निष्कल: सोम: * * * विजयता शङ्कर **काम** * न: ॥।

राजराजो * रसरत्नचक्रवर्त्तिजनार्द्दन: तारकाधिपति: स्वस्थो जयतात्तरणाङ्कुर: ॥।

श्रीमतोत्यन्तकामस्य द्विषद्दर्पापहारिण: श्रीनिधे: कामराजस्य हराराधन सङ्गिन: ॥।

अभिषेकजलापूर्णे चित्ररत्नाम्बुजाकरे आस्ते विशाले सुमुख: शिरस्सरसि शङ्कर: ॥।

तेनेदङ्कारितं शम्भो * * मन्दिरं शुभम् प्रजानामिष्टसिद्धयं —
* यदि * * शिवम् * येषामश्मनिहृदये कुपथगति विमो ।
क्षो रुद्रः ॥ अत्यन्तकामपल्लवेश्वर श्री —

† This line and the next down to ॥ occur on the floor of the Rámánuja Mandapa—pp. 95, 207. The words after ॥ occur also on the East face of the 3rd storey of the Southernmost (Dharmarája's) Ratha, but the ending is हा रणजय:

Inscription on the buried Siva temple—plate XV

श्रीमतोत्यन्तकामस्य द्विषद्

ध्वान्तहारिणः श्रीनिधेः काम

राजस्य हराराधन सङ्गिनः ॥

अभिषेकजलापूर्णे चित्ररत्नाम्बुजाकरे

आस्ते विशाले सुमुखः शिरस्सरसि शङ्करः ॥

तेनेदङ्कारितं शम्भोर्भवनं भूतये भुवः कै

लासमन्दिरनिभं भूभृताम् मूर्ध्नि तिष्ठता ॥ भक्तिप्रह्वे

ण मनसा भवं भूषणलीलया दीप्त्या च यो भुवन धत्ते

जीयात्स श्री भरद्विरं ॥। अतिरणचण्डः पतिरवनिभु

जां अतिरणचण्डेश्वरमकरोत् । चिमगिरितन

या गुहगणभक्तिरती नियतक्षतरतिर्भवतु पशु

पतिः ॥। गुर्वीमीशानभक्तिम् श्रीयमतिशायनीं दुरिवसम भारसुर्धा

निस्वमाच्याजदानं परमं अतिरणचण्डाज्ञया

स्थाने निर्मापितेस्मिन्विदिता * यथा ईशाने भर्त्ता भूतामा

नामष्टा मूर्तिश्चिरमतिरणचण्डेश्वरे यातु नित्यं * मिश्रः ॥

* * * * *

* * कमलासव ॥ समरधनञ्जयः संभ्रमधोरः ॥

Note.

It will be observed that in the Ganesa temple inscription Mr. Burrell reads Ramajaya instead of Jayarama. This agrees with Dr. Babington's own transcript (plate XIV.) though in the translation the name has been changed to Jayarama.

The following is a revised translation of Slokas 1, 2, and 5 of the Ganesa temple inscription:—

1. May Kāmamardana,* the cause of existence, continuance, and destruction, [himself] uncaused, be [propitious] to the boundless desires of the world.

2. May he, [himself] without illusion, [yet] of multiform illusion—without attribute, [and yet] the divider of attributes * * * be triumphant.

5. The king of fully satisfied desires and crowds of conquered enemies, known as Ranajaya—by him was this house of Sambhu† built.

Inscriptions on Dharmarâja's Ratha—p. 37 ff. and plate XVII.

Northern face—base.

श्रीनरसिंह: (*left hand.*)

Eastern face—base.

? भुवनभाजन: (*right hand.*)

त्रिधिविभार: [? पृथिवीभार:] श्रीभर: (*left hand.*)

Southern face—base.

अत्यन्तकाम: अनेकोमाय: (*right hand.*)

? अमेय: चैलोक्यनर्द्दन: विधि: (*left hand.*)

Northern face—second storey.

स्थिरभक्ति: मदनाभिराम: (*left hand.*)

विधि: (?)

* *Siva*, as "Slayer of Kāma," the god of love.—See Coleman's *Mythology of the Hindus*, p. 75 and Vans Kennedy's *Researches*, p. 297 ff.

† A name of *Siva*.

[illegible] TEMPLE [illegible]

श्रीनरसिंह: भुवनभाजन: श्रीमेघ:

अप्रतिहतशासन: (2)

कामललित: अमेयमाय:

सकलकल्याण: (3)

नयनमनोहरवाम: (right hand.)

अतिमान: (4)

Eastern face—second storey.

अनुपम: (right hand.) वाम: (left hand.)

? भयोत्तर: (right hand.) परावर: (left hand.)

Western face—second storey.

सत्यपराक्रम: (right hand.)

परावर: (1)

Southern face—second storey.

ललित (1—unfinished—left hand.)

नयनमनोहर:

सर्व्वतोभद्र: (2)

श्रीनिधि:

निरुत्तर: (3)

विधि: (right hand.)

विभ्रान्त: (1)

Eastern face—third storey.

* अत्यन्तकामपल्लवेश्वर श्री श (middle.)

रणजय: (1)

Annexed (plate XXIV.) is a sketch taken by Mr. Burnell of the buried *Siva* temple (Atira*n*a-cha*n*d*a* Ma*n*d*a*pa) at Sâ*l*uvan Kuppam, after it had been excavated for the purpose.

Arjuna's penance—p. 90 *and plate* I.

The following description is contained in slokas 1537—1542 of the Vanaparva of the Mahâbhârata (Calcutta edition, Vol. I., p. 463):—

रमणीये वनोद्देशे रममाणोऽर्ज्जुनस्तदा ।
तपस्युग्रे वर्त्तमान उग्रतेजा महामनाः ॥
दर्भचीरं निवस्याथ दण्डाजिनविभूषितः ।
शीर्णञ्च पतितं भूमौ पर्णं समुपयुक्तवान् ॥
पूर्णे पूर्णे त्रिरात्रे तु मासमेकं फलाशनः ।
द्विगुणेन हि कालेन द्वितीयं मासमत्ययात् ॥
तृतीयमपि मासं स पक्षेणाहारमाचरन् ।
चतुर्थेऽथ संप्राप्ते मासे भरतसत्तमः ॥
वायुभक्षो महाबाहुरभवत्पाण्डुनन्दनः ।
ऊर्द्ध्वबाहुर्निरालम्बः पादाङ्गुष्ठाग्रधिष्ठितः ॥
सदोपस्पर्शनाच्चास्य बभूवुरमितौजसः ।
विद्युदम्भोरुहनिभा जटास्तस्य महात्मनः ॥

Then Arjuna delighting himself in the pleasant forest, awful in his brightness, magnanimous, clothed in a *darbha** garment, adorned with a staff and deer-skin, performed severe penance and fed on the withered leaves which fell on the ground. He spent one month feeding on fruit once in three days; a second month eating at intervals of double the length; a third month also eating food once a

* Poa cynosuroides, a species of grass used in many solemn and religious observances (Wilson)—also called *Kusa*.

fortnight; when the fourth month arrived, the most excellent of the Bhâratas* feeding on air, having long arms, the son of Pâ*n*du,† with upraised arms, unsupported, stood on the point of his great toe. By constant ablutions, the matted locks of this man, of boundless brilliancy, lofty minded, were like lightning and the lotus.

Death of Mahishâsura—*p.* 101 *and plate* IV.

Extract from the Mârka*nd*eyapurâ*n*a—(Ed. Banerjea, p. 441 f.)—Devimáhátmya.

इति क्रोधसमाध्मातमापतन्तं महासुरं ।
दृष्ट्वा सा चण्डिका कोपं तद्वधाय तदाकरोत् ॥
सा क्षिप्त्वा तस्य वै पाशं तं बबन्ध महासुरं ।
तत्याज माहिषं रूपं सोऽपि बद्धो महामृधे ॥
ततः सिंहोऽभवत्सद्यो यावत्तस्याम्बिका शिरः ।
छिनत्ति तावत्पुरुषः खड्गपाणिरदृश्यत ॥
तत एवाशु पुरुषं देवी चिच्छेद सायकैः ।
तं खड्गचर्म्मणा सार्द्धं ततः सोऽभून्महागजः ॥
करेण च महासिंहं तञ्चकर्ष जगर्ज्ज च ।
कर्षतस्तु करन्देवी खड्गेन निरकृन्तत ॥

* Descendants of Bharata, from the extent of whose authority over the greater part of India, the country was called Bharatavarsha. —Wilson.

† So styled by courtesy only, Arjuna being in truth the progeny of Indra, the god of the firmament.—See Wilson's preface to Johnson's *Selections from the Mahâbharata*, and his note at p. 7, *ibid.*

ततो महासुरो भूयो माहिषं वपुरास्थितः ।
तथैव क्षोभयामास त्रैलोक्यं सचराचरं ॥
ततः क्रुद्धा जगन्माता चण्डिका पानमुत्तमं ।
पपौ पुनः पुनश्चैव जहासारुणलोचना ॥
ननर्द्द चासुरः सोऽपि बलवीर्य्यमदोद्धतः ।
विषाणाभ्याञ्च चिक्षेप चण्डिकां प्रति भूधरान् ॥
सा च तान् प्रहितांस्तेन चूर्णयन्ती शरोत्करैः ।
उवाच तं मदोद्धूतमुखरागाकुलाक्षरं ॥

देव्युवाच ॥

गर्ज्ज गर्ज्ज क्षणं मूढ मधु यावत् पिबाम्यहं ।
मया त्वयि हतेऽत्रैव गर्ज्जिष्यन्त्याशु देवताः ॥
एवमुक्त्वा समुत्पत्य सारूढा तं महासुरं ।
पादेनाक्रम्य कण्ठे च शूलेनैनमताडयत् ॥
ततः सोऽपि पदाक्रान्तस्तया निजमुखात्ततः ।
अर्द्धनिष्क्रान्त एवाति देव्या वीर्य्येण संवृतः ॥
अर्द्धनिष्क्रान्त एवासौ युध्यमानो महासुरः ।
तया महासिना देव्या शिरश्छित्त्वा निपातितः ॥
ततो हाहाकृतं सर्व्वं दैत्यसैन्यं ननाश तत् ।
प्रहर्षञ्च परं जग्मुः सकला देवतागणाः ॥
तुष्टुवुस्तां सुरा देवीं सह दिव्यैर्महर्षिभिः ।
जगुर्गन्धर्व्वपतयो ननृतुश्चाप्सरोगणाः ॥

Then Chan*d*ikâ seeing the great Asura thus coming, filled with anger, to fall upon her, became wrathful for his destruction. Throwing over him the noose, she bound that great Asura. Bound in the great battle, he relinquished the form of a buffalo and immediately became a lion. No sooner did Ambikâ cut off his head, than he appeared as a man, sword in hand. Then Devî quickly with arrows destroyed the man together with his sword and shield. He then became a great elephant. With his trunk he dragged the great lion and roared. Devî with her sword cut off the trunk of that dragging one. Then the great Asura again assumed the form of a buffalo, and as before agitated all things animate and inanimate in the three worlds. Then Chan*d*ikâ, the mother of the world, having become wroth, drank good wine again and again, laughed with her red eyes, and roared. That Asura also, filled with strength, valour, and pride, hurled mountains at Chan*d*ikâ. She crumbling his missiles with a cloud of arrows, her countenance inflamed with wine, spoke to him in confused accents thus: "Roar, roar, O fool, for a moment while I drink wine. The gods will soon roar when thou art slain here by me." Having thus spoken, she sprang upon the buffalo. Placing her foot on his neck, she struck him with her trident. Then trodden under foot by her he came half out of his own mouth,* and was overcome by the great valour of Devî. The great Asura doing battle was slain by Devî, who with a great sword cut off his head. Then with lamentations perished the whole army of Daityas,† and all the troops of Devatâs exceedingly rejoiced. The Suras‡ with the heavenly Maharshis§ praised Devî, the chief Gandharvas sang, and the troops of Apsarases danced.

* I. e. He came in his proper form out of the buffalo's mouth.

† Demons, Asuras, children of Diti, the mother of the Titan or giant race of Hindu mythology, by Kasyapa, grandson of Brahmâ.

‡ Deities, Devatâs. § The fourth of the seven orders of *Rishis*.

Notices of the SEVEN PAGODAS *will be found in the following works:—*

GENTIL, Voyage dans les mers de l'Inde, Vol. I. (Paris, 1779.)

Asiatic Researches, CHAMBERS (William) in Vol. I. (Calcutta, 1788); and GOLDINGHAM (J.) in Vol. V. (1798).

SONNERAT (M.), Voyage aux Indes orientales et à la Chine. (Paris, 1782). English translation, Voyage to the East Indies and China. (Calcutta, 1788-89.)

CRAWFURD'S (Quintin) Sketches of the Hindoos, Vol. I. (London 1792.)

HAAFNER, Reise längst der Küste von Coromandel, Vol. II.

BARTOLOMEO (Fra Paolino da San), Viaggio alle Indie orientali. (Roma, 1796). English translation, Voyage to the East Indies. (London, 1800.)

DANIELL'S (T. and W.) Oriental Scenery. (London, 1795—1808.)

VALENTIA'S (Lord) Voyages and Travels to India, &c., Vol. I. (London, 1809.)

Allgemeine Geographische Ephemeriden. EHRMAN in—1809, and DALBERG (Baron), 1810.

SOUTHEY'S (Robert) Curse of Kehama. (London, 1810.)

GRAHAM'S (Maria) Journal of a residence in India. (London, 1812.

GRAHAM'S (Maria) Letters on India. (London, 1814.)

HEYNE'S (Benjamin, M.D.) Tracts on India. (London, 1814.)

Oriental Magazine, Antiquarius (? Lieutenant John BRADDOCK) in Vols. I., II. (Madras, 1819—20.)

HAMILTON'S (Walter) East India Gazetteer. (London, 1815.)

CRAWFURD'S (Quintin) Researches. (London, 1817.)

HAMILTON'S (Walter) Description of Hindostan. (London, 1820.)

LANGLES (L.) Monuments Anciens et Modernes de l'Hindoustan. (Paris, 1821.)

HEEREN (A. H. L.), Historische Werke. (Göttingen, 1821—26). English translation, Historical Researches, Asiatic Nations, Vol. II. (London, 1846.)

FULLARTON (John) "Manuscript notes extracted from the Journal of his travels through Hindustan, during the years 1817, 1818, 1819, and 1820." (List of authorities in Hamilton's Gazetteer, edn. 1828.)

WILSON'S (Horace Hayman) Descriptive Catalogue of Mackenzie's Collection of Oriental Manuscripts. (Calcutta, 1828.)

HEBER'S (Bishop) Narrative of a Journey through the Upper Provinces of India; with an account of a Journey to Madras and the Southern Provinces. (London, 1828.)

CONDER'S (Josiah) Modern Traveller, Vol. X. (London, 1830.)

Transactions of the Royal Asiatic Society of Great Britain and Ire-

and, BABINGTON (Benjamin Guy, M.B., F.R.S.) in Vol. II. (London, 1830.)

BOHLEN (P. von), Das alte Indien mit besonderer Rücksicht auf Ægypten, Vol. II. (Koenigsberg, 1830.)

Calcutta Christian Observer, PERCIVAL (Rev. Peter) in—(Calcutta 1832.)

RITTER (Carl), Erdkunde, Vol. 6, Ost-Asien. (Berlin, 1836.)

Madras Journal of Literature and Science, TAYLOR (Rev. William) in Vol. VIII. (Madras, 1838); and MAHON (Rev. George William A.M.), BRADDOCK (Lieutenant John), TAYLOR (Rev. William), and ELLIOT (Walter) in Vol. XIII. (Madras, 1844.)

FERGUSSON'S (James) Rock-cut temples of India. (London, 1845.)

Journal of the Royal Asiatic Society of Great Britain and Ireland, FERGUSSON (James) and NEWBOLD (Captain T. J., F.R.S.) in Vol. VIII. (London, 1846.)

Journal of the Asiatic Society of Bengal, NEWBOLD (Captain T. J.) in Vol. XV. (Calcutta, 1846); and GUBBINS (Charles) in Vol. XXII. (Calcutta, 1853.)

LASSEN (Christian), Indische Alterthumskunde, Vol. I. (Bonn, 1847.)

FERGUSSON (James) Illustrations of Ancient Architecture in Hindostan. (London, 1847.)

PERCIVAL'S (Rev. Peter) Land of the Veda. (London, 1854.)

PHAROAH'S Gazeteer of Southern India. (Madras, 1855.)

GRAUL (Karl, D. Th.), Reise nach Ostindien, Vol. III. (Leipzig, 1856.)

BRUCE'S (James) Scenes and Sights in the East. (London, 1856.)

Murray's Hand-book of India, by EASTWICK (Edward B.) Part I.—Madras. (London, 1859.)

FERGUSSON'S (James) Rock-cut temples of India. (London, 1864.)

FERGUSSON'S (James, F.R.S., M.R.A.S.) History of Architecture, Vol. II. (London, 1867.)

ZIEGENBALG (Bartholomaeus), Genealogie der Malabarischen götter, erster, ungeänderter, nothdürftig erweiterter abdruck besorght durch Dr. Wilhelm Germann. (Madras, 1867.)

INDEX.

A

Abhaya 206*
Achyuta-râya 115, 117
Adam's Peak 20
Adiranadesvara 126
Âdiśesha 201, 211
Admetus 5
Adondai 69, 113 f.
Agastya 176, 181 ff.
Agrahâra 47, 117
Âhava Malla 132, 134 ff., 139, 143
Airâvata 104*, 204
Ajunta (Ajayantî) 37*
Alphabets, Ancient 56‡
Amasis 71 f.
Ambikâ 229
Âmûrkotta 133 f.
Âmûrnâd 133 f.
Ânandanilayam 181, 183
Anigiri 135
Aniruddha 13
Añjanâ 211§
Añjaneya 211
Annama-deva-râya 112*
Anurâdhapura 24
Apollo 5
Apsarases 180, 229
Arddhanârîśa 37‡
Argha 214*
Arian temples 157, 171*
Arjuna 30, 151, 226 f.
Arjuna's penance 4, 87, 89 ff., 200, 203 f., 208, 226 f.
Arjuna's Ratha 79*, 105*, 206
Armenia 71
Artaxata 70
Ârvâr 133, 216
Âryam 61†
Âryan temples 171†
Ashtâkshari 176*
Âśrama 176, 184
Asuras 47, 83, 99*, 101*, 229†
Asvatha 184
Atiranachanda 59
Atiranachanda Mandapa 120
Atiranachanda Pallava 120, 126, 128
Atiranachandesvara 59, 126*
Atri 176
Australia 71
Ayodhyâ 140

B

Bagistan 74
Bâlakrishna 94
Balarâma 206
Balhâra 26
Bali 3, 13, 47, 166, 169, 185
Bali, submersion of his city(?) 11, 15, 34, 46, 169, 185
Bali Chakravarti 202
Balicota Simcounnaidu 153*
Bamean 71
Bânâsura 13, 14

Banawasi (Banavâsi) 140
Behar 21, 98†
Beirout 73
Belnos' (Mrs.), Sundhya, referred to 183†
Belzoni's Egypt and Nubia, referred to 71
Be-Sitoon 73 f.
Bhadrakâli 56‡
Bhadrâ river 139
Bhâgavatapurâna, referred to 93
Bharata 227*
Bhâratas 227
Bhâravi 91‡
Bhava 102*
Bhavânî 101, 102*
Bhîma 200†, 204
Bhîmasena 200†
Bhîma's Ratha 10, 105†, 147*, 215
Bhonja family 114
Bhûdevî 216†
Bhûta 133
Bigandet's Life of Gautama, referred to 20*
Bodhi tree 20*
Bogahah 20
Bonomi's Egyptian Antiquities, referred to 73
Bo tree 20†
Braddock (Lieutenant J.) 63 ff.
Brahmâ 83, 84, 97, 149, 176, 180 184 f., 202, 208, 218, 229†
Brahmaloka 176
Brahmândapurâna 173
Brahmâsrama 176
Bricks 161
Bruce's Scenes and Sights in the East, referred to 11†, 77*; quoted 77†
Buddha 17*† 20‡, 21†, 22‡
Buddha, worship of 24
Budha 21†
Burrachur 171
Burckhardt's Travels, referred to 73
Burnell (Arthur) 221, 223, 225
Burnes (Sir Alexander) referred to 71
Burton's Excerpta Hieroglyphica, referred to 72
Buto 71

C

Canara 113
Carnatic 114, 117*
Cashmere (Kasmîr) 157, 171
Cat's penance 88§, 204
Cavery (Kâverî) river 136, 182
Ceylon 162 f., 166
Chakra 85*, 100, 201 ff., 208, 211, 214
Chalukya dynasty 139
Chalukya dynasty of Kalinga 126
Chalukya inscription 136
Chalukya Princes of Kalyân 127*, 135
Chalukyas 137, 138, 140
Châmara (chaurî) 100*, 209 f.
Chând 19†
Chandî 101*
Chandikâ 228 f.
Chandîpâtha 99*†, 101*
Chandra 19†, 203, 219‡
Châranas 208
Chhatra 209 f.
Chellambram (Chitambaram) 160
Cholas 127, 137, 140 f.
Churning of the Ocean 219‡
City of Bali, submerged (?) 11, 15, 34, 46, 109, 185
Clemens Alexandrinus 27
Clive (Lord) 200
Coins found at Mâvalivaram 16, 164, 169*

Coleman's Mythology of the Hindus, referred to 182†, 214*, 224*
Combaconum (Kumbhakonam) 166
Companra-udiyâr 117*
Conjeveram (Kâñchipura) 69, 112*, 113, 117, 127, 179*, 211, 220
Coromandel Coast 162, 169; encroachment of the Sea on 46, 52, 117 f.
Covelong (Kôvalam) 2, 178*
Ctesias 74
Çûḍâkoḍuta 216

D

Daityas 84, 229
Damaruka 203
Dânava 91†, 182
Dancing women 25
D'Anville, Antiquité géographique de l' Inde, quoted 20†
Darbha 175, 226
Date trees 155‖
De Havilland (Colonel) 58, 60, 120
Denon, Egypte, referred to 79
Devadâsi 23
Deva Malla-râja 111
Devanâgarî alphabet 9
Devanêri 119
Deva-râya 112*, 116, 117*, 118
Devatâs 23, 99*, 229
Devî 50§, 85, 101*, 229
Devîmâhâtmya 101*, 227 ff.
Dhâravaram 125
Dharmarâja 6, 36, 104, 204
Dharmarâja's Maṇṭapa 207
Dharmarâja's Ratha 106*, 216, 222, 224
Dharmarâja's throne 6, 7, 32, 86, 150, 212
Dharwar (Dhârwâḍ) 135, 139
Dîksha 183*
Diodorus Siculus 74
Dîpastambha 51‡, 158†
Diti 229†
Dolotsava Maṇḍapa 34, 30, 217
Doorkeepers 50*, 200, et al.
Dow's History of Hindostan, referred to 3
Draupadî 7, 104, 200
Draupadî's bath 7, 32, 86, 212*
Draupadî's Ratha 104†
Droṇâchârya 31*, 88‖, 203
Durgâ 33, 49, 77, 97, 99 ff., 149, 200, 202
Durgâpûjâ 99*, 101*
Duryodhana 89
Dvajastambha 11†
Dvârakâ 13
Dwârapâlas 50

E

Earth, the goddess 178
Eastwick's Prem Sâgar, quoted 93†; referred to, 94†
Ecbatana 74
Edrisi 26
Egypt 71, 73
Egyptian Architecture 8
Egyptian quarries 147*
Egyptian Ruins 79
Egyptians 71
Ehad 73
Elephanta 31, 37, 40, 45, 71, 148
Elephants 8, 35, 77, 87, 104, 202
Elliot's (Sir H. M.) History of India, referred to 26*
Ellis (Francis W.) 46, 60, 127†
Ellis' (Francis W.) Mirâsî Right, referred to 141
Ellora (Êlûra) 37*, 92*, 94‡, 115, 148, 150, 153, 171

F

Fa Hian's pilgrimage, referred to 166†
Fergusson (James), quoted 37*, 159; referred to 153
Fergusson's Ancient Architecture of Hindostan, quoted 106*
Fergusson's Rock-cut Temples of India (1846), quoted 150
Fergusson's Rock-cut Temples of India (1864) referred to 45
Ferishta, referred to 21

G

Gadâ 202 f., 208 f.
Gadiya 214
Gaja Lakshmî 50§, 202, 211
Gajapati princes 114
Ganda Deva-râya 117
Gandharvas 180, 204, 208 f., 220
Ganesa 30*, 76, 79, ff., 152
Ganesa temple 4, 56, 59, 61*, 69, 79, 154 f., 200, 221 ff.
Gangâ 182 f.
Ganges 13, 82, 93†, 166, 220
Gangondaram inscription 136, 138 f.
Garbhagriha 201, *et al.*
Garuda 184
Garuda-posture 183
Garudas 204, 208
Gautama 20*‡
Gentil, Voyage dans les Mers de l'Inde, referred to 11*; quoted 27 ff.
Ghantâ 209
Ghatikâ 214‡
Gibbon, quoted 162
Ginjee 115
Godâvarî **137**
Goddiliadenni **24**
Goldstücker's Sanscrit Dictionary, referred to 97†
Gopâla 5
Gopalas 49, 55
Gopikâs 206
Gôpîs 31
Gopîs' churn 77*
Gopura 181, 205*, 216, 218
Gothic Architecture **8**
Govarddhana 92 ff., 205 f.
Graham (Mrs.), referred to 45 ff., 52, 56*, 60
Granite at Mâvalivaram, Description of 146, 147*
Grantha alphabet 54*, 56‡
Gray (Captain), referred to 71
Guruparamparâprabhâvam, referred to 216‡
Guzerat 26

H

Haimavatî 102†
Hala Kannada alphabet 115
Hamalell 30
Hanumân 211§
Hanuman temple 217
Hari 98†, 178, 183, 220
Harinandana 179
Haripriya 179
Harisekhara 178, 211
Heber's (Bishop) Narrative, referred to 11†, 45, 52, 169
Heeren's Historical Researches, referred to 164†
Herodotus, referred to 71 f.
Heyne's Tracts on India, referred to 142*, 220*; quoted 153*
Himâlaya 89, 102
Himavat 102†, 182
Hiranyakasipu 12, 84*
Hiranyâksha 12, 84

Hobart (Lord) 56§
Howarth (Lieutenant), 141
Hudleston (Andrew), 45, 48 f.
Huli Honore 139

I

Idaiyan Pudal 119 f.
Indra 14 f., 89§, 92, 104*, 204, 227†
Indra Sabhâ, at Ellora 92*
Indra's heaven 180‡
Inscriptions 9, 32, 35, 37, 53 ff., 69, 95‡, 108, 113 f., 116, 120 ff., 132 ff., 138 f., 141, 221 ff.
Iradaipâdi 132, 134, 138 f.
Îsvara 89 f., 200, 206 f., 208
Îsvara temple 200

J

Jallipalli 154
Jain temple 106†
Jaina religion 113
Jâmbavat 202
Jananâthapura 132, 134, 141
Jayarasa (?) 223
Jayarasa Stambha (?) 57
Jayasimha 137
Jehangiri 98†
Job, Book of 73
Jones (Sir William), quoted 93, 102 f.
Journal of Royal Asiatic Society, referred to 135
Judges, Book of 73

K

Kadal Samgama 136, 139
Kadamba family 140
Kadamba Ganga 140
Kailâsa 67, 97*, 208
Kailâsa, at Ellora 160, 171
Kalasa 172*, 219
Kâlî 101*
Kalinga 126, 140
Kâlinga dynasty 127*
Kalpa 98†
Kalyân 127*, 135 f., 140
Kalyânapura 220†
Kâma 224*
Kâmamardana 224
Kâmarâja 58, 116*, 126, 128
Kanchi 211
Kâñchî 127, 211†
Kâñchipura Mâhâtmya 220
Kandy 24
Kapilavastu 17†
Karnâtakadesa 114 f.
Karnâtaka-râjâkal 115*
Kârtikeya 59, 107, 182*, 185; origin of name 107‡
Kasyapa 229†
Kauravas 31*
Kâverî 182
Kenerah (Kânhari) 62
Kennedy's (Vans) Researches, referred to 93*, 214*, 221*
Kerelko 70
Kermansboh 73
Kumârârya Srî Rangâchârya 128
Khadga 209
Kimpurushas 204
Kinnaras 204, 208
Kinnier (Macdonald), quoted 74
Kirâta 91*, 203
Kirâtârjuniya 91‡
Kîrti Varma 127*
Klings 138
Knox's History of Ceylon, referred to 19; quoted 23
Kôdai 216‡
Kolapûr 139*
Kongadesa 138
Kongus 138

Koppara-Kesari Varma 136
Kôril 23
Ko-Virâja-Kesari Varma 136
Krishna 5, 13 f., 30 f., 88, 92 ff., 151, 205 f.
Krishna Mandapa 5, 48 f., 53, 55, 92 ff., 205 f.
Krishna-râya 112b, 115, 117c, 153*
Krishna's butter ball 76, 77*, 147*, 200
Krishnasvâmi 203, 217
Krittikâs 107‡
Kudalgi Svâmi 129
Kulôttunga 125‡
Kulôttunga Cholan 113
Kumârasvâmi 208
Kurdistan 70
Kuntaladesa 136, 138, 140
Kurumbars 69, 113, 127, 141
Kusa, 226*
Kuvera 57, 97*, 180*, 204*

L

Laborde, referred to 71, 73
Lakshmesvar 136, 138 f.
Lakshmî 201, 211
Lakshmîsa 155
La Loubère, referred to 20 f.; quoted 17, 22
Land measure 123
Lankâ 18
Latona 71
Linga 11†, 30, 34, 56‡§, 96*, 107, 120, 126*, 157†, 159, 201, 210, 213, 214*, 218, 220†
Linga and Yoni 214
Lingavedî 214*
Lions 8, 104
Lotus-posture 203
Lycus river 73

M

Mábalipuram, the name 111
Mackenzie (Colonel) 46 f., 69, 75
Mackenzie MSS. referred to 111, 116, 118 f., 125‡, 127‡, 153, 169
Mâdhava 175
Madura 117c, 166‡
Madura Country 220
Mahâbali 47, 55, 81 f.
Mahâbalipura, the name 3, 55, 111, 165
Mahâbhârata 4, 6, 13, 31, 60, 91‡, 113, 220, 226 f.
Mahâdeva 77, 80, 89§, 96 f., 107
Mahâmalaipûr, the name 111
Mahâmalla race 127
Mahâmantra 176
Mahâmâyâ 21*
Mahâmuni 216
Maharshis 229
Mahendra Sânta 126
Mahimalu or Mavâlamu 112b
Mahishamardinî 209
Mahishâsura 33†, 49, 77, 97, 99 ff., 109, 149†, 200, 208‡, 209 f., 227 ff.
Mahishâsura rock 109, 159, 219
Malabar Coast 162 f.
Malayâlam alphabet 61†
Malcarpha 164
Malêcheren 14
Malla 111 ff.
Mallâdhipa 180
Malla family 113 f.
Mallâpurî 177 f., 181 ff.
Mallapurî, the name 165†
Mallâpurî Mâhâtmya 173 ff., 185
Mallapuri or Mallapuri-kshetram, the name 111a
Malla-râya 112b
Mallêrudu 14*, 111c, 170

Malleśvara 178, 180
Mâmallapuram, the name 111
Mâmallâ-puri 112*
Mâmallaipûr, the name 118
Mâmallai Perumâl 123, 141
Mandapa or Mantapa 200* et al.
Manmatha 57
Manu 97†
Maraga 70
Mârkandeyapurâna 99†, 101*, 227 ff.
Mathas 139
Maundrel, referred to 70
Mâvaligangâ, origin of the name 3
Mâvalipuram, the name 3
Mâvaliranam 112
Mâvalivaram, the name 111, 165†
Mavamalûr 112*
Mâvalivaram, its position 146
Max Müller, referred to 22‡
Mâyâ 21*
Media 70, 74
Mercury 20 f.
Meru 175
Mêlkôta 177
Monkeys 4*, 76, 77†, 200
Monkeys' Rocks 213
Moor's Hindu Pantheon, referred to 80, 93†, 94*, 102‡
Muir's Sanscrit Texts, referred to 83†, 84*, 89‡, 91‡, 97†, 101*, 107‡, 182†, 202, 214*
Mukundanâyanâr Kôvil 106†
Munis 175, 182 f.
Muralîdhara 94
Murray's Handbook, quoted 106*
Myas Hormas 162

N

Nâga-Maids 204
Nâgas 88‡, 154
Nahervalah (Nahrwâla) 26
Nakula and Sahadeva's Rath 103†
Nakula's Vimâna 215
Namuchi 13
Nanda 5, 31†
Nandî 97, 104, 109†, 155†, 159, 200, 206*, 218
Nandivaram 112*
Nârada 175 f., 184 f.
Naradîyapurâna, referred to 98*
Narasimha Avatâra 12
Nârâyana 97†, 99
Narmadâ (Nerbuddah) river 140
Nâyar (Nair) women 48
Nelatûr 128
Nelson's The Madura Country, referred to 220†
Nepaul 17†
Newbold, quoted 149
Newbold's Geology of Southern India, referred to 46†
Newbold's Notes on the Coast of Coromandel, quoted 147*, referred to 169*‡
Nîlamangainâchîyâr 216†
Nilgund inscription 139
Nile 71
Nîparana Mâhâtmya, quoted 220†
Nomius 5

O

Olakkanneśvarasvâmî 210
Ootramaloor (Uttaramallûr) 115*
Orissa 114

P

Pâlâr river 113‡
Pâli inscriptions 117 f.
Pâli language 9, 17 ff., 21, 61*
Pallava 126
Pallava Mardu 127
Pallavas 128

Palmyra trees 22, 78, 155‖
Pânavattamo 214*
Pañchâgni 183
Pândavas 31*, 103*†, 200, 205, 212
Pându 46, 89, 151, 227
Pându princes 200†
Pândya kingdom 114, 166
Paramesvara 208, 218
Paramesvara Mahâvarâha Vishnu 133 f., 141
Parasu 209
Parghur 139
Pârvatî 33, 50‡§, 59, 78, 80, 85, 96 f., 102*†, 107, 149, 157, 177, 208, 214*, 218
Pâsa 100
Pâsupata 208
Pâsupatâstra 89, 91, 203
Pâtâla or Pâtâlaloka 57, 82, 204
Pavarakkâran's choultry 124, 125, 128
Peacock 77
Pennâr river 113
Periya Âlvâr 216‡
Persia 73
Petra 71
Pharoah's Gazetteer, referred to 149§
Pihan 21
Pillaiyâr 76
Pillar in front of Shore Temple 91, 108 f., 158 f., 218
Pithâpur 126
Pleiades 107‡
Poodan 21
Porter (Sir R. K.) referred to 70
Prâbât 19
Pradakshina 216
Prahlâda 12
Pramathas 204, 209
Prem Sâgar, quoted 93†, referred to 94†
Prinsep, referred to 127§
Ptolemy 164
Pûdattâlvâr 217
Pulikara-nagara 136
Pulikesi 127*
Pundarîkapushkarini 217
Pundarîka pond 182 ff.
Pundarîka Rishi 170, 177 ff., 216
Pundarîkasaras 181
Punyakotivimâna 179, 211, 220

R

Râjamalla 127
Râja Râja Chola 138
Râja Râja Narendra 157
Râjendra Deva 132, 134, 136
Râmânujiyyar Mandapa 95‡, 207, 222
Râmatâraka 183*
Râmesvaram 137
Ranajaya 223 f.
Ranganâyaka 209
Rathas 7†, 8, 35, 52, 60, 71, 103 ff., 126, **147***, 155, 213, 214§
Râvana 57
Rattakula 138 f.
Rattehalli 139
Râyala Gopura 95, 205, 212, 217
Râyalu 205*
Relandus, Dissertationes, quoted 27
Remesses 73
Renaudot, Anciennes Relations, quoted 24
Rishis 90, 182, 204, 229§, *et al.*

S

Sadras (Sadurangapattanam) 2, 146, 163
Sahadeva 100†

Sahadeva's Vimâná 215
Sais 71
Saivas 56†
Sakti 209, 211, 214 f.
Salsette (Sâshthi) 37*, 62
Salt-marsh 163, 213
Sâluvan Kuppam 69 f., 119, 140 f., 221, 225
Samana Kodam 17 ff., 21, 22‡
Sambhu 224
Samdutty 139
Samvartana 181
Sani 80†
Sankara Bhârati 139*
Sankesvar 139*
Sankha 201 ff., 208 f., 211, 213
Sanscrit, Ancient Alphabets of 60
Sanscrit language 54*
Sanscrit Sloka 13, 166, 230
Sassanian era 74
Sâstrakâran 99
Satânanda 178
Saturn 80†
Satyaloka 175
Satya *Srîya* 127*
Savanâr 136
Sculptures and Excavations, Unfinished state of 9 f., 150, 153 f.
Sea, The god of the 15
Sea of Milk 177, 179
Semiramis 74
Sesha 7, 33, 98, 159
Seshadharma, quoted 220
Setu (Bridge of rocks at Ramesvaram) 140
Seven Pagodas, the name 2, 167
Shanmukha 182
Shaw's Travels, referred to 4†
Shamgar 73
Shore temple 10, 35, 51, 107 f., 156 ff., 218 f.
Siamese 9, 17
Siamese priests 22
Sidon 70
Siddhas 204, 208
Simha 7 ff., 31 ff., 35, 120
Simhama or Singama Nâyadu 76, 115*, 116*, 153, 207
Simhâsana 7
Simhikâ 13*
Sinaí 73
Singalam 136*
Singhalese 23
Siva 10, 32, 34, 57 ff., 79 f., 89, 91‡, 97, 101 f., 104 ff., 149, 157, 176 f., 181, 185, 201, 204, 208, 214*, 218, 224
Sivan lake 70
Sivânî 149
Skanda 107‡, 182†
Skândapurâna 99*
Smârta sect 139*
Soma 19†, 21†
Somesvara Deva I. 137 f.
Somesvara Deva Chalukya I. 135
Sonitapura 13§
Spence Hardy's Manual of Budhism, referred to 19§, 20‡, quoted 21†
Southey's Curse of Kehama, referred to 66
Sphynx 94
Sramana Gautama 17*, 22‡
Srî Hanumân 217
Srî Mahâ Vishnu 218
Sringeri 139*
Srî Râma 211
Srîrangam 209*, 216‡
Srî Sailam 113
Srî Vallabha 127
Srî Vîra Mârtanda 139
Steel, Indian 147*
Sthalapurâna 173 ff., 185, 218
Sthalasâyî 160, 185

Sthalasayana 180, 217
Sthalasayanasvâmî 183, 216
Sthalasayanasvâmi temple 156†, 216
Sthalasekharasvâmî temple 205 (see Sthalasayanasvâmî)
Stone couch 33, 96
Subrahmaṇya 97, 107, 218; origin of name 107‡
Suddhodana 17†
Sukra 83
Sukrâchârya 12, 203
Sultan Ganj 98†
Sumeru 175
Suras 229
Sûrya 203
Sûta 176, 181
Svarga 170, 180‡, 184
Syene 71
Syria 73

T

Tailapa Deva Chalukya 138
Tâlapât 22
Taldanga 171
Tamil alphabet 3, 126*; Ancient forms of 54*
Tâṇḍavarâya Mudaliyâr 132, 141
Tanjore (Tañjâvûr) 115, 160
Tanjore pagoda 105*
Tapta Mudrâ 183*
Târaka 182
Târksha 184
Tel-et-mai 72
Telingâna 113 f., 137, 141
Têr of Arjuna 56*
Tilavanam 182 f.
Tîrthas 182
Tiruvaḍandai 178*
Tiruvâkêrvi 121[6]
Tiruvalikkêṇi 214
Tiruverichi 134 f.
Tiruviḍichûr 126*
Tiyyattis (Tier women) 45
Todavera 121[6]
Tomara 209
Toṇḍamaṇḍala 127
Ton-pô 20§
Treta yuga 81
Tribhuvana Malla 125‡, 140
Tribhuvana Viradeva 121
Trichinopoly 117[c]
Trilochana Pallava 126*
Tripalore (Tirupôrûr) reef 163
Tripati (Tirupati) 69, 113
Triplicane 214†
Trisûla 203
Trivikrama 82, 202
Tulasî 216‡
Tuluva 113
Tungâ river 139
Turmeric 212*

U

Umâ 67, 102†

V

Vaigai river 220†
Vaikuṇṭha 181
Vaishnavas 56†
Vâmana Avatâra 50†, 81 f.
Varadarâjasvâmi 211
Varâha Avatâra 50, 55, 83 f.
Varâhakshetra 177 f.
Varâhasvâmî 178, 201 f., 210 f.
Varâhasvâmî temple 53 ff., 69, 132 ff., 185*, 210
Varuṇa 219†
Varuṇa temple 219
Vedas 22
Vegavatî 220
Vegidesam or Vengidesam 137, 140
Vellâras 113

Vellore (Vêlûr) 113, 115[c]
Vellugôtivâru 115[c], 153
Velugoti Singama Nâyadu 207
Venginâdu 136
Venkatapati Srîdevarâya 128
Venus (planet) 83
Vidyâdharas 204, 205
Vihâra 21, 27
Vijayâditya 126
Vijayanagara princes 205
Vijayanagaram 112[b]
Vijayanagaram dynasty 114 f., 117, 126
Vijayapûr 26
Vikkilan 136
Vikrama Deva 125
Vikramâditya 127
Vikramâditya II. 137
Vimâna 108*, 161, 210, 213*, 214 ff., 214§
Vinâyaka 201, 216
Viprachitti 13*
Vîra Chola Deva 125 f, 140
Vîrapatam 28
Vîra Râjendra Chola 136 ff., 140
Virochana 13*
Vishnu 12, 33 f., 50, 77, 80 ff., 85, 97 ff., 101, 105 f., 108, 149 f., 159, 170, 176 ff., 183 f., 202, 206 f., 211*, 216‡, 218
Vishnu, Recumbent figure of 7 (See Nârâyana)
Vishnupurâna, quoted 93†; referred to 84, 97†
Vishnusarma 177
Vishnu Varddhana 125‡
Vishnu's heaven 181*
Visvakarma 203
Vrishabhesvara 206
Vyâsa 89§

W

Wady Mokatteb 73
Wardah (Varadâ) river 139
Wheeler's History of India, referred to 89*
Williams' Indian Epic Poetry, referred to 89§
Wilkins, referred to 101
Wilkins' Hitopadesa, quoted 98†
Wilson's Essays, referred to 183*, 214*
Wilson's Meghaduta, referred to 182†
Wilson's Sanscrit Dictionary, referred to in the notes, *passim.*
Wilson's Vishnupurâna, referred to 84*, 97†; quoted 92†, 101* 102*
Woden 21

Y

Yachama-nâyadu 115[c]
Yadugiri 177
Yakko 23
Yaksha 23*, 180
Yalamanganâchâra 621
Yama 181†, 208‡
Yamapuri Mandapa 208
Yamarâja 33, 149, 159
Yogis 176
Yojana 13, 166, 220
Yoni 214*, 218
Yudhishthira 6

Page 11, note †. *For* "More probably", *read* "Some have supposed it to be". (Cp. note† p. 159.)

Page 65. *For* "Mâhâmalaipûr", *read* "Mahâmalaipûr".

Page 96, note*. *For* "Arâkkennei (அராக்கெண்ணெய்) temple", *read* "Urakkennei (உழக்கெண்ணெய்) Îsvara temple"; and *for* "one ollock (about 1½ gill)", *read* "one *urakku* (about 3 gills)".—(Cp. p. 210.)

Page 114. "Vijayanagaram ascendancy" appears to be a misprint in the original for "Vijayanagaram dynasty."

Page 115, note. *For* "Vellugôtivâru", *read* "Velugôtivâru".

Page 116. *For* "a clue", *read* "as a clue".

Pages 124, 126, 128. "Pavarakkâran's (prop. Pavalakkâran's) Choultry" signifies "Coral-monger's Choultry." (Korallenhändler-Sattiram—Graul.)

Page 126. *For* "Mahendra Shanta", *read* "Mahendra Sânta."

Page 126, note*. With reference to Sir Walter Elliot's remark on the Tamil alphabet, it will be observed that the Grantha letter ஶ, not the Tamil letter ச, is used in the word "Adisandesvara," in the inscription referred to. (See p. 128.)

Page 129. [illegible] is probably an error in the transcript for [illegible].

Page 133. *For* "Mâhavarâha" read "Mahâvarâha."

Page 141. "36th year" appears to be an error for "37th year." (Cp. p. 121.)

Page 143, line 14 from the bottom. *For* [illegible], *read* [illegible].

Page 173, Sloka 4. *For* उपोयुषा, *read* उपेयुषा.

Page 173, note*. A fourth MS. reads—

दिक्षु सर्वासु च ततो मेरौ निश्चयमेयुषा ।
संतुष्टया धिया तस्य लाभतो मुनिरैधत ॥

Page 174, Sloka 13. *For* चक्रुत्वा, *read* चकृत्वा.

Page 178. *For* "Harisekara," *read* "Harisekhara."

Page 181. "Pundarîkasaras", *read* "Pundarîkasaras."

Page 184. For *Asrâma*, read *Âsrama*.

Page 185. *For* "Sthalasayi", *read* "Sthalasâyî".

Page 216, note‡. *For* "Peria", *read* "Periya."

Page 217. *For* "Pundarîkapuskarinî", *read* "Pundarîkapushkarinî."

Additional Note.

Mr. Fergusson (*History of Architecture*, Vol. II., p. 502 ff.) thus describes three of the five *Rathas*:—

The Southernmost, No. 43 in the Sketch, he remarks "imitates a Buddhist monastery of five storeys. The time at which it was executed was very little removed from that of Buddhism in this part of India. There is little or none of the extravagance of later Hindu styles in the sculptures. Neither the Jains nor the Hindus introduced anything like a new style of architecture. They adapted the Buddhist style to their own purposes."

No. 41, Mr. Fergusson describes as being "the only free-standing monolithic representation I know in India of such a temple [Chaitya] as those excavated in the rock at Ajunta and elsewhere.
But in this, as in all more modern structures of this class, we find considerable confusion between the forms of the temple and those of the monastery. This is no more than might be expected when we consider that the original purposes to which those forms were adapted had ceased to exist, and that in these late copies what were originally essential constructive necessities have become mere ornamental appendages."

And No. 42, the same authority states, "evidently belongs to the same system. There can be little doubt that it is the copy of a variety of the Buddhist temple or Chaitya, of which we have no exact representation in the caves—probably of a built Buddhist temple."

ADDENDUM.

Since the foregoing pages were printed, Mr. R. Bruce Foote, F. G. S., of the Geological Survey of India, has kindly favoured the Editor with the following—

Notes on the Geology of Mahâvalipuram.

The rock in which the temples at Mahâvalipuram are cut is a low ridge of quartzo-felspathic gneiss, an extension of which occurs at the fishing village of Padari, nearly three miles to north, and also at Cullatoor, three miles to the S. S. W.

The bedded character of the rock is but very rarely seen, hence it has often been described as a granite. The strike of the bedding is N. by 5° E.—S. by 5° W. and coincides with that of the grain of the rocks and with the general direction of the hilly ridges further inland. The dip of the beds appears to be westerly but is very obscure and nearly obliterated by excessive metamorphic action.

The texture of the rock suggests the idea of a coarse gritty bed having been exposed to severe lateral pressure, the quartz and felspar having an irregular flakey arrangement and not forming distinctly continuous laminæ as in typical gneiss rock. The color of the rock when freshly quarried is a rich pinkish grey weathering to a drab or pale dirty flesh color. Where exposed to the sea spray, as in the walls of the Shore Temple, the stone acquires a black color and decays far more rapidly than where merely exposed to wind and weather further inland. This gneiss has been, and is still, largely quarried, as it splits very easily into blocks of useful size and shape, and has a decidedly handsome appearance.

The ridge of rocks to the East of the Shore Temple on which the fury of the surf is broken, consists also of gneiss, but probably belongs to another bed running in a parallel direction. The East foot of the Mahâvalipuram gneiss ridge is covered by the beach or by blown sands, but at its West side are beds of sand and clay abounding in Marine and Œstuarine shells of recent species, but in a subfossil condition. These beds are cut through in many places by the Coast Canal.

www.ingramcontent.com/pod-product-compliance
Lightning Source LLC
Chambersburg PA
CBHW030815230426
43667CB00008B/1228
9783337413989